BRAXTON BRAGG AND CONFEDERATE DEFEAT
Volume II

Braxton Bragg
and Confederate Defeat

VOLUME II

JUDITH LEE HALLOCK

The University of Alabama Press

Tuscaloosa and London

Frontispiece: Braxton Bragg, Courtesy of the Library of Congress

Library of Congress Cataloging-in-Publication Data

Braxton Bragg and Confederate defeat
    p. cm.
Vol. 1: Reprint with new pref. and new maps. Originally published:
New York : Columbia University Press, 1969 / Grady McWhiney.
Vol. 2: Judith Lee Hallock.
Vol. 2 originally presented as thesis (doctoral)—State University
of New York at Stony Brook.
Includes bibliographical references and indexes.
ISBN 0-8173-0543-2 (alk. paper)
1. Bragg, Braxton, 1817–1876. 2. Generals—Confederate States of
America—Biography. 3. Confederate States of America. Army—
Biography. I. Hallock, Judith Lee, 1940-   . II. Title.
E467.1.B75M3 1991
973.7′13′092—dc20   91-3554
[B]

British Library Cataloguing-in-Publication Data available

To Grady McWhiney

The future Historian in chronicling the events and the lives of our great men, will hoist on high the name of Braxton Bragg, as synonymous with cool courage, consummate bravery, and determined devotion to the cause he espoused and served so well.

Major Simon Mayer, 1863

CONTENTS

MAPS AND ILLUSTRATIONS

ACKNOWLEDGMENTS

It is with deep gratitude and great pleasure that I thank Grady McWhiney for his many contributions to the completion of this book. His first contribution was the fact that he did not write it himself after completing the first volume on Braxton Bragg in 1969. He generously shared all of the material he had gathered on Bragg during his own study and made available to me a set of the *Official Records* for use in my home. These two sources provided the core of the material from which this book was written. Professor McWhiney has been a constant source of encouragement, support, and advice throughout the research and writing of this second volume.

For their assistance and encouragement, I thank Wilbur R. Miller, Nancy Tomes, Michael Barnhart, and John Pratt of the State University of New York, Stony Brook. I am grateful also to the staff at the SUNY Stony Brook Library, and especially the Inter-Library Loan Department, for their cheerful help.

Donald S. Frazier, proprietor, Computer Cartography Co., worked patiently, painstakingly, and cheerfully to produce the maps. He also revamped those for Volume I under the direction of Grady McWhiney.

I acknowledge the permission of the Western Reserve Historical Society to quote from their extensive collection of Braxton Bragg Papers, Manuscript Collection No. 2000. This collection was previously part of the William P. Palmer Collection, and has been cited as such in Volume I. Other assistance has been provided by the staffs of the Henry E. Huntington Library; Chickamauga National Military Park; Tulane University Library; the Southern Historical Collection at the University of North Carolina at Chapel Hill; the University of the South in Sewanee, Tennessee;

the Eugene C. Barker Texas History Center at the University of
Texas, Austin; the Rosenberg Library in Galveston, Texas; the
Museum of the Confederacy and the Virginia Historical Society
in Richmond; the Library of Congress; and the National Archives
and Records Administration.

My family has always been supportive of whatever I choose to
do. My parents, stepfather, sisters, and brothers have provided a
background of caring and acceptance for all of my endeavors. My
sister, Sharon Hallock Boutcher, read and critiqued the manuscript for me, as did my son Ernest Albee. My other son, David
Hallock, and daughters-in-law Bella Christ and Annmarie Di-
Stefano Hallock also made my task easier in many ways. All four
of my children are a continual source of pride and joy.

Judith Nelson Fleming, friend and colleague, has been a constant supporter and meticulous proofreader. Along with Judy,
Carolyn Kaitz proofread my final draft. The late Mildred E.
Richards spent hours walking and talking with me, helping me to
unwind after a long day of writing. She is sorely missed. Daniel
Jacobs and E. A. "Bud" Livingston, members of the Civil War
Round Table of New York, read and commented on some of the
chapters and have been generous with their interest and support
throughout the project. I also acknowledge friends in Great Brit-
ain who have been supportive: John Ventura, Roland Grimer,
Barry Martin, Margaret Sillwood, and especially Barrie Almond,
who kept up a voluminous correspondence on Bragg over the
years I have worked on this project. My colleagues at North
Coleman Road Elementary School, Middle Country Schools,
Centereach, New York, my students, and their parents have
maintained an interest in this project. A former supervisor, by
example, provided insight into Bragg's character and relationships
with people.

A special thank you goes to my closest friend, Ingeborg Linsen-
barth Kelly. I owe her more than she suspects.

BRAXTON BRAGG AND CONFEDERATE DEFEAT

Recently, Richard M. McMurry published a book of essays explaining why the eastern armies of the Confederacy have received more attention than those of the West. One of the reasons, he contended, is that the western armies simply did not have charismatic generals, and he used Braxton Bragg's biographer to support his point. "[Grady] McWhiney found his subject so nauseous that he abandoned the project after completing only the first of a projected two volumes," McMurry wrote. "At last report he had turned the disgusting Bragg over to a graduate student." [1]

I was that graduate student.

McMurry overstated the case on Bragg. Some of his contemporaries may indeed have viewed Bragg as disgusting, but many others admired and respected him. One who served under him, while discussing the merits of the upper-echelon officers of the Army of Tennessee, declared Bragg "the greatest & best man amongst them all," and in 1873, a former staff officer believed Bragg "the peer . . . of any officer of the late war." But Bragg also produced ambivalence among his compatriots. "I could not avoid a feeling of reverence when he . . . acknowledge[d] the salute of the Colors of the regiment," testified a soldier, "although . . . I am not an admirer of his, by any means."[2]

A contemporary believed that if the true history of the Civil War is ever known, "no man will occupy a higher position than

[1]Richard M. McMurry, *Two Great Rebel Armies: An Essay in Confederate Military History* (Chapel Hill, N.C., 1989), pp. 7–8; Grady McWhiney, *Braxton Bragg and Confederate Defeat*, vol. 1 (New York, 1969).

[2] Thomas Ruffin, Jr., to My dear Sister, December 15, 1863, Cameron Family Papers, Southern Historical Collection, University of North Carolina, Chapel Hill; Kinloch Falconer to E. T. Sykes, February 7, 1873, Southern Historical Society Collection, Eleanor S. Brockenbrough Library, Museum of the Confederacy, Richmond; Joshua K. Callaway to My Dear Wife, April 16, 1863, Joshua K. Callaway Papers, University of Texas, Austin.

. . . [Bragg] will, & none more deservedly." Bragg, however, has not gained such recognition. He was severely criticized during the war, and this condemnation has continued to the present. Some historians, in an effort to promote their own favorites, have taken Bragg to task, overlooking many of his accomplishments, particularly when he served as President Davis's military adviser. Others have repeated these opinions without carefully surveying the data. One student charges that most people today have fallen into the "Bragg syndrome," believing everything they have heard "without having sound foundation to justify the view."[3] This study is an attempt to give Bragg his due, to present fairly the facts of his life and career, thus giving a more balanced view of a man central to the Confederate cause and to its defeat.

Braxton Bragg's experiences during the Civil War provide a key to understanding many of the things that went wrong for the South. He suffered from myriad illnesses, many of them psychosomatic, a trait he shared with some of his Southern peers. The assignments he received highlight Confederate failure to make the most of human resources. His problems during the command of the Army of Tennessee illustrate the neglect of the West by the Richmond authorities. The many controversies swirling about him demonstrate the inability of Southerners to put their differences aside during their efforts to achieve independence.

Bragg's present-day reputation is based upon his many controversies. He did indeed have poor relationships with many of his subordinates and peers. In an effort to understand him, I focus this study on these relationships, trying to determine how much of the controversy was indeed the fault of Bragg, and how much was sour grapes, jealousy, and ambition on the part of those he had to deal with. Bragg's battlefield experiences are told primarily from his point of view, and the reader will be referred to other sources for more detailed discussion of the key battles.

[3] Thomas Ruffin, Jr., to My dear Sister, December 15, 1863, Cameron Family Papers; for example, see Clifford Dowdey, *Lee's Last Campaign: The Story of Lee and His Men against Grant—1864* (New York, 1960); Barrie Almond to author, May 10, 1988.

On November 14, 1863, Braxton Bragg waxed lyrically on the view from his headquarters on Missionary Ridge, a position he would lose in just ten days. He explained that the two armies lay beneath his perch; beyond were their outposts and signal stations, with a series of mountains creating a magnificent background. "At night all are brilliantly lit up in the most gorgeous manner, by the . . . camp fires," he wrote to his wife, Elise. "It surpasses any sight . . . ever witnessed, and . . . it is worth a trip of a thousand miles."[4]

Bragg had traveled many thousand miles to arrive at the position he now occupied, atop the heights overlooking Chattanooga, and in command of the Army of Tennessee. Born in North Carolina in 1817, he was now forty-six years old. After graduating from West Point, fifth in a class of fifty, he served in the Seminole War before becoming a heroic public figure during the Mexican War. Sinking into relative obscurity after the war in Mexico, Bragg resigned from the U.S. Army in 1856 to develop a Louisiana sugar plantation. This move was made possible by the usual expedient for a relatively moneyless young man—he married a wealthy woman, a set goal that he had managed to accomplish in 1849, when he wed Eliza "Elise" Brooks Ellis. On March 7, 1861, shortly before the actual outbreak of the Civil War, Bragg was commissioned brigadier general and assigned to command the Gulf Coast from Pensacola to Mobile. Promotion to major general came on September 12, 1861, and to full general on April 12, 1862, after acting as Albert Sidney Johnston's chief of staff and commanding the Second Corps at Shiloh. When General G. T. Beauregard took an unauthorized leave of absence,[5] Bragg replaced him as commander of the Army of Tennessee on June 27, 1862. Bragg invaded Kentucky from August to October 1862,

[4] Bragg to Elise, November 14, 1863 (photostat), Braxton Bragg Papers, Library of Congress.
[5] Throughout this volume I refer to General Pierre Gustave Toutant Beauregard as G. T. Beauregard, rather than using the three given names as some authors do. Beauregard dropped the use of Pierre as a young adult and thereafter always signed himself G. T. Beauregard.

when General Don Carlos Buell defeated him at Perryville. At Mufreesboro in late December 1862 to early January 1863, he again suffered defeat, this time by General William S. Rosecrans.[6]

In the summer of 1863 a soldier described Bragg as "a tall, fine looking man and very stern." Another observer, after asserting Bragg was "mild and agreeable in manner," went on to say that his "peculiar conformation of eyebrows . . . and a cold, steel-grey eye, which exhibited much of the white when animated, gave him . . . when aroused, a very ferocious aspect, which made him a terror to all who incurred his displeasure." In early autumn 1862 a woman in Chattanooga was impressed with his tall, soldierly bearing, but she thought the "peculiar way he had of showing his lower teeth when he laughed or talked gave him . . . a rather grim look." Another contemporary also described Bragg as grim. An artillery officer who received a humorous letter from Bragg declared he intended to keep it to prove that the man thought of as "Grim visaged War" could on occasion "relax his Wrinkled front." When he chose, Bragg could be charming. "His manner delighted all of us," a woman asserted, and English colonel James Fremantle reported him as being "extremely civil."[7]

Bragg's delightful manner and civility, however, were often overshadowed by his sour temper and petulant manner, caused no doubt by his chronic sickness. Beginning with his service in Florida, Bragg continually complained of ill health. His ailments,

6 McWhiney, *Bragg*, pp. 26, 101, 118, 139, 141, 154, 190, 216, 253, 319, 371.
7 Robert Draughon Patrick, *Reluctant Rebel: The Secret Diary of Robert Patrick, 1861–1865*, ed. F. Jay Taylor (Baton Rouge, 1959), p. 34; William Preston Johnston, *The Life of Gen. Albert Sidney Johnston, Embracing His Service in the Armies of the United States, the Republic of Texas, and the Confederate States* (New York, 1879), p. 547; Henry C. Semple to My dear Wife, June 8, 1863, Henry C. Semple Papers, Southern Historical Collection; Lizzie Hardin, *The Private War of Lizzie Hardin: A Kentucky Confederate Girl's Diary of the Civil War in Kentucky, Virginia, Tennessee, Alabama, and Georgia*, ed. G. Glenn Clift (Frankfort, Ky., 1963), p. 203; Arthur James Lyon Fremantle, *The Fremantle Diary; Being the Journal of Lieutenant Colonel Arthur James Lyon Fremantle, Coldstream Guards, on His Three Months in the Southern States*, ed. Walter Lord (New York, 1960), p. 115.

which included migraine headaches, boils, dyspepsia, and rheumatism, tended to increase proportionately with his responsibilities and, as with most people, usually occurred when he became despondent or frustrated. During the early months of 1863 Bragg's depression caused by the failure of the Kentucky campaign, and the controversies raging within his high command, once again brought on bouts of illness. His general physical breakdown was evidenced by an outbreak of boils and chronic diarrhea. His staff found him without "the slightest epicurean proclivity," forcing them to remind him to take nourishment. His emotional and physical states were in such turmoil while at Tullahoma that, according to biographer Grady McWhiney, Bragg had "lost confidence in himself," was "disoriented," and "had lost touch with reality."[8]

Bragg's unpopularity aggravated his physical and mental strain. His early Civil War career had pushed this extremely ambitious man once again into the public view, where he received praise and applause. By early 1863, however, following the disastrous Kentucky campaign and the retreat from Murfreesboro, his fragile ego was no longer bolstered by success; instead, he was now under severe criticism by some of the most influential and vocal segments of the Confederacy—the press, the Congress, and the generals under his command. Throughout his six-month stay in the Tullahoma area, controversy raged among the high command as to whom to blame for the failure of the Kentucky campaign. Bragg began the controversy when he attempted to put himself in a better light by blaming his subordinates, none of whom would allow him to denigrate their own reputations. An ambiguously worded circular to his subordinates merely exacerbated the situa-

[8] Thomas Robson Hay, "Braxton Bragg and the Southern Confederacy," *Georgia Historical Quarterly*, IX (1925), 295; Fremantle, *Diary*, p. 115; *War of the Rebellion: A Compilation of the Official Records of the Union and Confederate Armies* (128 vols., Washington, D.C., 1880–1901), Series 1, LII (pt. 2), 499–500, hereinafter cited as *OR* (unless otherwise noted, all citations are to Series 1); St. John R. Liddell, *Liddell's Record*, ed. Nathaniel C. Hughes (Dayton, Ohio, 1985), p. 128; L. H. Stout, *Reminiscences of General Braxton Bragg* (Hattiesburg, Miss., 1942), p. 7; McWhiney, *Bragg*, pp. 27, 28, 94, 179, 377, 384, 389.

tion when some generals chose to interpret the document in its broadest sense and advised Bragg that the Army of Tennessee would benefit from his resignation.[9]

Bragg was not the only one in trouble as 1863 began. Southerners' attempts during 1862 to extend their northern frontiers had all met with failure. Bragg had been driven from Kentucky, and Robert E. Lee from Maryland. The Confederates found themselves more on the defensive than ever before. General William S. Rosecrans watched over Bragg's Army of Tennessee, while General Ambrose B. Burnside prepared to attack Lee at Fredericksburg, Virginia, and General U. S. Grant planned to take Vicksburg, Mississippi, in order to open the Mississippi River to Federal invasion. On sea, the blockade of Southern ports continued to tighten. On top of all else, Abraham Lincoln's Emancipation Proclamation went into effect on January 1, 1863.[10]

[9] See McWhiney, *Bragg*, pp. 374–92, for a full discussion of the controversy surrounding the Kentucky invasion and the battle at Murfreesboro.

[10] E. B. Long and Barbara Long, *The Civil War Day by Day: An Almanac, 1861–1865* (Garden City, N.Y., 1971), pp. 283, 291, 306.

I am utterly broken down

January–July, 1863

THE TULLAHOMA CAMPAIGN during June–July 1863 illuminated the ambiguities surrounding Braxton Bragg and his career as a field officer. The months leading up to the retreat from Tullahoma to Chattanooga saw the Army of Tennessee beset with quarrels and its commander ill much of the time. Against the counsel of his subordinates and others, Bragg insisted on holding his position at Tullahoma, but when the Federals advanced, he turned to his generals for advice. The Richmond authorities neglected the Army of Tennessee and even lost all contact with it during its most critical days. And yet, Bragg managed to save his army from capture or serious damage, which was more than the Confederacy's other two major army commanders accomplished during this critical period.

"Finding my communication seriously endangered by movements of the enemy, I last night took up a more defensible position, . . . losing nothing of importance," Bragg cavalierly informed his superior officer in Richmond, Virginia, Adjutant General Samuel Cooper. "The whole army has crossed the Tennessee. . . . Our movement was attended with trifling loss of men and materials."[1] Thus Bragg dismissed his abandonment of Middle Tennessee and North Alabama as the result of the Tullahoma campaign of June 23 to July 3, 1863. But his loss composed a good chunk of the region characterized by historian Thomas Connelly as the heartland of the South, its largest concentrated area for the production of war materials (including wheat, corn, horses,

---

[1] *OR*, XXIII (pt. 1), 583, 584.

mules, pork, wool, and iron), in addition to providing soldiers for the Southern armies.[2]

Others recognized the disaster, but Bragg continued to minimize the loss, largely by ignoring it in his official communications. On July 3 he reported that although he and his troops had wanted to fight, the Federals held a position Bragg could not attack with success, while they outflanked his army and severed his communications. In this, the only official report on Tullahoma he submitted, Bragg seemed to suggest that his opponent, General William S. Rosecrans, had not fought fairly when he moved his army around the flanks of the Army of Tennessee while Bragg had his attention occupied elsewhere.[3]

Several months later, Bragg had further thoughts on the disastrous evacuation of Middle Tennessee. In a draft memorandum on the Battle of Chickamauga, he again complained about Rosecrans's behavior ("taking advantage of our weakness") but went on to blame others, too. He denounced "the traitors about Shelbyville" who informed the Federals of his attempt to deceive the Federals into believing the Confederate forces were stronger than they actually were. By the time he submitted his final Chickamauga report, however, Bragg decided to ignore the Tullahoma disaster. Thus his reports to Richmond on the campaign comprised only three short telegraphic dispatches and a 300-word "explanation."[4]

The Tullahoma campaign, remarkable for its confusion and indecision,[5] revealed that stress undermined Bragg's noted organizational abilities. The extended stay in the Tullahoma area following Bragg's retreat from Murfreesboro, rather than providing

[2] Thomas Lawrence Connelly, *Autumn of Glory: The Army of Tennessee, 1862–1865* (Baton Rouge, 1971), pp. 4, 8, 9.
[3] *OR*, XXIII (pt. 1), 584.
[4] Braxton Bragg, "Memorandum on the Battle of Chickamauga," n.d., Braxton Bragg Papers, Western Reserve Historical Society, Manuscript Collection No. 2000, Cleveland, Ohio; *OR*, XXIII (pt. 1), 583, 584.
[5] Connelly. *Autumn of Glory*, p. 112, contends there was a complete communications breakdown among Bragg's high command during the campaign.

an opportunity for resolving internal army problems, was marked by continuous squabbling among the high command.

Bragg's Army of Tennessee naturally included a range of personalities. In June 1863 he had two infantry corps, commanded by Lieutenant Generals Polk and Hardee. The cavalry also consisted of two corps, under Major General Wheeler and Brigadier General Forrest.[6]

Bragg's senior infantry corps commander was Leonidas Polk, a fifty-seven-year-old native of North Carolina who had graduated from West Point in 1827. But in October of that same year Polk resigned from the army to study for the ministry. Ordained in 1830, he combined the ministry with planting and in 1838 became Episcopal Bishop of the Southwest, a position which required him to leave his wife, Frances Ann Devereux, and their children to manage on their own for extended periods of time. Despite Polk's lack of military experience, President Jefferson Davis appointed him a major general in June 1861. Promoted to lieutenant general in October 1862, Polk by early 1863 had become a seasoned campaigner, seeing action at Shiloh, in Kentucky, and at Murfreesboro. During this time, Polk had twice threatened to resign over what he imagined were slights to his prestige, but each time he allowed himself to be dissuaded. Contemporaries described him as tall, soldierly, good-looking, and gentlemanly, "with all the manners and affability of a 'grand seigneur,'" considerate of the men, fearless in battle, dignified, imposing, and loved by his staff. However, another contemporary assessed Polk's military aptitude as "more theoretical than practical," and a historian concluded he did not make his mark as a combat leader.[7] In supreme self-confidence, he retained his bishopric while serving as a general.

Benjamin F. Cheatham and Jones M. Withers commanded Polk's divisions. Cheatham, a forty-two-year-old Tennessee farmer,

---

[6] *OR*, XXIII (pt. 2), 873.

[7] Joseph H. Parks, *General Leonidas Polk, C.S.A.: The Fighting Bishop* (Baton Rouge, 1962), pp. 21, 43, 54, 77, 170, 375; Fremantle, *Diary*, p. 111; Mark Mayo Boatner III, *Civil War Dictionary* (New York, 1959), p. 658.

had served as a colonel of Tennessee volunteers in the Mexican War. Appointed major general in the Confederate army on March 10, 1862, he was a veteran of several battles. Withers, a forty-nine-year-old Alabamian, graduated from West Point in 1835, but his only army service was during the Mexican War. As a private citizen in Mobile, he pursued law, merchandising, and politics. His Civil War career encompassed fighting in the western theater. His rank of major general became effective April 6, 1862.[8]

Bragg's junior infantry corps commander was General William J. Hardee, a forty-seven-year-old native of Georgia. Graduating in 1838 from West Point, Hardee served in various positions within the U.S. Army. An assignment in 1840–1841 to study at the French Royal Cavalry School demonstrated to Hardee the importance of military instruction and rigorous discipline, and during the Mexican War his superiors noted his talent for drilling and organizing troops. In 1853 the War Department assigned him to prepare a new manual, *Rifle and Light Infantry Tactics*. Although largely a translation of the French manual of tactics, it soon became known as Hardee's *Tactics* and was used extensively by both Union and Confederate officers. From 1856 to 1860 Hardee served as commandant at West Point, during which time he assiduously cultivated the friendship of Jefferson Davis, who served as Secretary of War from 1852 to 1856. After leaving West Point in 1860, and while still an officer of the U.S. Army, Hardee became Governor Joseph Brown's purchasing agent of arms and munitions for the state of Georgia. On January 29, 1861, Hardee resigned his commission in the U.S. Army, and by early 1863 he had seen action at Shiloh, in Kentucky, and at Murfreesboro. Promoted to lieutenant general on the same day as Polk, Hardee conveyed an air of command and sternness. His compatriots described him as handsome and muscular, and although exacting in discipline and drill, he appeared to some as kind and solicitous for the welfare of his soldiers. One contempo-

---

[8] Ezra J. Warner, *Generals in Gray: Lives of the Confederate Commanders* (Baton Rouge, 1959), pp. 47–48, 342–43; Boatner, *Dictionary*, pp. 147–48, 944–45.

rary, however, described Hardee as "ever grasping" for recognition, even to the "detriment or injury" of his subordinates. In his personal life, after the death of his first wife, Elizabeth Dummett, Hardee passed responsibility for his four children onto Elizabeth's sister Anna and, eleven years later, married a woman twenty-three years his junior, nearly the age of his daughters.[9]

Hardee's division commanders were Alexander P. Stewart and Patrick R. Cleburne. Stewart, a forty-two-year-old native of Tennessee, graduated from West Point in 1842. He spent three years in the army before resigning in order to teach. Fighting in several of the battles in the West, Stewart received promotion to major general on June 2, 1863. Cleburne, a native of Ireland, immigrated to the United States in 1849. He had received some military training in Ireland, but at the outbreak of the Civil War he was a fairly wealthy entrepreneur and lawyer in Arkansas. After joining the Confederate forces, he rapidly established a reputation as a superb combat officer and fought at Shiloh, in Kentucky, and at Murfreesboro. His promotion to major general came on December 13, 1862, making him one of only two foreign-born officers to attain that rank.[10]

Bragg's cavalry had undergone many changes just prior to the start of the Tullahoma campaign. It had consisted of two corps, commanded by Generals Earl Van Dorn and Joseph Wheeler. In February 1863 Van Dorn had been sent to Spring Hill, Tennessee, on Bragg's far left, in command of an interdepartmental cavalry force expected to serve the needs of both Bragg in Tennessee and Pemberton in Mississippi. In May 1863, however, after

[9] Nathaniel Cheairs Hughes, Jr., *General William J. Hardee, Old Reliable* (Baton Rouge, 1965), pp. 6, 12, 21, 40, 41, 46, 55, 68, 188; Fremantle, *Diary*, p. 110; Basil W. Duke, *Reminiscences of General Basil W. Duke, C.S.A.* (New York, 1911), pp. 67–68; E. J. Warner, *Generals in Gray*, p. 125; E. T. Sykes, *Walthall's Brigade: A Cursory Sketch, with Personal Experiences of Walthall's Brigade, Army of Tennessee, C.S.A., 1862–1865* (n.p., n.d.), pp. 540–41.

[10] E. J. Warner, *Generals in Gray*, pp. 293–94, 53–54; Boatner, *Dictionary*, pp. 798–99, 158–59; Howell Purdue and Elizabeth Purdue, *Pat Cleburne, Confederate General* (Hillsboro, Tex., 1973).

an outraged husband murdered Van Dorn, the command was split, some going to Mississippi and the rest to Alabama.[11]

Wheeler, a native of Georgia, was promoted to major general in January 1863 at the age of twenty-six. He had graduated from West Point in 1859, near the bottom of his class. Serving as an officer of infantry at Shiloh, he transferred to cavalry in July 1862 and saw action during the Kentucky campaign and at Murfreesboro. Generals John A. Wharton and William T. Martin commanded Wheeler's divisions. Wharton was a thirty-five-year-old Tennessee native, practicing law in Texas at the outbreak of the war. As captain in the Eighth Texas Cavalry, he took command after the deaths of his superior officers. Wounded at Shiloh, Wharton returned to duty for the Kentucky campaign. Promoted to brigadier general on November 18, 1862, he distinguished himself at Murfreesboro. Forty-year-old Martin had been a district attorney in Kentucky when the war began. Raising a company of cavalry, he took them to Richmond, Virginia, where they joined J. E. B. Stuart in his famous ride around McClellan's army, in the Seven Days' Battle, and at Sharpsburg. Martin received promotion to brigadier general on December 2, 1862, and was sent to the West.[12]

Under Van Dorn and Wheeler were two of the Confederacy's most colorful cavalry commanders—Generals John Hunt Morgan and Nathan Bedford Forrest. Morgan, a thirty-seven-year-old Alabamian, had served in the Mexican War before setting himself up as a merchant in Kentucky. His battle experience included Shiloh, the Kentucky campaign, and Murfreesboro. Fond of the spectacular raid, Morgan was off on an unauthorized and ill-fated jaunt into Ohio when the Tullahoma campaign began. Forrest, a forty-one-year-old Tennessean, had been a wealthy planter, for-

---

[11] E. J. Warner, *Generals in Gray*, pp. 314–15; Boatner, *Dictionary*, p. 867; Connelly, *Autumn of Glory*, p. 106; Robert G. Hartje, *Van Dorn: The Life and Times of a Confederate General* (Nashville, 1967).

[12] John P. Dyer, *"Fightin' Joe" Wheeler* (Baton Rouge, 1941); E. J. Warner, *Generals in Gray*, pp. 214–15, 331–33; Boatner, *Dictionary*, pp. 515, 909–10.

mer slave trader, and businessperson in 1861. Footing the bill for the raising of his own battalion of cavalry, he fought at Fort Donelson (escaping with his command before its surrender), at Shiloh, and in West Tennessee. Assessed by some military critics as the foremost cavalry officer produced in America, Forrest often had problems with his superiors. During the army's stay at Tullahoma, his inability to get along caused his transfer from Wheeler to Van Dorn; upon Van Dorn's death, Forrest assumed control over the area commanded by his late superior.[13]

Bragg lacked the tact and diplomacy necessary to meld these subordinates into a cohesive, cooperative unit, and it had been a difficult winter for him. His subordinates tried and failed to have him removed from command of the army; Rosecrans had forced him to retreat from Kentucky and now awaited the right opportunity to strike again. With these pressures on Bragg, enemies within and without, it is not surprising that he remained ill most of the winter, even at times disoriented. Thus, when the Federals advanced, Bragg found himself sick, befuddled, and beleaguered.

Bragg's decision to concentrate his army at Tullahoma was criticized when he made it in January. Tullahoma did form an important road junction, but after studying the topography, Hardee pointed out that the position was vulnerable to both direct and flank attack, with no advantages to outweigh its faults. Others agreed with him. In April President Davis sent Colonel William Preston Johnston to inspect the Army of Tennessee. He soon reported that the advantages of the ground were not obvious. Polk, however, who knew the area intimately through prewar activities on behalf of a proposed Episcopal university, appears to have

[13] E. J. Warner, *Generals in Gray*, pp. 220–21, 92–93; Boatner, *Dictionary*, pp. 566, 288–89; Connelly, *Autumn of Glory*, p. 125; James A. Ramage, *Rebel Raider: The Life of General John Hunt Morgan* (Lexington, Ky., 1986); Cecil Fletcher Holland, *Morgan and His Raiders: Biography of the Confederate General* (New York, 1943); Howard Swiggett, *The Rebel Raider: A Life of John Hunt Morgan* (Garden City, N.Y., 1937); Robert Selph Henry, *"First with the Most" Forrest* (New York, 1944); John Allan Wyeth, *That Devil Forrest: Life of General Nathan Bedford Forrest* (New York, 1959).

made no recommendations on where or how the army should be disposed.[14]

The military arrangements around Tullahoma indicated the severity of Bragg's disorientation. Colonel Johnston reported that Bragg believed Rosecrans would attempt to flank the Confederate right, but Bragg posted the bulk of his army on the left. After describing the fortifications Bragg had ordered constructed, including an abatis of felled timber, Johnston commented that the works were not strong enough to rely upon for defense but were too strong to allow them to fall into enemy hands. Bragg's reasoning for constructing fortifications as he did confirms his confused mental state. "General Bragg says heavy intrenchments demoralize our troops, and that he would go forward to meet the enemy, in which case that abatis would be an obstruction, to say the least." In addition, Johnston reported, although Bragg had been at Tullahoma for over three months, there appeared to be no plans for meeting a Federal advance, or for mounting an advance himself.[15] Bragg seemed content to wait for Rosecrans to decide when and where a battle would take place.

Besides being a difficult area to defend, Tullahoma offered little in the way of subsistence for Bragg's army. Since much of the produce of the region was raked off to supply the eastern armies, the Army of Tennessee had to survive the best it could. Colonel Johnston confirmed reports of shortages when he wrote to Davis that the army was living "from hand to mouth." Not only humans suffered from lack of sustenance: the transport horses and mules and the artillery horses were without long forage. The cavalry horses, with a wider ranging area in which to forage, were doing better.[16]

[14] Bragg to Hardee, January 1863, J. Stoddard Johnston Military Papers, Filson Club, Louisville, Kentucky; *OR*, XXIII (pt. 2), 617–18, 760–61; J. Stoddard Johnston Diary, March 15, 1863, Johnston Military Papers.

[15] *OR*, XXIII (pt. 2), 760–61.

[16] Thomas Lawrence Connelly, *Army of the Heartland: The Army of Tennessee, 1861–1862* (Baton Rouge, 1967), pp. 11–12; *OR*, XXIII (pt. 2), 759–60.

Railroad
Hill

10 Miles

N

Murfreesboro

Bellbuckle
Gap
Liberty
Gap
McMinnville

Guys
Gap

Hoovers
Gap

Shelbyville

Wartrace
Manchester
Hillsboro

Duck River

Tullahoma
Bethpage
Bridge
Allisona
Bridge
Tracy
City

Elk River
Decherd
Winchester
Brakefield
Point
Sewanee

Cowan
Battle
Creek

Tennessee
Kellys Ferry

Alabama
Bridgeport
Chattanooga

Stevenson
Georgia

Tennessee River

Donald S. Frazier

THE TULLAHOMA CAMPAIGN

The vulnerability of Tullahoma and the uncertainty of subsistence did not detract from the generally good condition of Bragg's army. The soldiers were all armed, with reserves on hand, and ammunition, clothing, and shoes were in adequate supply. Bragg had received some conscripts, bringing his aggregate present on June 10, 1863, to about 55,000, as opposed to Rosecrans's 82,000. After praising Bragg's organizational talents and his attention to detail, Johnston hedged his overall opinion of the army's fitness for a campaign with a qualifying adjective: "The army lacks no physical element of success." [17]

The army may have lacked no "physical element" for success, but its commander was another matter. "Our darkest hour may now be upon us," Bragg wrote Elise just three days prior to Rosecrans's advance into Middle Tennessee. Bragg explained that his demonstrations against the enemy were merely to hold them in check and to conceal the fact that some of his units were being sent to Mississippi with General Joseph E. Johnston to aid Pemberton, beseiged in Vicksburg. "My efforts were perfectly successful," he claimed, "until our newspapers were received by the enemy when all of course, became known," a comment revealing his bitterness toward newspapers. He concluded his letter by assuring Elise, "I am better than I have been for a month."[18] The events of the next two weeks, however, were to prove disastrous to this temporary improvement of his always-fragile health.

There were several roads by which Rosecrans could advance. In front of the Confederate center was a series of rugged hills with four gaps cutting through them: Hoover's Gap, through which ran the road from Murfreesboro to Manchester, on Bragg's right; Liberty Gap, five miles to the west of Hoover's, carried a wagon road leading to Wartrace, where Hardee was headquartered; Bellbuckle Gap, one mile to the west of Liberty, through which the railroad ran on its way through Wartrace; and, six miles further west, Guy's Gap, through which ran the pike to Shelbyville, the site of Polk's headquarters. Besides these routes, Rosecrans could also opt for a wide sweep to either the left or the right of Bragg's army. To cover all bases, Bragg had his army stretched nearly seventy miles, with the bulk of it concentrated on the direct routes to Chattanooga—Hoover's, Liberty, and Guy's gaps.[19]

Although the gaps and roads ran north and south, three rivers

[17] *OR*, XXIII (pt. 2), 759–60, 873, 378, 758.

[18] Bragg to Elise, June 20, 1863, Braxton Bragg Papers, William K. Bixby Collection, Missouri Historical Society, St. Louis.

[19] Parks, *Polk*, p. 309; Shelby Foote, *The Civil War: A Narrative, Fredericksburg to Meridian* (3 vols., New York, 1963), II, 666; Connelly, *Autumn of Glory*, p. 113.

flowed generally east to west through the region between Murfreesboro and Chattanooga: the Duck, the Elk, and the Tennessee. Mid-June found most of Bragg's army encamped north of the Duck River, which would have to be crossed to reach the Tullahoma fortifications.

The center of Bragg's line appeared to be the focus of the Federal advance on June 23, 1863. For three days Rosecrans kept Polk's Corps busy at Liberty and Hoover's gaps. But while Bragg focused attention on his center, the bulk of the Union army marched around Bragg's right, through McMinnville to Manchester, with virtually no opposition. Fortunately for the Confederates, heavy rains delayed Rosecrans's advance, affording Bragg additional time to plan and organize his response.[20]

Bragg, who had been completely outfoxed by Rosecrans's brilliant maneuver, reacted slowly. Three days after the Union advance began, Bragg ordered Forrest to observe and harass the enemy; next he instructed Polk to attack the Federals in flank and rear at Liberty Gap at daylight on June 27, while Hardee's Corps pressed them from the east. Polk objected, pointing out that the character of the country made the position "nothing short of a man-trap." Despite Polk's opposition, Bragg insisted. At 4:00 P.M., however, Bragg abandoned the plan when he learned that the right flank of Stewart's Division had been turned. He then ordered both Polk and Hardee to retreat to Tullahoma.[21]

Bragg spent June 27 and 28 moving his army across the Duck River and into Tullahoma. At 5:30 A.M. on the twenty-seventh he advised Polk to put his troops in motion immediately, as the Federals threatened to get ahead of them. Bragg left his Shelbyville headquarters a half hour later, arriving in Tullahoma about noon, when he ordered a brigade from Cleburne's Division to determine the enemy's strength on the roads leading into Tullahoma from Manchester. At 10:00 P.M. Bragg found it necessary to order Polk

[20] *OR*, XXIII (pt. 1), 449, 406–7.
[21] Bragg to Forrest, June 26, 1863, Bragg Papers, Western Reserve; *OR*, XXIII (pt. 1), 618; (pt. 2), 886; Bragg, Letter Book, June 26, 1863, pp. 395–96, Bragg Papers, Western Reserve.

to move his baggage wagons because they were holding up Cleburne's troops and trains. Polk's tardiness, Bragg asserted, endangered Cleburne as well as the entire army. But it was not until 4:00 P.M. on June 28 that the wagon trains finally made their way into town, owing partly to the heavy and continuous rains, which made road conditions terrible.[22]

Bragg spent June 29 preparing for battle, but even as he made tentative plans to defend Tullahoma, he and his corps commanders discussed whether to make their stand there or to retreat along their line of communications. Although the enemy had destroyed the railroad at Decherd, interrupting communications with the rear, Bragg remained determined to give battle at Tullahoma. Polk apparently made no protest at this time to Bragg, but after leaving Bragg's headquarters he told Hardee that Bragg's decision was "injudicious." Bragg met again with Polk and Hardee at 3:00 P.M. to discuss their opinions regarding the present condition of the army. Polk adamantly advised instant retreat, even suggesting that they take only the mules, leaving the wagons behind. He argued that, not having sufficient cavalry to cover their communications, Rosecrans would cut their lines and Bragg would find his army in the same position as Pemberton's in Vicksburg. If Bragg did manage to escape across Tennessee, he would end up in the hills of North Alabama without food, forcing the army to disperse. In the meantime, Polk declared, Rosecrans would have taken possession of the "heart of the Confederacy." And, he added for good measure, it was his opinion that Davis did not favor their fighting at Tullahoma. After Polk finished his predictions of doom, Hardee gave his opinion. Having learned that the railroad at Decherd was not, after all, seriously damaged and needed only a few hours' work to repair it, Hardee advised that they await further developments. Polk quickly modified his original position, but he still believed it necessary to retreat to save their communi-

[22] *OR*, XXIII (pt. 1), 619, 578, 620; Bragg, Letter Book, June 27–28, 1863, pp. 397–401, Bragg Papers, Western Reserve; *OR*, XXIII (pt. 2), 887, 888, 890, 891.

cations. Bragg decided to reserve his decision, in effect adopting Hardee's wait-and-see position.[23]

By now the news of Bragg's dilemma had spread. "We do not know the moment that we may hear of a disaster to our army," Confederate nurse Kate Cumming confided in her diary. Despite her anxiety, she pitied Bragg, believing he always fought "under great disadvantages," and he was confronting one of the best Union generals. Others, she lamented, were not as understanding as she: "Every body is now against him."[24]

By early afternoon on June 30 Bragg knew that he must abandon Tullahoma. That morning Forrest's command, posted on the Manchester and the Hillsboro roads, had been pressed by the advancing enemy, and Bragg had also learned that Rosecrans had troops moving toward Bethpage, the location of a bridge vital to the Confederate retreat. Bragg ordered the corps commanders to move the men out quickly, and by 7:00 P.M. the last units were headed south.[25]

"Citizens of Tullahoma tell us that the Rebels so hastily left on our approach, that every fellow just skedaddled on his own hook," a Federal reported in a letter home. "A perfect Panic seized them—and they gathered up all the cars they could and piled in and on them and moved their army beyond Elk River, the rag and tag following as rapidly as possible." He also claimed the Confederates left 500 tents, along with provisions, cooking utensils, and several seige guns. Meanwhile Rosecrans boasted to his wife that he had achieved a decided advantage over the Confederates at very little cost.[26]

By 11:00 P.M. on June 30 Bragg had crossed the Elk River,

[23] OR, XXIII (pt. 1), 621–22; David Urquhart, Memorandum, June 29, 1863, Bragg Papers, Western Reserve.
[24] Kate Cumming, Kate: The Journal of a Confederate Nurse, ed. Richard Barksdale Harwell (Baton Rouge, 1959; orig. ed., 1866), p. 111.
[25] Wyeth, That Devil Forrest, p. 210; OR, XXIII (pt. 2), 892–93; (pt. 1), 622–23.
[26] J. M. Todd to Mrs. Mary Sterling, July 14, 1863, Civil War Collection, Henry E. Huntington Library, San Marino, California; William S. Rosecrans to My dearest, June 30, 1863, William S. Rosecrans Papers, Special Collections, Research Library, University of California, Los Angeles.

issuing orders from his temporary headquarters at Decherd, twelve miles southeast of Tullahoma. He directed Wheeler to cross the Allisona Bridge immediately, Hardee to destroy the bridge the instant Wheeler's cavalry had crossed, and Polk to destroy the Bethpage Bridge. Bragg asked for an estimate as to when the Elk River would be fordable—in other words, when he could expect Rosecrans to be in hot pursuit.[27]

The next day Bragg suffered indecision and panic. He sent his engineers to inspect the road over the mountain, an indication he was considering a retreat into Chattanooga. At the same time his concern about the Elk River crossing prompted a frantic dispatch to Polk: "Is the river now fordable? Is it so falling as to be fordable by morning? Is the railroad bridge destroyed? Are all the troops and trains this side?" Polk replied that Wheeler estimated the river would not be fordable until the next evening at the earliest, the railroad bridge was burned, and all trains and troops were on the south side, except the cavalry, which would not need a bridge. At 7:00 P.M. an even more distraught communication from Bragg reached Polk: "The question to be decided instantly, Shall we fight on the Elk, or take post at foot of mountain at Cowan?" It appears Bragg was either unable to make a decision or wanted someone to share the responsibility for the abandonment of Middle Tennessee. Polk favored falling back to Cowan and also recommended that as many wagons as possible be started over the mountain. Hardee concurred with Polk, and Bragg set the move in motion.[28]

Having started the infantry toward the foot of the mountain, Bragg began earnestly preparing for flight over it. He directed Forrest to examine the mountain roads, and he instructed Wheeler to block the road leading over the mountain from Winchester to Stevenson.[29]

By this time Bragg's subordinates expressed serious doubts

[27] *OR*, XXIII (pt. 2), 894.
[28] *Ibid.* (pt. 1), 623–24; (pt. 2), 894–95.
[29] Bragg, Letter Book, July 1, 1863, pp. 402–4, Bragg Papers, Western Reserve.

about their commander's ability to cope with the situation. At
8:30 P.M. on July 1 Hardee wrote to Polk concerning Bragg's enfeebled health. If there should be a fight, Hardee feared that
Bragg would be "unable either to examine and determine his line
of battle or to take command on the field." He suggested that he
and Polk meet with General Simon B. Buckner, who had joined
Bragg for the emergency from East Tennessee, but when Bragg
decided to concentrate at Cowan, Hardee canceled the meeting.
However, Hardee believed that, considering Bragg's feeble state of
health, it would be more prudent to retreat than to fight. Hardee
anticipated criticism; if he came under censure along with Bragg
for the abandonment of Middle Tennessee, he could now prove
that he had distrusted his commanding general's mental and physical fitness for battle.[30]

Very early the next morning, on July 2, Bragg began abandoning Middle Tennessee. Just after midnight he ordered Wheeler to
cross and destroy the Elk River bridge at Allisona. Besides covering the army's rear and blocking the road, Wheeler would also
harrass the enemy's right and defend the railroad. At 1:30 A.M.
Bragg directed Polk and Buckner to move to Cowan at daylight,
while Hardee moved to Brakefield Point. By 5:20 A.M. Polk had
his corps on the move, drawing up in line of battle when it
reached Cowan. Enemy cavalry, however, having crossed at fords
near Allisona, pressed Bragg's troops, and at 4:00 P.M. Bragg ordered Polk to start his wagons over the mountain immediately.[31]

Bragg spent July 3 on the run, prompting one of his soldiers to
write, "One thing is certain, if Bragg cannot whip Rosencrantz he
can OUT-RUN him badly." In the late afternoon Wheeler reported
his cavalry obstructing the road slowly (having only six axes), but
the work soon ended completely when a large force of the enemy
appeared. Wheeler suggested there be no delay in crossing the
Tennessee River. Consequently, Bragg ordered the engineers at
Bridgeport and Battle Creek to be sure the pontoon bridges were

[30] *OR*, XXIII (pt. 1), 623–24.
[31] *Ibid.* (pt. 2), 896; (pt. 1), 624–25.

ready to be thrown across the Tennessee at a moment's notice.[32]

That moment occurred on July 4. "Unable to obtain a general engagement without sacrificing my communications," Bragg wired Cooper, "I have after a series of skirmishes, withdrawn the Army to the River." By the end of the day all of Bragg's army had retreated across the Tennessee.[33]

Now that his army had gained a measure of safety, Bragg began to put it back in order, a task he thoroughly enjoyed. After positioning his various units to protect the likely routes of attack, Bragg turned to the serious problem of desertion. "Stragglers and deserters from Bragg's army continue to come in," a Union soldier at Tullahoma recorded. "Many thousands of Bragg's Army deserted him," wrote another, "swearing they would never cross the Tennessee River." Most of the deserters came from Kentucky and Tennessee and were making their way back home. On July 7 Bragg ordered Wheeler and Forrest to prevent deserters from crossing at Kelly's Ford. In addition, on July 15 he requested regular reports from the corps commanders on their effective total and aggregate present and absent, and he directed subordinate officers to investigate the reasons for absenteeism in their commands.[34]

Although Bragg optimistically summed up the Tullahoma campaign for Cooper on July 7, on the same day he wrote more pessimistically to Buckner, who had returned to Knoxville. After thanking Buckner for his aid, Bragg admitted, "I did not succeed

[32] W. W. Heartsill, *Fourteen Hundred and Ninety-One Days in the Confederate Army: A Journal Kept by W. W. Heartsill for Four Years, One Month, and One Day; or, Camp Life; Day by Day, of the W. P. Lane Rangers from April 19, 1861, to May 20, 1865*, ed. Bell Irvin Wiley (Jackson, Tenn., 1953), p. 136; *OR*, XXIII (pt. 1), 615–16; Bragg, Letter Book, July 3, 1863, p. 404, Bragg Papers, Western Reserve.

[33] Bragg to Cooper, July 4, 1863 (telegram), Jefferson Davis Papers, Duke University Library, Durham, North Carolina.

[34] *OR*, XXIII (pt. 2), 900; Bragg, Letter Book, July 5–6, 1863, pp. 407–8, Bragg Papers, Western Reserve; John Beatty, *Memoirs of a Volunteer, 1861–1863*, ed. Harvey S. Ford (New York, 1946), p. 218; Todd to Sterling, July 14, 1863, Civil War Collection, Huntington Library; Special Orders No. 179, Headquarters, Army of Tennessee, July 7, 1863; Kinloch Falconer to Hardee, Polk, Wheeler, Forrest, and Jackson, July 15, 1863, Bragg Papers, Western Reserve.

in striking the enemy," and foresaw condemnation of the retreat.
Bragg had, however, succeeded in gaining control over his earlier
hysteria, during which he had confessed, "This is a great disaster."[35]

In a much lengthier report, Rosecrans complained to his superior
that his operations had been severely hampered by the unusually
heavy rains. He pointed out that his nine days' campaign had
driven Bragg from two fortified positions and given the Federals
possession of Middle Tennessee. Although the objective should
have been the destruction of Bragg's army, Rosecrans boasted that
the results were far more than he had anticipated. He reported his
losses as 85 killed, 462 wounded, and 13 missing. He made no
estimate of his opponent's casualties but reported he had a total of
1,634 Confederate prisoners.[36]

Union observers, who had found Bragg "as slippery as an eel,"
believed the weather was the only reason Bragg escaped relatively
unscathed. "The weather prevented us from crushing Bragg,"
Rosecrans complained to his wife, and soldier Michael S. Bright
told his uncle, "The only thing that saved [Bragg] and his army
was the condition of the weather and the roads. . . . [I]t rained
every day for two weeks, and the roads got so bad that it was
almost impossible to get the Artillery and Wagon trains along."[37]

Throughout the campaign, Bragg had been poorly served by
his cavalry, a serious drawback, as Civil War generals relied upon
the cavalry to keep them informed of enemy movements. Morgan's ill-fated raid into Ohio against orders constituted only the
first instance of the cavalry's poor performance. The cavalry on

[35] *OR*, XXIII (pt. 1), 584; Bragg, Letter Book, July 7, 1863, p. 412, Bragg Papers, Western Reserve; Charles Todd Quintard, *Doctor Quintard, Chaplain C.S.A. and Second Bishop of Tennessee, Being His Story of the War (1861–1865)*, ed. Arthur Howard Noll (Sewanee, Tenn., 1905), p. 87.

[36] *OR*, XXIII (pt. 1), 408–9.

[37] Constantin Grebner, trans., and Frederic Trautmann, ed., *"We Were the Ninth": A History of the Ninth Regiment, Ohio Volunteer Infantry, April 17, 1861, to June 7, 1864* (Kent, Ohio, 1987), p. 130; Rosecrans to My Sweet Wife, July 11, 1863, Rosecrans Papers; Aida Craig Truxall, ed., *"Respects to All": Letters of Two Pennsylvania Boys in the War of the Rebellion* (Pittsburgh, 1962), p. 94.

the scene left much to be desired. In one request for information, Bragg admonished Wheeler, "Try and get it soon and accurate." After being surprised by the enemy early in the campaign, a regimental commander sarcastically reported, "I had been led to believe that this cavalry was vigilant and would give timely notice of the approach of an enemy. The enemy surprised this invincible cavalry, and (to use their language) rode over them." General Arthur M. Manigault speculated that the blame for the results of the Tullahoma campaign could be placed on the cavalry. He believed that Bragg did not give battle because of the cavalry's failure to furnish him with reliable information. Manigault concluded his critique of the cavalry with a sweeping condemnation: "It often appeared to me that many of our failures or misfortunes arose from our lamentable deficiency in this branch of the service."[38]

Historians as well as contemporaries have recognized the weakness of Bragg's cavalry. Wheeler serves as a case in point. A student of the Army of Tennessee accused Wheeler of neglecting his duties on Bragg's right. Instead of remaining in the area to which he was assigned, Wheeler moved west into the Shelbyville front, leaving only one regiment to cover the Confederate right, which Rosecrans easily outflanked.[39]

The views on the army commander proved less consistent. Although one Confederate soldier believed Bragg had no alternative but to retreat, he also thought his commander would be censured for it. He pointed out that Bragg deserved high praise for bringing off most of his stores and wagons. Kate Cumming believed that some people were satisfied that Bragg had made the only move possible under the circumstances, but she admitted that many did not agree. "If he had enemies before, they can be numbered now by the score." Her own thoughts were mixed; she admitted that

[38] *OR*, XXIII (pt. 2), 892; (pt. 1), 600; Arthur Middleton Manigault, *A Carolinian Goes to War: The Civil War Narrative of Arthur Middleton Manigault, Brigadier General, C.S.A.*, ed. R. Lockwood Tower (Columbia, S.C., 1983), pp. 76–77.
[39] Connelly, *Autumn of Glory*, p. 126.

he had much to contend with and that she was incompetent to judge his command abilities.[40]

Others did not hesitate to judge Bragg's competence. A Confederate soldier told his parents that he had heard the war department ordered the retreat, and he was "inclined to think it an order from Lincoln's war department." He lamented that what little confidence he had had in Bragg was now gone. "I have lost hopes of our gaining our indipendance," wrote a minimally educated, and certainly ill-informed, civilian. "General Bragg has give up every place he has had & . . . if he was not Jef Daveis' brother in law he would be put out of ofis." A generally sympathetic diarist was forced to note many soldiers no longer trusted Bragg and concluded that he should resign from command.[41]

Bragg made mistakes in Middle Tennessee, the first of which was choosing Tullahoma as his point of concentration after retreating from Murfreesboro. It did form an important road and rail junction, but it was also nearly indefensible, especially for an outnumbered army. In an effort to cover all avenues of attack, Bragg stretched his army too thin and, in the end, did not have the actual route of invasion covered at all.

Bragg's poor health may have contributed to his mistakes. He had informed Elise three days before the retreat began of his improved health, but within a week he fell ill again. He did not describe his ailments in detail, but on July 7 Bragg complained to Buckner that he had been sick since June 29. The continuous and heavy rains during the entire campaign exacerbated his usual ill health under stress. On July 1 Hardee confided to Polk his concern about Bragg's "enfeebled state of health," and two days later Bragg admitted to a sympathetic listener, "I am utterly broken

[40] Frank Batchelor and George Turner, *Batchelor-Turner Letters, 1861–1864, Written by Two of Terry's Texas Rangers*, annotated by H. J. H. Rugeley (Austin, Tex., 1961), p. 59; Cumming, *Kate*, pp. 114–15.

[41] J. P. Kendall to His Parents, July 12, 1863, W. D. Kendall Papers, Huntington Library; E. S. Metts to Alexander Tilghman, July 19, 1863, E. S. Metts Papers, Duke University Library; Cumming, *Kate*, p. 115. See also John Euclid Magee Diary, typescript (copy), Chickamauga National Military Park, Chickamauga, Georgia.

down." Several weeks after reaching Chattanooga, his condition forced him into the hospital.[42]

Ill and enfeebled, Bragg also contended with unsupportive and unreliable subordinates prone to interpreting orders to their own satisfaction and convenience. Bragg's difficulties with his cavalry were one indication of this problem, and his infantry corps commanders proved no more trustworthy. When he ordered Polk to move his corps to Chattanooga "without delay," Polk in turn directed his division commanders to remain where they were for the night and to move toward Chattanooga the next day, "as expeditious as you can with convenience."[43] This response hardly complied with the intent of Bragg's order. Hardee's correspondence with Polk on July 1 regarding Bragg's health revealed Hardee as willing to oust his commander if he could obtain his peers' connivance in doing so.

Bragg's superiors in Richmond proved as unreliable and unsupportive of Bragg as did his subordinates, partially because of other military activity. This was indeed, as Bragg had written to Elise, "our darkest hour," not only for Bragg's army, but for the Confederacy. On July 4, as Bragg retreated across the Tennessee River, General Robert E. Lee pulled his defeated Army of Northern Virginia out of Gettysburg, Pennsylvania, and Pemberton surrendered his entire army to General Ulysses S. Grant at Vicksburg, Mississippi.

Richmond's full attention had been focused on these two trouble spots for weeks. In late May one of Bragg's divisions had been sent to Mississippi to support Pemberton, and on June 25, two days after the Tullahoma campaign opened, Davis asked Bragg to reinforce further the armies in Mississippi. Additional evidence of Richmond's lack of attention to Bragg's needs was an order on July 4 from the office of the adjutant general in which an infantry captain was directed to report to Bragg at Tullahoma. Bragg, however, had left Tullahoma four days earlier. Since the telegraph made communications during the Civil War speedier than in ear-

[42] Bragg, Letter Book, July 7, 1863, p. 412, Bragg Papers, Western Reserve; Quintard, *His Story*, p. 87; Cumming, *Kate*, p. 129.

[43] *OR*, XXIII (pt. 2), 900–901.

lier wars, it is almost inconceivable that Richmond could have so
lost contact with one of its major armies that they remained un-
aware of its difficulties for so long.[44]

Despite his errors, his illness, and his lack of support from both
superiors and subordinates, Bragg performed creditably during
the retreat from Tullahoma. One soldier correctly declared that
Bragg had exhibited "masterly skill" in extricating his army from
"the very jaws of destruction." Bragg suffered few casualties, and
his losses in matériel were slight. His opponent's report of captured goods boasted only an undetermined number of small arms,
"3 field pieces, 6 caissons, 3 limbers, 3 rifled seige pieces without
carriages . . . 89 tents, 89 flags, and 3,500 sacks corn and corn
meal."[45] This small booty does not bear out the Union reports of
Confederate panic and disorganization. Throughout this arduous
campaign, under daunting circumstances, Bragg managed to preserve his army and to establish it intact at Chattanooga, more than
could be said for Pemberton, and with far fewer casualties than
Lee, through his poor command decisions (especially Pickett's
Charge), had inflicted upon his own army.

The Union army developed an inflated view of its success.
"Scouts and spies report that the Panic stricken crew didn't even
halt at Chattanooga," wrote a Federal soldier, and he added that
civilians were fleeing the town, "while Bragg is skedaddling, as
fast as possible, southward." "Every day furnishes us proofs of his
terrible scare," Rosecrans told his wife, and predicted only a few
days' detainment while the army rebuilt the railroad bridges.[46]

As it turned out, it took Rosecrans considerably longer than a
few days to repair the railroad and gather supplies. And when he
did move forward in late August, Rosecrans discovered that Bragg
had more bite than he had expected.

[44] *Ibid.*, 849; Davis to Bragg, June 25, 1863 (telegram), Braxton Bragg Papers,
Samuel Richey Confederate Collection, Miami University, Oxford, Ohio; Special
Orders No. 158, Adjutant and Inspector General's Office, July 4, 1863, Bragg
Papers, Western Reserve.
[45] Joshua K. Callaway to My Dear Love, July 7, 1863, Callaway Papers; *OR*,
XXIII (pt. 1), 409.
[46] Todd to Sterling, July 14, 1863, Civil War Collection, Huntington Library;
Rosecrans to My Sweet Wife, July 11, 1863, Rosecrans Papers.

CHAPTER II

Simple fighting would be refreshing recreation

July–August, 1863

B RAGG'S HASTY RETREAT from Tullahoma to Chattanooga left the Union army unable to pursue immediately. Although Rosecrans settled down in Middle Tennessee to await supplies, Bragg had no respite. His administrative duties and his interpersonal relationships during the next six weeks proved nearly as frustrating as his failure in the field.

Within two weeks of his army's arrival in Chattanooga, Bragg seemed to have recovered his fighting spirit, if not his health and his wits. On July 17 he informed General Joseph E. Johnston in Mississippi that he had no orders from Richmond, and furthermore, he did not believe Rosecrans could advance for at least six weeks (a two-week miscalculation, as it turned out). Bragg suggested that he and Johnston concentrate under Johnston's command and hit the Federals at once.[1]

Bragg's proposal was unrealistic. His intention to leave Chattanooga in the hands of his inefficient and unreliable cavalry, strengthened by just a few brigades of infantry, indicates lack of discernment. Aware of the importance of Chattanooga as the gateway to the deep South, Bragg knew President Davis could not approve a plan which left it virtually unprotected. Too, having coordinated the movement of a substantial army over a long distance, Bragg knew his troops could not reach Johnston and be prepared to fight within the five days he proposed for the maneuver. As it was, he had difficulties with supplies and transporta-

---

[1] *OR*, LII (pt. 2), 508.

tion, and his suggesting that such a move was feasible reveals
Bragg's disorientation.[2]

If overly optimistic in his view of strategic possibilities, Bragg
nevertheless managed to cope with the usual routine of army administration. On July 12 he turned his attention to the placement
of supply depots. Should Rosecrans seize the hills beyond the
Tennessee River, Bragg's Chattanooga railroad depot would be
within Federal artillery range. He therefore directed that his main
depot be located beyond this danger at the Chickamauga station.[3]

What Bragg intended to store in this depot was another matter
demanding his attention. He was short of both ammunition and
food. Bragg's chief of subsistence informed him on August 25 that
he could not expect to provide the army with meat past the end of
September. The following day Bragg forwarded the report to the
War Department, noting that the situation injured the morale of
the army and contributed to desertions. The War Department
sent the report on to the commissary general, Colonel Lucius B.
Northrop, an unpopular man considered by many to be a particular favorite of Davis. Northrop returned a scathing reply to
the secretary of war. Addressing Bragg's assertion that soldiers
were deserting because of insufficient food, Northrop charged
that Bragg had "fallen into a delusion." Northrop believed the
true cause of the heavy desertion rate could be attributed to the
fact that many of Bragg's soldiers came from areas known to be
"lukewarm, if not disloyal," and others were from areas now
within Federal control. In conclusion, Northrop could not resist a
sharp dig at Bragg and other western generals. It was "justly supposed that the armies of the west and southwest could hold the
country, which was amply sufficient to subsist them."[4]

Bragg may have been deluded as to its cause, but the problem of

   [2] *Ibid.*; McWhiney, *Bragg*, pp. 384, 388.
   [3] Bragg, Letter Book, vol. 2, July 12, 1863, p. 425, Bragg Papers, Western Reserve.
   [4] *OR*, XXIII (pt. 2), 927; Special Orders No. 189, Headquarters, Army of Tennessee, July 17, 1863, Bragg Papers, Western Reserve; *OR*, XXX (pt. 4), 548–49;
E. J. Warner, *Generals in Gray*, p. 225; *OR*, XXX (pt. 4), 550.

desertion proved very real indeed. A Union staff officer reported a constant stream of deserters from the Army of Tennessee into his lines. "We had yesterday 11 men from one Company of Louisianians come to us," he asserted; "they all say that thousands would come if they dared make the attempt." Northrop's assessment of the cause had been partially correct. Most of Bragg's soldiers were westerners, their homes close by, and as the army retreated, they saw their families falling under Federal control. "Oh God," one soldier cried as the retreat from Tullahoma got under way, "must we leave our homes and our loved ones to the mercy of the ruthless foe again?" Some, unable to ignore the plight of their loved ones, simply left the army to go home.[5]

Some who did not actually desert were not always where they should have been. Bragg repeatedly prodded his subordinates to make prompt and accurate reports of their numbers and to investigate thoroughly and report the circumstances of all absences. He ordered investigation into the exact location of soldiers on extra duty or detached service, complaining of the "frightfully large" details from the army.[6]

A good part of Bragg's forces spent the summer rounding up deserters. In July officers of the Thirty-ninth Alabama went to Pike and Russell counties to arrest deserters from the regiment, and in August a detail from the Twenty-eighth Alabama visited Walker and Blount counties for the same purpose. Bragg ordered Wheeler's cavalry to arrest stragglers and deserters, and part of an escort company scouted the Tennessee River from Chattanooga to the mouth of the Chickamauga, arresting soldiers absent from their commands. Colonel J. M. Hughes of the Twenty-fifth Tennessee Volunteers received permission to track down deserters in Middle Tennessee, and an officer inspected the post at Kelly's

[5] Alfred Lacey Hough, *Soldier in the West: The Civil War Letters of Alfred Lacey Hough* (Philadelphia, 1957), p. 129; D. Coleman Diary, June 30, 1863, Southern Historical Collection.

[6] Bragg, Letter Book, July 15, 24, 1863, pp. 427, 443, Bragg Papers, Western Reserve.

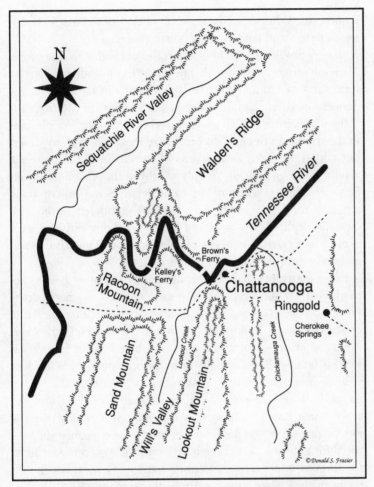

VICINITY OF CHATTANOOGA , TENNESSEE

Ferry to determine how the boats were guarded to prevent deserters from using them to cross the river. Polk detailed part of his
cavalry escort to patrol the banks of the Tennessee River after a
large number of his people deserted during the night of August
16–17. Some deserted before they even reached the army,
prompting General Gideon Pillow, in charge of conscription, to

request that Wheeler send a regiment of cavalry to assist in arresting deserters and conscripts in North Alabama.[7]

Bragg's problems with his soldiers did not end with desertions. Many deserters joined with one another or with civilians to form gangs of marauders. In late July Bragg sent a force across the Tennessee River towards Bersheba Springs to destroy the "bushwhackers & tories" and to protect the property of civilians in the region. Even closer to hand were those who did not desert but raided the fields and gardens of citizens in the area. "Such conduct," Bragg scolded, "is only worthy of the Abolition barbarians. . . . Shall soldiers of the Confederate States imitate these inhuman monsters, and become the base plunderers of the widows and orphans, the aged and helpless?" Apparently so, as it became necessary to send out patrols and provost guards day and night to round up offenders for punishment.[8]

Bragg's attempts to deal with desertions and other lawless activities earned him a reputation in some quarters as a harsh disciplinarian. The execution of Kentuckian Asa Lewis after the Battle of Murfreesboro, despite protests from General John C. Breckinridge and other Kentucky officers, may have laid the foundation for this infamy. Breckinridge's biographer contends this incident created a breach between Bragg and Breckinridge that never mended. Bragg's renown as a disciplinarian spread beyond the army. Nurse Kate Cumming related an incident whereby two majors visiting the hospital jestingly requested some eggnog she prepared for patients. "I told them they must first get an order from the surgeon under whose care they were, as General Bragg . . . might put me *under arrest* for disobedience of orders."[9]

Bragg's repute may have exceeded his deeds. One soldier admit-

[7] Special Orders No. 193, Headquarters, Army of Tennessee, July 21, 1863; Bragg Letter Book, August 14, July 22, August 10, 15, 8, 17, 3, 1863, pp. 498, 440, 486, 502, 480, 504, 460, Bragg Papers, Western Reserve; *OR*, XXX (pt. 4), 502.

[8] Bragg, Letter Book, July 29, 1863, p. 445, Bragg Papers, Western Reserve; *OR*, XXIII (pt. 2), 954.

[9] William C. Davis, *Breckinridge: Statesman, Soldier, Symbol* (Baton Rouge, 1974), pp. 332–33; Cumming, *Kate*, pp. 130–31.

ted that though he had heard of several executions for unbecoming conduct, none had occurred in his brigade, nor had he witnessed any executions. At least twice in July Bragg revoked the sentenced punishment of soldiers, and in August he offered a general amnesty to those absent without leave who returned at once, extending it to include those already under arrest for or convicted of desertion.[10]

Not all considered Bragg's methods harsh, and many regarded highly his abilities as a disciplinarian. In July a soldier, reporting a rumor that Beauregard would replace Bragg as commander of the Army of Tennessee, opined that although Beauregard would end the disasters in the Western theater of the war, the army still needed Bragg for discipline. This soldier firmly believed that Bragg was one of the Confederacy's greatest leaders.[11]

Bragg's strict measures of duty also applied to the military hospitals under his jurisdiction. An inspection in July declared them nearly perfect. The inspector found the clothing, food, medicine, and stores in ample supply and assured Bragg he had every reason to be satisfied with the hospitals. Their fine condition may be attributed in part to Bragg's personal attention; whenever possible, an observer noted, Bragg visited and talked with the patients.[12]

Perhaps Bragg's own health, "anything but good," increased his sensitivity to the needs of his sick soldiers. "Long continued and excessive labor of mind and body," he complained, "have produced its natural result on a frame not robust at best." On July 22 Bragg informed Cooper that if affairs allowed, he planned to spend some time at Ringgold, Georgia, twenty miles away, par-

---

[10] Hannibal Paine to Mary L. Paine (copy), February 24, 1863, Chickamauga National Military Park; Special Orders No. 187, July 15, 1863; Special Orders No. 193, July 21, 1863, Headquarters, Army of Tennessee, Bragg Papers, Western Reserve; *OR*, XXIII (pt. 2), 954–55.

[11] E. John Ellis to Dear Steve, July 10, 1863, E. John, Thomas C. W. Ellis and Family Papers, Louisiana State University Archives, Baton Rouge.

[12] A. J. Foard to Bragg, July 24, 1863, Bragg Papers, Western Reserve; Fannie A. Beers, *Memories: A Record of Personal Experience and Adventure during Four Years of War* (Philadelphia, 1889), p. 89.

taking of the mineral water in an effort to regain a measure of health.[13]

His own health was not Bragg's only source of concern, nor was mineral water the only attraction at Ringgold. Elise, staying near Ringgold, had been ill for some months. Throughout the summer, she convalesced at the cottage of a Dr. and Mrs. Gamble, a local woman reported, "but she was quite too feeble to come into town very often." Elise was recuperating now and wrote to Braxton on July 28, "I continue well but still have those pains in my limbs." She worried more about her husband's health than her own. "I am truly glad to hear you have been allowed to *rest well*— I am more concerned just now about your health than anything else."[14]

Illness had not prevented Elise from keeping abreast of Bragg's military concerns. She reported to her husband, "It is currently believed . . . Rosecrans is only keeping you in check, & may not fight at all." She later commented, "The weather is deliciously cool & fine for the movement of troops," perhaps implying that Bragg himself should make a move.[15]

Elise missed Braxton. "If there is no immediate probability of a battle, can you not come down & see me? or if that is not possible, can I not visit you?" she asked. "You are out of the range of the enemy's guns, & at a very nice place." Bragg opted instead to visit Elise at Cherokee Springs for a few days.[16]

Spending time with Elise at the springs did not free Bragg from army problems, particularly those of the cavalry. On July 30 he reported that Wheeler's units encamped at Cherokee Springs were "doing some harm and no good." Although he gave no particulars, it was typical that the cavalry needed reprimanding. Both Wheeler and Forrest submitted sloppy reports. Bragg reproved Wheeler for "certain inaccuracies," which he listed "in order to prevent the same in future reports." Pointing out that General

---

[13] *OR*, XXIII (pt. 2), 925.
[14] Beers, *Memories* pp. 88–89; Elise to Bragg, July 28, 1863, Braxton Bragg Papers, University of Texas, Austin.
[15] Elise to Bragg, July 28, 1863, Bragg Papers, University of Texas.
[16] *Ibid.*; *OR*, XXIII (pt. 2), 938.

Orders No. 137 detailed the requirements, Bragg asked Wheeler to follow its provisions. However, a month later Wheeler received a similar communication, with another list of his errors. His flagrant disregard for proper reporting prompted Bragg's assistant adjutant general to "enclose a copy of G[eneral] O[rders] No. 137 thinking you may never have received it." Forrest, meanwhile, got scolded for filing no report whatsoever on his unit's loss of arms and ammunition during the retreat from Tullahoma.[17]

The cavalry also displayed other faults. On August 13 General Pillow learned that some of his people encouraged Bragg's soldiers to desert in order to join the cavalry, a more desired branch of service. Bragg advised Pillow to check this evil practice, and he recommended that any officer who knowingly accepted such a volunteer be cashiered. Some cavalry soldiers, on the other hand, apparently did not view their position as any more desirable than that of the infantry; so many were gone from their commands without authority that Bragg ordered them dismounted and reassigned.[18]

As the cavalry spent the summer guarding fords, scouting enemy positions, and driving cattle to feed the army, Bragg kept them under constant supervision. He reminded Wheeler of the importance of knowing the enemy's position and movements. He chided General Philip D. Roddey for not keeping his command in hand and urged Forrest to maintain vigilance. The cavalry's extensive carelessness and dereliction of military duties prompted Elise to hope that "your scouts may prove more attentive, & give you the correct information," but on August 28 General William W. Mackall, Bragg's chief of staff, admitted that "inspection of Wheeler's cavalry shows it worse than even we thought."[19]

[17] *OR*, XXIII (pt. 2), 938; Bragg, Letter Book, July 17, 19, August 13, 1863, pp. 432, 512, 495, Bragg Papers, Western Reserve.
[18] Bragg, Letter Book, August 13, 1863, p. 494, Bragg Papers, Western Reserve; *OR*, XXIII (pt. 2), 956; XXX (pt. 4), 656.
[19] *OR*, XXX (pt. 4), 557; Bragg, Letter Book, July 9, 13, 18, 19, 22, August 14, 17, 18, 1863, pp. 416, 423, 433–35, 440, 502, 505, 508; Special Orders No. 189, Headquarters, Army of Tennessee, July 17, 1863, Bragg Papers, Western Reserve; Elise to Bragg, July 28, 1863, Bragg Papers, University of Texas; *OR*, XXX (pt. 4), 561.

If Bragg was not entirely satisfied with his cavalry commanders, at least one of them returned the feeling. In August Forrest began a campaign for an independent command with which he planned to obstruct the navigation of the Mississippi and to recruit a large force from behind enemy lines. Ten days after submitting his request through channels, Forrest wrote directly to Jefferson Davis. Davis referred the matter back to Bragg, who demurred, insisting that Forrest's unit composed one of the army's greatest assets. Davis accepted Bragg's recommendation. This incident did not endear Bragg and Forrest to one another, and matters would worsen before their relationship ended.[20]

Bragg also had problems with other subordinates. During the summer his relationship with General Buckner deteriorated. Simon B. Buckner had already seen widely varied service. He was forty years old, with a compact, medium build, his gray hair worn long, and "quite active looking." A native of Kentucky, Buckner graduated from West Point in 1844 and then served with the U.S. Army in the Mexican War, on the frontier, and as a teacher at West Point before resigning in 1855 to become a Chicago real estate entrepreneur. When the Civil War began, both the Union and the Confederacy offered him appointments; he accepted the Confederate appointment to brigadier general on September 14, 1861. On February 16, 1862, his superiors, Generals Pillow and John B. Floyd, left Buckner to surrender Fort Donelson while they sneaked off. Promoted to major general on August 16, 1862, Buckner led a division during the Kentucky invasion and at the Battle of Perryville. From December 1862 to April 1863 he fortified Mobile, and from May to July 1863 commanded the Department of East Tennessee.[21]

In late July Davis extended Bragg's command to include Buckner's department, although Buckner continued to report directly

[20] *OR*, XXX (pt. 4), 507–10.
[21] Joab Goodman to My dear Niece, September 28, 1863 (copy), Chickamauga National Military Park; E. J. Warner, *Generals in Gray*, pp. 38–39; Boatner, *Dictionary*, pp. 95–96; Arndt Mathias Stickles, *Simon Bolivar Buckner: Borderland Knight* (Chapel Hill, N.C., 1940).

to Richmond. The ambiguities of this arrangement became more
confusing with Bragg's announcement on August 6 that Buckner's
troops would now constitute the Army of Tennessee's Third
Corps, to be known as Buckner's Corps.[22]

Although Buckner had cheerfully aided Bragg during the
Tullahoma campaign, the vagueness of the orders merging his department with Bragg's caused him to fret about his actual authority. He spent a good deal of time composing long, testy letters
to Bragg and to Richmond. Richmond provided no help. On August 28 the adjutant general's office attempted to clarify its original merger order. "The Department of East Tennessee will be
continued in its former limits so far as the administrative duties of
the command are regarded. In strategic operations it will be subordinate to and a part of the Department of Tennessee." This
merely inspired further letters from Buckner. In late September,
when Buckner and his troops were in Chattanooga, Bragg assigned some of Buckner's soldiers to another officer. "Does administration of the Department of East Tennessee as a department
still exist with me, subject to the orders of General Bragg for
strategic combinations?" Buckner queried Cooper. Cooper's reply
should have left no doubts—"The administration of Department
of East Tennessee does not exist with you so long as you are
beyond the limits of that department and are under the orders of
General Bragg for strategic combinations." Despite the clarity of
this reply, Buckner continued to yammer.[23]

Bragg discovered that he had problems similar to Buckner's.
Although Atlanta was within his department and served as his
primary supply depot, Richmond failed to consult him on the
appointment of Colonel G. W. Lee as city commandant. Bragg
objected to Lee's appointment because, having known him since
the first days of the war, Bragg had been "unable to find his merits." In March Bragg had informed Johnston of Lee's un-

[22] *OR*, XXIII (pt. 2), 924, 954.
[23] *Ibid.*, 962–63; XXX (pt. 4), 561–62, 703; Buckner to Bragg, November 3,
1863; Buckner to Brent, October 20, 1863; Buckner to Cooper, October 31, 1863;
Simon Boliver Buckner Papers, Huntington Library.

savoriness—"without education or character," the man could not sign his own name. While serving with Bragg at Pensacola in 1861, Lee had been arrested on serious charges and then left the army with money intended to purchase clothing for his men.[24]

Colonel Marcellus H. Wright, commanding the forces in Atlanta, agreed with Bragg's assessment of Lee. On July 28 Wright reported that he had retained Lee as commandant of the post, but by August he complained about Lee's flagrant abuses of power, citing as an example the conduct of the railroad guards. "They succeed," he wrote, "pretty well in annoying all respectable travelers and letting all villians pass, the latter always protected by papers." He wished to know from whom Lee received his instructions. "I have tried in vain to learn from him his orders, &c.," Wright complained, "but for the life of me I can get nothing from him." Wright sought permission to relieve Lee from command, "for so long as he has authority to sign passes things will go loose."[25]

This situation further exacerbated Bragg's relations with Richmond. Notifying Davis that Atlanta was in great danger, Bragg protested, "[As I am] forbidden to interfere with arrangements . . . at that place, [it] is my duty to say they are totally inadequate and unreliable." Davis's reproof came immediately, informing Bragg that, although they differed on the choice of the commandant at Atlanta, it remained Bragg's responsibility to protect his own supply depot. About the same time Bragg wrote a lengthy letter to Cooper, grumbling that, as "these arrangements have been made by the War Department without consulting me, and my efforts on two occasions to improve them have been disapproved and my orders countermanded, I feel unwilling to incur the displeasure of the Department again." Bragg then tried to protect himself from future criticism. "I should not be held blameless in case of disaster, though my correspondence will show my en-

[24] J. B. Jones, *A Rebel War Clerk's Diary at the Confederate States Capital*, ed. Howard Swiggett (2 vols., New York, 1935), II, 4; *OR*, XXIII (pt. 2), 924, 656.
[25] *OR*, XXIII (pt. 2), 935; XXX (pt. 4), 520.

deavors to bring about some change." Secretary of War James A. Seddon pointedly reminded Bragg three days later that Lee's retention as commandant did not interfere with Bragg's command, and he expected Bragg to defend Atlanta, regardless of Lee's presence there. In an effort to demonstrate his understanding of his responsibilities and duties, Bragg informed Cooper that before receiving Seddon's reprimand he had already dispatched troops to Atlanta.[26]

In addition to his problems with subordinates and superiors, the newspapers provided another irritant to Bragg. "I am advised that General Rosecrans has the fullest information [on our strategic sites], derived in a great measure from our own newspapers," he lamented. A main culprit was the *Chattanooga Daily Rebel*, a publication highly popular among Bragg's soldiers, edited by Henry Watterson, a former aide to Forrest. Besides revealing Bragg's troop dispositions, Watterson relentlessly attacked Bragg's generalship. The commander's January contretemps with his subordinates over their lack of confidence in his abilities had been prompted by an editorial in the *Rebel*, resulting in Bragg's lasting enmity toward the paper. During the Tullahoma campaign Bragg further exacerbated the situation by imposing a censorship over press coverage of the army's movements. Never having met Bragg, Watterson unwittingly criticized him in person at a tea party. After expressing his opinion on "Bragg's almost supernatural ineptitude," he exchanged some "pointed words" with an officer who defended Bragg, only to discover the officer was Bragg himself.[27] Hostilities between the two men continued throughout the fall.

Frustration with unsympathetic people did not prevent Bragg from working to increase his forces. At times, though, he seemed

[26] *Ibid.*, LII (pt. 2), 511–12; XXIII (pt. 2), 924–25. Although the *OR* tentatively identifies the recipient of Bragg's letter on pages 924–25 as General R. E. Lee, Seddon's reply on page 930 makes it clear that it was sent to Cooper.

[27] *Ibid.*, XXIII (pt. 2), 924; Roy Morris, "That Improbable, Praiseworthy Paper: The *Chattanooga Daily Rebel*," *Civil War Times Illustrated*, XXIII, no. 7 (1984), 18, 21–22.

to argue against his need for more troops. At the end of July Seddon requested some soldiers from Johnston for Bragg. Richmond, however, wanted assurances from Bragg as to how the troops would be used. Asked whether he would attack if he was given Johnston's men, Bragg equivocated. "I should look for success if a fight can be had on equal terms. The difficulties," he cautioned, "in reaching the enemy's position and the time necessary must be considered." Three days later Bragg proved even less disposed to attack, stating, "I feel it would be unsafe to seek the enemy where he now is, in Middle Tennessee." To Johnston, Bragg suggested that after crossing the "rugged and sterile" country and "a river difficult of passage" to reach Rosecrans, "the simple fighting would be refreshing recreation." Bragg did not, however, decline to confront Rosecrans under all circumstances. "Whenever he shall present himself on this side of the mountains," he boasted, "the problem will be changed."[28]

Finally, as Rosecrans advanced, Bragg began to receive reinforcements. As the army expanded, new personalities appeared on the scene. Polk's Corps had only one change in top personnel, Withers being replaced by General Thomas C. Hindman on August 3, while Hardee's Corps underwent several changes.

Hardee left to join Johnston in Mississippi, and General Daniel Harvey Hill took over the corps command. Hill was forty-two years old, a native of South Carolina, and an 1842 graduate of West Point. His antebellum military service, part of which he spent in Bragg's battery, included the Mexican War. When he married Isabella Morrison in 1848, he resigned from the army to teach mathematics. Having joined the Confederates at the start of the war, when he came to Bragg he had already held a variety of positions in the eastern theater. On July 11 he received promotion to lieutenant general and shortly thereafter went to Bragg's army. "Inconspicuous—five feet ten, thin . . . slightly bent from spinal affection and cursed with an odd humor," Hill never minced words. Generous with praise when he thought it merited, he nev-

[28] *OR*, XXIII (pt. 2), 936, 948, 952–53; LII (pt. 2), 514.

SIMPLE FIGHTING WOULD BE REFRESHING RECREATION   41

ertheless freely criticized—"harsh, abrupt, often insulting in the
effort to be sarcastic"—what he perceived as military blunders on
the part of his superiors. On the other hand, Hill had an easy and
informal manner with the soldiers in his command, always willing to expose himself to the same dangers they faced. Although he
and Isabella had nine children, there were frequent conflicts in
their marriage, particularly when Hill volunteered for combat duties. Her fear of his death in battle physically prostrated Isabella,
and she felt great relief when he took an administrative post in
early 1863. Volunteering for field duty in the western armies in
the spring of 1863, Hill lied to Isabella, leading her to believe it
was Davis's doing rather than his own.[29]

Hill enjoyed no better health than Bragg. Sick since childhood,
his condition deteriorated during the war. In early 1863 he wrote,
"I [have] never been free for a single moment [during my twenty
months of war service] from pain and that too, often of the most
excruciating character." His condition declined noticeably when
he became mentally depressed, as he often did over the ill fortunes
of the armies.[30] His temperament, his propensity for criticism,
and his bouts of illness boded ill for relations between himself and
Bragg, particularly on occasions when both men felt sick and
testy.

Hill's replacing Hardee was just one of the changes in the corps.
By the end of August, Hardee retained Patrick Cleburne as division commander, but A. P. Stewart's Division was sent to reinforce Buckner. To replace Stewart, General John C. Breckinridge
returned from Mississippi, where he had been sent as a result of
the feuding in the Army of Tennessee after Murfreesboro. Born in
1821, Breckinridge was forty-two years old, a Kentucky lawyer
and politician. Tall, with a "martial figure . . . and huge, dark,

[29] *OR*, XXIII (pt. 2), 912; XXX (pt. 4), 495; XXIII (pt. 2), 908–9, 918; Douglas
Southall Freeman, *Lee's Lieutenants: A Study in Command* (3 vols., New York, 1943),
I, 20; Robert Garlick Hill Kean, *Inside the Confederate Government: The Diary of
Robert Garlick Hill Kean, Head of the Bureau of War*, ed. Edward Younger (New York,
1957), p. 81; Hal Bridges, *Lee's Maverick General: Daniel Harvey Hill* (New York,
1961), pp. 16, 18, 20, 23, 27, 28–32, 146–47, 149–54, 162, 167, 189, 194, 277.
[30] Bridges, *Lee's Maverick*, p. 162.

drooping mustachios," he married Mary Cyrene Burch in 1843, with whom he had six children. Breckinridge's pre–Civil War military service consisted of six months' occupation duty at Mexico City in 1847–1848. Elected to the U.S. Congress in 1851, he served as Buchanan's vice president from 1856 to 1860, and in the 1860 presidential race he ran against Abraham Lincoln, Stephen Douglas, and John Bell, returning to the U.S. Senate upon losing the presidential election. When Kentucky declared its neutrality, Breckinridge became the leader of the Southern sympathizers in the state, resulting in his ouster as Kentucky's representative in Washington. On November 2, 1861, he received commission as Confederate brigadier general and assignment to command the Kentucky units serving with Albert Sidney Johnston. At Shiloh he commanded a division, received promotion to major general on April 14, 1862, and that summer operated in Mississippi and Louisiana. Upon Bragg's decision to invade Kentucky, Breckinridge reluctantly joined him. In his official report on the battle at Murfreesboro, Bragg questioned not only Breckinridge's command abilities but also the fighting qualities of the Kentucky soldiers. It is not surprising that when Bragg asked his high command what they thought of Bragg's generalship, Breckinridge concurred with his brigade commanders in believing Bragg no longer useful to the Army of Tennessee. Hill, on the other hand, found his new subordinate most congenial, an important factor in Hill's developing anti-Bragg stance.[31]

When Buckner joined Bragg from East Tennessee, he brought more new faces to the Army of Tennessee. Generals A. P. Stewart, William Preston, and Bushrod Rust Johnson commanded the three divisions of Buckner's Corps. Stewart and his division were returning after a brief absence, but the other two division com-

[31] OR, XXX (pt. 4), 578, 547; McWhiney, Bragg, pp. 369, 378; Bridges, Lee's Maverick, p. 199; Lucille Stillwell, John Cabell Breckinridge (Caldwell, Idaho, 1936), pp. 16, 19, 20, 39, 67–68, 77–78, 98, 100–101, 103–4, 109, 110, 111–12, 115, 118, 146–48; Frank H. Heck, Proud Kentuckian, John C. Breckinridge, 1821–1875 (Lexington, Ky., 1976), pp. 22, 107, 111, 112–13; W. C. Davis, Breckinridge, pp. 37, 40, 295, 315, 368.

manders had been away since Murfreesboro. Preston was a forty-seven-year-old Kentuckian, a graduate of Harvard Law School and a practicing lawyer and politician when he became involved in the attempt to have Kentucky secede. Preston saw action in the Mexican War, and when the Civil War began, he joined the staff of his brother-in-law, Albert Sidney Johnston, until Johnston's death at Shiloh. Preston received appointment to brigadier general on April 14, 1862, and served at Corinth, Murfreesboro, and Vicksburg. Johnson was a native of Ohio, forty-six years old, and an 1840 graduate of West Point. After active duty in the Seminole War, the Mexican War, and on the frontier, he resigned from the army in 1847 to teach in Kentucky and Tennessee. His appointment to brigadier general came on January 24, 1862. He escaped Fort Donelson (leaving his division behind), was wounded at Shiloh, and led a brigade in the Kentucky campaign and at Murfreesboro.[32]

John Pegram, a brigadier general of cavalry, also returned to Bragg's army with Buckner. Pegram was a thirty-one-year-old Virginian, and an 1854 graduate of West Point. His army career included frontier duty, service as cavalry instructor at West Point, and the Utah Expedition. Pegram resigned from the U.S. Army on May 19, 1861. In Confederate service, he was captured at Rich Mountain. After his release he served as staff officer for Beauregard and Bragg, and as chief of staff to Kirby Smith during the Kentucky campaign. On November 7, 1862, he received appointment to brigadier general and assignment to command a cavalry brigade, which he led at Murfreesboro.[33]

General Philip D. Roddey, another addition to the cavalry forces, sported brand new brigadier insignia as of August 3, 1863. Officially listed as part of Martin's Division, Roddey often served on detached duty. A thirty-seven-year-old tailor, sheriff, and steamboater from Alabama, Roddey raised a cavalry company in

[32] E. J. Warner, *Generals in Gray*, pp. 157–58, 246; Boatner, *Dictionary*, pp. 437, 668.
[33] E. J. Warner, *Generals in Gray*, pp. 231–32; Boatner, *Dictionary*, pp. 629–30.

1861, serving as its captain. Commissioned colonel in December 1862, he then recruited and organized the Fourth Alabama Cavalry. Sometimes working alone, and sometimes under Wheeler or Forrest, Roddey served primarily in northern Alabama.[34]

As August drew to a close and Rosecrans began advancing, the Army of Tennessee had failed to become a tight unit. Bragg's relations with his subordinates promised little. Of his three corps commanders, only Polk, who had already requested that Davis replace Bragg, had served with him during the retreat from Tullahoma. Hill arrived in July expecting to work well with Bragg but found his initial meeting with his commander unsatisfactory. Buckner continued quarreling with Bragg and with Richmond over the new limits to his authority. Of the new division commanders, Breckinridge awaited a court of inquiry on his conduct at Murfreesboro, and Preston, who had served under Breckinridge, was also a firm anti-Bragg man.[35]

In addition to these quarrels, Bragg had the army poorly positioned to meet the enemy advance. Polk's Corps held Chattanooga, while Hill's stretched along 100 miles of riverfront to Loudon, where Buckner's Corps encamped. General Patton Anderson's Brigade alone covered the area west of Chattanooga from their post at Bridgeport, Alabama.[36]

Bragg also had his cavalry poorly positioned. He believed the real threat would come from a move by Federal general Ambrose Burnside toward Knoxville, despite Anderson's reports of enemy activity to the west of Chattanooga. Supposing that Rosecrans would wait until Burnside took Knoxville and then maneuver for a concentration of their forces, Bragg neglected to cover his left flank. Forrest guarded the river crossings northeast of Chattanooga, while Wheeler, centered in Gadsden, Alabama, proved

[34] E. J. Warner, *Generals in Gray*, p. 262; Boatner, *Dictionary*, p. 706.

[35] *OR*, XXIII (pt. 2), 729–30; Daniel Harvey Hill, "Chickamauga—the Great Battle of the West," in *Battles and Leaders of the Civil War*, ed. Robert Underwood Johnson and Clarence Clough Buel (4 vols., New York, 1956), III, 639; Connelly, *Autumn of Glory*, p. 159.

[36] Connelly, *Autumn of Glory*, pp. 164–65; *OR*, XXIII (pt. 2), 911–12, 913–16, 918, 923, 926, 928, 932, 933–35, 938.

WESTERN THEATER, 1863

too far out of position to control the river west of Chattanooga. Wharton and Martin guarded the river from Chattanooga to Gunter's Landing, while Roddey's brigade covered from that point to Florence. Bragg thus had his cavalry so positioned that it would be impossible for them to discover Rosecrans's route of advance. Troop placements around Chattanooga were so loose and ineffective, in fact, that on August 9 Bragg received a report from the inspector general's office stating, "I traveled from the other side of 'Lookout Mountain' after dark last night into this town without being halted by anyone."[37]

---

[37] Bragg, Letter Book, August 17, July 22, 1863, pp. 505, 440, Bragg Papers, Western Reserve; Connelly, *Autumn of Glory*, p. 163; Special Orders No. 189, Headquarters, Army of Tennessee, July 17, 1863; Bragg, Letter Book, August 10, 1863, p. 484, Bragg Papers, Western Reserve.

On August 21, after several days of rumor and alarm, Rosecrans gave Bragg irrefutable notice of his advance by shelling Chattanooga from across the river. Wavering among possible reactions, Bragg took stock of what the summer had brought him. His army continued to be poorly rationed and supplied; his soldiers continued to desert; Elise was convalescent, and his own health precarious; command problems at Atlanta remained unresolved; newspapers persisted in criticizing; the army had been hastily reinforced with little opportunity to organize and discipline; and, worse, many of those sent to strengthen the army were decidedly anti-Bragg.[38] Although one soldier reported, "The Confidence of our Army is still unshaken in Bragg," another believed the Army of Tennessee was "dissatisfied, badly fed, badly used and disheartened." Hill later attributed the army's mood to Bragg's many retreats, which had destroyed the enthusiasm of the soldiers.[39] In truth, Bragg's only uncontested accomplishment of the summer was the near perfection of his hospitals.

Foremost in his mind as he considered his response to Rosecrans's advance must have been the question of just what he could expect from this disparate collection of jealous, quarreling, subversive subordinates. Discovering the answer made Bragg ill once again.

[38] Thomas Lawrence Connelly and Archer Jones, *The Politics of Command: Factions and Ideas in Confederate Strategy* (Baton Rouge, 1973), pp. xiv, 63. These historians contend that there was a powerful, although informal, anti-Bragg bloc of Confederates established primarily "upon local antipathy for Bragg within the Army of Tennessee." This antipathy was largely, but not only, among the Kentucky officers, who were enraged by the loss of Kentucky and by the charges Bragg made after the campaign that Kentuckians were cowards who would not join his army. In late summer Bragg's three corps commanders were active in this coalition.

[39] Batchelor and Turner, *Letters*, p. 68; Hough, *Soldier in the West*, p. 129; Hill, "Chickamauga," p. 639.

CHAPTER III

The responsibilities weigh heavily upon him

August–September, 1863

THE NEXT FOUR WEEKS found Bragg increasingly disconcerted. As he tried to bring Rosecrans's divided army to battle, disobedience and lack of coordination ran rampant through the upper echelons of the Army of Tennessee. The cavalry's poor performance left Bragg in the dark regarding Federal movements, and although Richmond finally decided to reinforce Bragg from the East, the troops arrived slowly. Meanwhile, Bragg's frustration mounted, and his health declined.

In late August Bragg appeared, to one Texas Ranger, "content to wait there at Chattanooga long enough for the enemy to get supplies and concentrate a force sufficient to come out, attack, and clean up his army"—which is just about what Rosecrans did. Since late July the Federal general had received repeated messages from Washington reminding him of the tremendous political pressure for him to move on Bragg's army. Finally, on August 15, 1863, Rosecrans advanced.[1]

A week later Bragg stumbled into activity, following Rosecrans's shelling of Chattanooga from across the Tennessee River. Bragg had been entirely ignorant of the Federal advance. Such a surprise indicated the inadequacy of the intelligence service as well as Bragg's poor positioning of troops. Bragg had boasted to Hill that he intended to allow Rosecrans to make the first move and then planned to jump on him with the entire Army of Ten-

---

[1] R. M. Collins, *Chapters from the Unwritten History of the War between the States* (St. Louis, 1893), p. 174; Henry W. Halleck to Rosecrans, Washington, D.C., July 24, 25, 1863, Rosecrans Papers.

nessee. But the next day, Bragg was so upset that he informed Davis of the impossibility of saving Chattanooga.[2]

Confusion reigned. Bragg moved his headquarters a mile out of town on August 23, but the army remained in and around Chattanooga for more than a fortnight as Bragg recalled, reshuffled, and rearranged his troops. On August 21 he ordered Hindman to send troops to the west side of Lookout Creek, but the following day they returned; on August 29 Bragg sent him to Chickamauga Bridge, but three days later he returned to Chattanooga, where he remained until the army abandoned the city. Buckner moved in stages from Loudon to Chattanooga between August 21 and September 7, with orders to destroy all the bridges and trestles as he moved over them and to collect whatever stores of subsistence there were. As he traveled, Buckner received conflicting orders: at times Bragg wanted him to attack the enemy, but at other times Bragg ordered him to concentrate with the Army of Tennessee at Chattanooga.[3]

Hill found little in his conflicting orders to improve his dour disposition. Posted near Chickamauga Bridge, he received orders on August 29 to dispose his troops as he thought best, but to be prepared to concentrate with the rest of the army at a moment's notice. In the same dispatch Bragg informed Hill that Wharton's cavalry division was being sent to his front but warned that this unit was the only division from Wheeler's corps fit for duty. The dispatch concluded with a plea: "If you have any influence in Richmond, beg for arms." On August 31 Bragg directed Hill to attack the Federals when they crossed the Tennessee River, but orders the following day called for him to concentrate at Chattanooga.[4]

[2] George William Brent Diary, August 21, 1863, Bragg Papers, Western Reserve (although the diary has been catalogued as the diary of J. Stoddard Johnston, June I. Gow has identified it as Brent's in "The Johnston and Brent Diaries: A Problem of Authorship," *Civil War History*, XIV [1968], 46–50); *OR*, XXX (pt. 4), 531; LII (pt. 2), 517.

[3] Brent Diary, August 23, 24, 30, 31, September 1, 4, 5, 6, 1863, Bragg Papers, Western Reserve.

[4] *OR*, XXX (pt. 4), 563–64; Brent Diary, August 31, September 6, 1863, Bragg Papers, Western Reserve.

Three days later Hill expressed his uneasiness about the delay. Urging Bragg to take the initiative, Hill nevertheless confessed that, not knowing the country, he had too little confidence in his own judgment to offer a specific plan of action.[5]

Hill's own opportunity to take the initiative came the next day. On September 4 he received notice of a Federal corps across the river from his position. "Now is our time to crush the corps opposite," Bragg prodded. "What say you?" Advised to consult with Cleburne, whom Bragg considered "full of resources, and ever alive to a success," Hill received little encouragement from his subordinate. After a delay of a full eighteen hours, Cleburne warned Hill that he had just over 5,000 men, he did not know how the artillery could cross the river, and the men had had little rest. These excuses allowed Hill to forget the attack, and two days later his corps marched safely into Chattanooga.[6]

Meanwhile, Bragg received reinforcements. Between August 27 and 31 Walker's Division arrived from Mississippi, poorly equipped and missing many stragglers. Bragg issued chaotic orders to Walker. After ordering him to support Buckner, Bragg next sent him in the opposite direction. Finally, after dispatching one of his brigades to Rome, Georgia, the remainder, consolidated with Liddell's troops, became Walker's Reserve Corps.[7]

William H. T. Walker was new to corps command. A forty-six-year-old Georgian, he graduated from West Point with Bragg in 1837. On May 25, 1861, he received a brigadier general appointment in the Confederate army but resigned on October 29, probably because of dissatisfaction with his rank, since he immediately accepted appointment to major general of Georgia's state troops. In February 1863 Joseph E. Johnston had him reappointed brigadier general in the Confederate army, and on May 23 his promotion to major general came through.[8]

[5] *OR*, XXX (pt. 4), 588.
[6] *Ibid.*, 594, 601.
[7] Brent Diary, August 27, 28, 31, September 4, 5, 1863, Bragg Papers, Western Reserve.
[8] E. J. Warner, *Generals in Gray*, pp. 323–24; Boatner, *Dictionary*, p. 886.

Walker's Reserve Corps consisted of two divisions commanded by Generals States Rights Gist and St. John R. Liddell. The thirty-two-year-old Gist, a graduate of the Harvard University Law School, was a practicing attorney in his native South Carolina when the war came. At the First Battle of Manassas he acted as volunteer aide to General Bernard E. Bee (who gave Thomas J. Jackson the name "Stonewall"), succeeding to Bee's command upon the latter's death in battle. As brigadier general, Gist served with Johnston in the Vicksburg area until sent to Chattanooga with Walker, under whom he commanded a brigade. With Walker's assignment to corps command, Gist moved up to command the division. Liddell was forty-eight years old, a native of Mississippi who had settled in Louisiana after attending West Point. He was in Bragg's class until expelled after one year for dueling. Liddell's promotion to brigadier general came on July 17, 1862, and he fought as brigade commander at Corinth, Perryville, and Murfreesboro. Chickamauga would be his debut as division commander. Liddell viewed his appointment to Walker's Reserve Corps as a punishment meted out by Bragg for outspokenness at a council of generals in mid-August. Walker, Liddell asserted, was "a crackbrained fire-eater, always captious or cavilling about something[,] whimsical and changeable and hardly reliable. . . . [H]is orders were often destitute of common sense."[9]

Bragg's orders to the cavalry proved as chaotic as those issued to the infantry. Forrest, ordered to picket from Loudon to Chattanooga, soon received instructions to unite with Pegram. Four days later, Bragg directed Forrest to picket from the Hiwassee to Chattanooga, but the following day Bragg ordered the entire command to Chattanooga, where it arrived lacking many who had deserted. On September 3, Forrest, now commanding Pegram's cavalry as well as his own, resumed picketing the river in Buckner's front.[10]

[9] E. J. Warner, *Generals in Gray*, pp. 106–7, 187–88; Boatner, *Dictionary*, pp. 344–45, 482; McWhiney, *Bragg*, p. 10; Liddell, *Record*, pp. 135–37.
[10] Brent Diary, August 25, 27, 31, September 1, 3, 1863, Bragg Papers, Western Reserve.

Wheeler's cavalry corps also raced from position to position. On August 31 Bragg ordered Wheeler from Gadsden, Alabama, where he had been posted on the twenty-first, to Chattanooga to cooperate with Roddey. By September 4 Wheeler had arrived in, and left, Chattanooga, headed for Will's Valley to learn the strength and position of the Federals. Bragg's assistant adjutant general urged Wheeler, "This must be done even at the sacrifice of troops." The staff officer knew his man. Wheeler decided to spend September 4–5 blocking the passes over the mountain to Will's Valley and then discovered he had obstructed it so well that it would require some time to clear it before he could carry out his intelligence assignment. Instead of performing this duty with his main body of troops, he chose instead to send out a small party of scouts. As a capstone to his general disregard of orders, Wheeler reported that the passes down the mountain were so strongly picketed by the enemy that he would have great difficulty in fighting his way down. So much for the stipulation that "this must be done even at the sacrifice of troops."[11]

Bragg, meanwhile, attempted to explain his situation to Richmond. On September 4 he complained to Cooper of his inability to mount an offensive, caused by the lack of subsistence in the area and the subsequent need to cling to his line of communications. Davis queried Bragg closely on his plans for meeting Rosecrans's advance and again urged Bragg to act. But Bragg continued to equivocate, telling Davis he intended to attack Rosecrans but warning, "We are obliged to make great sacrifices and abandon territory." Davis did not choose to press for an advance under such circumstances. "However desirable a movement may be," he lectured, "it is never safe to do more than suggest it to a commanding general, and it would be unwise to order its execution by one who foretold doom."[12]

In truth, the uncertainty of Bragg regarding Rosecrans's move-

[11] *Ibid.*, August 31, September 4, 1863; *OR*, XXX (pt. 4), 602, 614–15.
[12] *OR*, XXX (pt. 4), 2, 21; LII (pt. 2), 521, 522; XXX (pt. 2), 21; XXIII (pt. 2), 953.

ments and intentions made it difficult to respond in an effective manner. On August 22, the day after the Federals first shelled Chattanooga, Colonel George W. Brent, Bragg's assistant adjutant, complained, "Our Scouts bring in but little definite or reliable intelligence. Our Secret Service Corps gives us nothing tangible." And so it continued for days. "Movements of the enemy are still *nubilus* [*sic*]," although it was generally believed Rosecrans intended to effect a junction either in Bragg's front or on his right flank. With a note of rising hysteria and confusion, Brent reported on successive days: "The position of the enemy & his designs unknown"; "Spies & Scouts report that the enemy will cross in force below this point, & will amuse us in our front"; "Enemy reported to have crossed the Tennessee . . . & Rosecrans has crossed his main force at Bridgeport & below." On September 3 Brent reported, with great constraint, "a little restiveness as to the situation of the Army. . . . [T]he enemy . . . disappeared, & altho' a week has elapsed, we have little or no information concerning him."[13]

Bragg's great fear was that Rosecrans would move rapidly around his army and sever the Confederate communications. A spate of telegrams from army headquarters beginning at 2:00 A.M. on September 1 alerted the army to be ready to move. Still, through September 4, no one could tell Bragg whether Rosecrans's activities on Bragg's left flank were a feint or not. Bragg's worst fears were confirmed on September 5 ("the enemy has passed to our left in force"), and indications pointed to an enemy move towards Rome, the loss of which would expose Bragg's line of communications to Federal depredations. The situation became even more critical with communications broken through Knoxville and East Tennessee, occupied now by Burnside.[14]

[13] Brent Diary, August 22, 24, 28, 29, 30, 31, September 1, 2, 3, 1863, Bragg Papers, Western Reserve; *OR*, XXX (pt. 4), 554.
[14] Brent Diary, September 3, 4, 5, 6, 1863; telegrams, Brent to Hill, Liddell, McDonald, and Rice, 2:00 A.M., September 1, 1863; Brent to Polk, Martin, Buckner, Forrest, Wharton, and Roddey, September 1, 1863; Brent to Wharton and Mauldin, September 2, 1863, Bragg Papers, Western Reserve; *OR*, XXX (pt. 4), 566.

Bragg decided to abandon Chattanooga but, as usual, pondered on it a bit before acting. On September 6 he issued orders for the Army of Tennessee to be ready to move, but that same night he suspended them. On the seventh he continued to receive conflicting reports as to Rosecrans's whereabouts and intentions on Bragg's left and rear: Wheeler believed the Federals were there in force, while another officer contradicted him. Yielding to the views of Polk and Hill, Bragg continued to delay the orders for the abandonment of Chattanooga throughout the day.[15]

Although the army remained temporarily in Chattanooga, Bragg ensured Elise's safety. Through August she had stayed with the Gambles near Ringgold, but on September 3 Kate Cumming reported that both Mrs. Gamble and Mrs. Bragg had left the area. She thought this "ominous, as we think the general intends making an important move, and has given them time to get out of the way." Staying now at a cottage in Warm Springs, Georgia, Elise complained of being lonely and homesick. Her greatest worry, though, was for her husband. "As yet there is no battle," she wrote on September 8, "—a probability of there being none for some days— . . . I feel easier for the present & have some respite from anxious fears."[16]

Elise's respite from anxiety did not last long; three days after giving the first order to leave Chattanooga, Bragg's army finally got off, moving south in two columns: Hill, followed by Polk, on the Lafayette Road, and Walker and Buckner on the Summerville Road. "The day was hot & dust was intolerable," Brent reported, but despite the discomfort, another observer found "the army marching in the very best of spirits under the conviction that we are to have a fight." On the road at 6:00 A.M., Bragg headquartered that night and the next on Chickamauga Creek, near Lee and Gordon's Mills. About midnight of September 8–9 he or-

---

[15] Brent Diary, September 7, 1863, *ibid.*
[16] Cumming, *Kate,* p. 136; Elise to Bragg, September 8, 1863, Bragg Papers, University of Texas.

dered a concentration at or near Lafayette, Georgia, but circumstances soon caused him to change his mind.[17]

On September 9, Bragg glimpsed an opportunity to attack
Rosecrans's army in detail. Both armies operated over moun-
tainous terrain, great ranges stretching for miles generally north
and south, with occasional gaps allowing for movement east and
west. "The river & mountains afford a safe and sure screen,"
Brent explained while complaining of the lack of knowledge as to
Rosecrans's whereabouts. Bragg's description was more colorful.
"A mountain is like the wall of a house full of rat-holes. The rat
lies hidden at his hole, ready to pop out when no one is watching." Bragg, however, was watching, and the rat he spied popping
out on the ninth proved to be General George Thomas's Corps.[18]

Using Sand and Lookout mountains as a screen, Rosecrans had
moved his army in three widely separated columns in an effort to
get behind Bragg's army. One column marched southeasterly,
another southwesterly, and Thomas's Corps had taken the middle
route. About twenty-five miles from Chattanooga, one of
Thomas's divisions crossed Lookout Mountain through Steven's
Gap and entered McLemore's Cove. Here the road continued
across the cove and through Pidgeon Mountain at Dug Gap, then
on to Lafayette, a key point in Bragg's line of communications. By
blocking both Steven's and Dug gaps, the Confederates had an
opportunity to trap and destroy Thomas's Corps.[19]

This is precisely what Bragg attempted to do. Suspending the
midnight order to concentrate at Lafayette, he directed Hindman
to move his division into McLemore's Cove. Entering the cove at
the northern end, Hindman would be joined by Cleburne's Division at Davis's Cross Roads. Bragg ordered Hindman to hold

[17] Brent Diary, September 9, 10, 1863; Circular, Headquarters, Army of Tennessee, September 6, 1863, Bragg Papers, Western Reserve; OR, XXX (pt. 2), 71.
[18] Brent Diary, August 24, 1863, Bragg Papers, Western Reserve; Hill,
"Chickamauga," p. 641n.
[19] Emerson Opdycke, "Notes on the Chickamauga Campaign," in Battles and
Leaders, III, 668; Connelly, Autumn of Glory, p. 144. For a full discussion of the
activity at McLemore's Cove, see Connelly, Autumn of Glory, pp. 174–85, and
Glenn Tucker, Chickamauga: Bloody Battle in the West (Dayton, Ohio, 1961),
pp. 60–71.

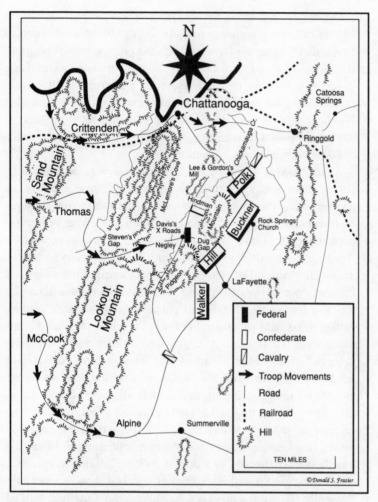

THE CHICKAMAUGA LINE

himself available to act in whatever capacity his seniority entitled
him to. Hill's orders gave him discretionary powers—hence the
question as to Hindman's position—either to send or to take
Cleburne's Division to the crossroads himself.[20]

[20] Brent Diary, September 9, 1863; Kinloch Falconer to Hindman and Hill,
11:45 P.M., September 9, 1863, Bragg Papers, Western Reserve.

On the morning of September 10 Bragg's trap developed hitches before it even began to snap closed. Hill belatedly notified Bragg that Cleburne's Division, because of its scattered position, the illness of its commander, and the obstructions in Dug Gap, would not be able to cooperate with Hindman. Hill recommended that Bragg suspend the movement, but Bragg notified Hindman at 8:00 A.M. that instead of Cleburne or Hill, Buckner would join him. His seniority over Buckner made the command, and the responsibilities, Hindman's.[21]

As the ranking officer in this crucial military action, Hindman fell far short of ideal. A thirty-five-year-old Tennessee lawyer, he had served in the Mexican War and as Arkansas's congressional representative from 1858 to 1860. Appointed brigadier general on September 28, 1861, Hindman advanced to major general on April 14, 1862. After seeing action at Shiloh, he commanded the Trans-Mississippi Department for one month, then fought at Prairie Grove in December 1862. Hindman cut quite a figure: he was five feet one inch tall and partial to close-fitting clothing, ruffled shirts, and patent-leather boots. The men of his new command were not impressed. "All I have to fear now is our new general," wrote soldier Thomas Hall. "Hindman has proven himself to be a regular low life rowdy by what he done the other night. Our division was on the march until about two o'clock in the night. When we halted Gen. Hindman found Polk's staff camped on the spot where he had picked and he went up and roused them calling them a set of 'unprincipled curs.' To say the least he was challenged to a duel, which he did not accept."[22]

The next two days highlighted Hindman's incompetence and cowardice. He moved quickly into McLemore's Cove but stopped within four miles of his destination, spending the rest of the day pondering the communications he received and planning his route

[21] Brent Diary, September 10, 1863; Brent to Buckner and Hindman, 8:00 A.M., September 10, 1863, *ibid*.
[22] E. J. Warner, *Generals in Gray*, pp. 137–38; Boatner, *Dictionary*, p. 402; Charles T. Jones, Jr., "Five Confederates: The Sons of Bolling Hall in the Civil War," *Alabama Historical Quarterly*, XXIV (1962), 179.

of retreat. When Buckner arrived in the late afternoon, Hindman
ordered him to bivouac where his troops could secure a second
route of retreat. That evening Hindman received two orders from
army headquarters to move forward. At 6:00 P.M. Bragg urged,
"It is highly important that you should finish the movement now
going on as rapidly as possible," and at 7:30 P.M. he prodded,
"The enemy is now divided. . . . It is important now to move
vigorously and crush him."[23] But Hindman declined to fight.

The night of September 10–11 saw further deterioration of
Bragg's plans to defeat Rosecrans piecemeal. A council of his subordinates, convened by Hindman, unanimously agreed to disobey
Bragg's orders. Enumerating a number of remote and conflicting
possibilities, the council concluded that an advance would be hazardous and chose to maintain their safer position. After the meeting Hindman dispatched an unsavory staff officer who spoke poor
English, with whom Bragg had already quarreled, to request a
modification of his orders. Upon hearing the officer's garbled account, and ascertaining that Hindman had based his suggestions
upon unreliable information, Bragg again ordered Hindman to
attack early in the morning. Bragg later confessed that during this
conference he was so "greatly vexed" that his staff accused him of
speaking harshly.[24]

Bragg's plan required that Hindman be at Davis's Cross Roads
before Hill attacked the Federals through Dug Gap. Believing the
enemy to be approaching the gap, Bragg hoped to block the line of
retreat through McLemore's Cove, thus trapping the Federals between Hindman and Hill and destroying them completely. The
sound of Hindman's guns would be the signal for Hill's advance.
Bragg left Hindman no doubts as to his expectations—Hindman
was "to attack the enemy [even] if he lost his command in carrying

[23] OR, XXX (pt. 2), 292–93, 301; Brent Diary, September 10, 1863, Bragg Papers, Western Reserve.
[24] OR, XXX (pt. 2), 29, 294; Connelly, Autumn of Glory, p. 181; William T.
Martin to Bragg, August 13, 1867, William T. Martin Letters, University of
Texas; Bragg to E. T. Sykes, February 8, 1873 (copy), Leonidas Polk Papers, University of the South, Sewanee, Tennessee.

out the order." Somehow, though, Hindman convinced himself
that Bragg "considered my position a perilous one, and therefore
expected me not to capture the enemy, but to prevent the capture
of my own troops."[25]

The following day proved one of the most frustrating of Bragg's
career. Proceeding to Dug Gap at daylight on September 11,
Bragg spent the day anxiously awaiting the attack by Hindman's
column. He dispatched several couriers and two staff officers at
various times throughout the day urging Hindman "to move with
promptness and vigor," but to no avail. "His impatience at not
hearing Hindman's guns," reported one observer, "was manifested
by his restless walking back and forth on the top of the hill overlooking the enemy in the Cove, and occasionally he would stop
and irritably dig his spurs in the ground."[26]

Hindman, meanwhile, cowered in the cove. At 2:00 P.M.,
Bragg ordered Colonel Taylor Beatty to find Hindman and insist
that he attack, but upon arriving at Hindman's position, Beatty
found the general had already made preparations for a withdrawal. Before he could begin his retreat, however, Hindman received reports that the enemy was swiftly withdrawing from
McLemore's Cove through Steven's Gap. Thus assured that an advance posed little danger, Hindman immediately ordered his line
to move forward as rapidly as possible but called off the ineffectual pursuit about dark. Patton Anderson later asserted that his
division only regretted "the failure of the enemy to stand and confront them."[27] The Federals had, in fact, waited nearly the entire
day, but Hindman had chosen not to confront them.

Bragg passed this unhappy day with Hill's Corps, which held
itself in readiness to attack as soon as Hindman's guns announced
his movement under way. Wanting to bag all of the Federals in the

[25] OR, XXX (pt. 2), 29, 294, 295; David Urquhart, Statement, Headquarters,
Army of Tennessee, November 21, 1863, Bragg Papers, Western Reserve.
[26] OR, XXX (pt. 2), 295; Irving A. Buck, Cleburne and His Command, ed.
Thomas Robson Hay (Jackson, Tenn., 1959), p. 120.
[27] Taylor Beatty Diary, September 11, 1863, Southern Historical Collection;
OR, XXX (pt. 2), 296, 317.

cove and having amassed a superiority of numbers with which to do so, Bragg felt reluctant to begin an advance from Hill's position. He feared the enemy would take alarm and withdraw through Steven's Gap before Hindman was in position, thus rendering the victory "less decisive than intended to be." As it happened, the Federals took alarm anyway and adroitly removed themselves from danger, thanks largely to Hindman's procrastination. "Hill's Corps," one Confederate reported, "was in ecstasies of grief. Men and officers swore, some were almost in tears, many were in despair"—an accurate reflection of Bragg's mood. A cavalry officer described Bragg as "indignant & excited," expressing "in the most emphatic manner . . . [his] disappointment." He also recalled that when Hindman and Buckner arrived, Bragg's greeting was "by no means cordial."[28]

Many blamed Hindman for the unconscionable failure at McLemore's Cove. Beatty believed "prompt obedience was all that was wanted to insure success. . . . We can never get a better chance & perhaps never again one as good." Two days after the affair, Brent reported complaints throughout the army about Hindman's delay in attacking. General William B. Bate told Bragg in 1867 that he and others thought "the campaign immediately preceding the movement into McLemore's Cove *which ought to have been* its culmination was one of, if not, the best military schemes of the war." General Arthur Manigault wrote, "The opportunity for [Hindman] distinguishing himself and striking a terrible blow was favorable in the extreme," but, he asserted, Hindman "was not up to the work, it being far beyond his capacity as a general."[29]

Although Manigault later contended that Bragg never forgave Hindman, Bragg did in fact appear to exonerate Hindman when he dropped the charges of disobedience filed against him on Sep-

[28] Buck, *Cleburne*, pp. 120–22; Martin to Bragg, August 13, 1867, Bragg Papers, University of Texas.
[29] Beatty Diary, September 11, 13, 1863, Southern Historical Collection; William B. Bate to Bragg, September 29, 1867, Bragg Papers, Western Reserve; Manigault, *A Carolinian*, p. 93.

tember 29. In a letter to Jefferson Davis on November 15, Bragg explained that "the necessity for uniform discipline prevented me overlooking the [McLemore's Cove] affair," and he assured Davis that Hindman "possesses my fullest confidence as a most gallant soldier and excellent disciplinarian," very high praise indeed from Bragg. Nevertheless, Bragg's later efforts to defend his own reputation over McLemore's Cove led him once again to blame Hindman.[30]

Although Beatty believed "Rosecrans was completely outgeneralled," others proved less kind to Bragg. Hill blamed Bragg's "lack of knowledge of the situation" and "lack of personal supervision of the execution of his orders" for the McLemore's Cove debacle. Bragg's "want of definite and precise information had led . . . him more than once to issue 'impossible' orders," Hill maintained, and "those intrusted with their execution got in the way of disregarding them."[31] Hill thus condoned the deliberate disobedience of subordinates.

Historians have also criticized Bragg. Connelly contended that Bragg failed to give positive orders and "entrusted an important task to a subordinate whose judgment was questionable." Bragg remained within eight miles of Hindman's position throughout the day but gave no indication that he ever considered personally directing the attack. At the crucial moment courage gave way to indecision and cowardice throughout the upper echelons of the Army of Tennessee.[32]

Bragg's hesitation and lack of confidence at McLemore's Cove may be ascribed in large part to the unreliable information provided by his badly scattered and uncoordinated cavalry. Forrest and Wheeler had ridden continually about the countryside. "This constant moving about without an object," complained Brent, "can accomplish nothing"—which is exactly what the

[30] Manigault, *A Carolinian*, p. 94; *OR*, XXX (pt. 2), 298, 310–11; Bate to Bragg, September 29, 1867, Bragg Papers, Western Reserve.
[31] Beatty Diary, September 22, 1863; Hill, "Chickamauga," pp. 641, 646.
[32] Purdue and Purdue, *Cleburne*, p. 214; Connelly, *Autumn of Glory*, p. 184.

cavalry did. On September 11, even as Hindman cowered in McLemore's Cove, Bragg's staff complained of the cavalry's conflicting reports on the strength and position of the enemy.[33]

The one thing Bragg knew for certain on September 12 was the location of General Thomas L. Crittenden's Corps, so he turned his attention there. Having lost the opportunity to trap a division of Thomas's Corps, as well as the knowledge of its position and movements, and never having been sure at all of General Alexander M. McCook's whereabouts and intentions, Bragg decided to go for the enemy he could find. At 8:30 A.M. Bragg ordered Polk to take position at Rock Spring in preparation for a move against Crittenden. That evening Bragg informed Polk there existed "a fine opportunity of striking Crittenden in detail" and ordered him to "attack at day-dawn tomorrow." At 12:30 A.M. on September 13 Bragg again instructed Polk, "It is highly important that your attack in the morning should be quick and decided. Let no time be lost."[34]

Clear and peremptory though his orders were, Polk failed to obey them. At 8:00 P.M. on September 12, Polk informed Bragg he needed additional forces and that he could not have his troops in position by dawn. However, he assured his commander, "If I find he is not going to attack me I will attack him without delay." Bragg sent Buckner's troops in support and rode to Polk's headquarters himself early on the thirteenth, only to find that no battle line had yet been formed. At 7:00 A.M., some time after the stipulated "day-dawn," Polk sent a circular through his corps stating that the attack would be made "so soon as the division commanders are ready for it." Finally, after 8:30 A.M., Polk ordered brigades forward on three roads, "in order to develop the enemy."[35] The enemy, however, was no longer there to be developed; alerted

[33] Brent Diary, September 10, 11, 1863; Brent to Wheeler, 10:30 A.M., September 10, 1863, Bragg Papers, Western Reserve.
[34] Brent to Polk, 8:30 A.M., 8:00 P.M., 6:00 P.M., September 12, 1863, Bragg Papers, Western Reserve; *OR*, XXX (pt. 2), 30.
[35] *OR*, XXX (pt. 2), 45; Brent Diary, September 13, 1863, Bragg Papers, Western Reserve; *OR*, XXX (pt. 4), 645.

to his exposed position, Crittenden had withdrawn. Once again, a disobedient subordinate frustrated Bragg's plans.

As with Hindman's excuses at McLemore's Cove, explanations for Polk's dilatoriness actually clarified little. Polk himself reported that "Crittenden's whole Corps was in his front advancing with steady step to attack him." Consulting with his subordinates, Polk "determined to await the enemys [sic] attack . . . and when he did move the bird had flown." Polk's son, on the other hand, maintains the bird had flown the evening of September 12 and blamed Bragg for not ordering the attack that morning. He fails to explain how Bragg could be informed of the enemy's retirement when the general on the scene reported the enemy to be "advancing with steady step," or how the attack could possibly have been made a day earlier, when his father was not ready to attack at the stipulated time on the thirteenth. The fact is, once again a council of his subordinates had determined to disobey Bragg's orders. Commenting on the lack of "zealous cooperation" on the part of Bragg's subordinates, Liddell declared, "If he had caused one or two of us to be shot, I firmly believe the balance would have done better."[36]

Bragg's opportunities to defeat Rosecrans's army in detail lasted another few days—days that Bragg frittered away. "The truth is," Hill explained, "General Bragg was bewildered by 'the popping out of the rats from so many holes.'"[37] Bragg did indeed appear too confounded by the widely separated points of contact between the armies to decide where to attack next.

Rosecrans used the respite offered by Bragg's indecision to concentrate his forces. His decision to disperse his army had been based upon the arrogant assumption that Bragg would flee Chattanooga as he had Tullahoma. "I don't suppose that we will stop," one of Rosecrans's soldiers boasted, "until we drive old Bragg into

[36] Brent Diary, September 14, 1863, Bragg Papers, Western Reserve; W. M. Polk, "General Polk at Chickamauga," in *Battles and Leaders*, III, 663; Liddell, *Record*, p. 114.
[37] Hill, "Chickamauga," p. 644.

the Ocean for when Old Rosey gets started he never stops while there is a rebel within reach." Faced now with evidence that Bragg's retreat from Chattanooga was not the panicked flight he had imagined, Rosecrans recalled his far-flung army corps. "Our army is fearfully scattered," a Federal private reported. "If Bragg should attack us now, he could whip us in detail. . . . If he will keep his hands off for a few days, we will be in better condition to cope with him."[38]

Bragg obliged. On September 14 he maintained his headquarters at Lafayette, but Brent believed, "We cannot stay here much longer, we must beat the enemy or get back to our communications." Bragg believed likewise. After a meeting with his corps commanders the next morning, he notified Cooper: "The Enemy has retired before us at all points. We shall now turn on him in the direction of Chattanooga." Although Bragg's corps commanders were reportedly unanimous in their approval of his decision, his staff was not. "A bad plan," Brent complained. "Something better and more promising of success might have been devised." Bragg also seemed in no hurry to carry out his plan, as two days passed before the Army of Tennessee turned toward Chattanooga.[39]

Bragg's army, meanwhile, began receiving additional reinforcements. "Troops from Virginia for this Army are said to have arrived at Atlanta," Brent noted on September 13. "No official intelligence of this unexpected aid has reached us from Richmond." There may have been no official notification, but the arrival of the eastern soldiers seemed to be common knowledge. Kate Cumming observed the passage of the Virginia troops, and

[38] William Pyle to Dear Uncle, September 16, 1863, Bragg Papers, Western Reserve; Opdycke, "Notes on Chickamauga," p. 669; Private Smith, *Private Smith's Journal: Recollections of the Late War*, ed. Clyde C. Walton (Chicago, 1963), p. 89.
[39] Brent Diary, September 14, 10, 13, 15, 1863, Bragg Papers, Western Reserve; Bragg to Cooper, September 15, 1863 (telegram), Braxton Bragg Letters, Duke University Library; Special Orders No. 245, September 16, 1863; Brent to Wheeler, Walker, Polk, Buckner, and Hill, September 17, 1863 (dispatches), Bragg Papers, Western Reserve.

even the Federals were aware of the reinforcements. One Union soldier wrote to a friend on September 16, "It is said that the rebels are being strongly reinforced from Richmond," and to a cousin he sent more particulars: "They have brought Longstreet's Corps from Richmond." By the sixteenth, Brent reported the Virginia soldiers arriving on the field, but, he believed, "They come after the damage has been done, a lock and key on the stable door after the horse has been stolen—such has been the action of Jeff Davis in the Western Campaign, always too late."[40]

Opinions on Bragg's intentions and abilities to use these reinforcements in battle ranged widely. "Gen'l Bragg may get us out 'right side up with care' but we have our doubts," wrote a Confederate soldier. "Bragg promises to give battle," a newspaper editor announced, "but we do not forget that generalship may paralyze the greatest bravery and render abortive the most strenuous exertion." From Richmond, Josiah Gorgas complained, "Bragg has shown his usual readiness for retreating and has *retreated* us out of the whole of East Tennessee." Shortly after the evacuation of Chattanooga, a soldier feared, "If . . . Bragg is maneuvering, then we will not be surprised to wake up one of these September mornings and find the entire Army at or near Atlanta instead of Nashville as we all so much desired."[41]

Others seemed certain there would be a battle, but did not agree on the victor. Federal soldier William Pyle believed the Confederates would make a desperate effort to recover their lost territory, but he assured his correspondent, "You need not fear for the result. Old Rosey commands an army that have never been defeated." Kate Cumming found Southerners had as much confidence in Bragg as Pyle had in Rosecrans. Reporting on the rein-

[40] Brent Diary, September 13, 16, 1863, Bragg Papers, Western Reserve; Cumming, *Kate*, p. 142; William Pyle to My Dear Friend, and to Dear Cousin, September 16, 1863, Bragg Papers, Western Reserve.

[41] Heartsill, *Journal*, pp. 149, 147; *Daily Richmond Whig*, September 21, 1863; Josiah Gorgas, *The Civil War Diary of General Josiah Gorgas*, ed. Frank E. Vandiver (University, Ala., 1947), p. 62. See also Benjamin M. Seaton, *The Bugle Softly Blows*, ed. Harold B. Simpson (Waco, Tex., 1965), p. 39.

forcements from Virginia, she noted, "Many are now predicting great things, saying that all [Bragg] needed was plenty of men, which he has never had." One of Bragg's officers believed the army, not Bragg, would achieve the victory. "I think we shall gain a decisive victory," he boasted to his wife. "The spirit of the men is good, & they know the importance of the conflict." The newspaper editor who had questioned Bragg's abilities had no such doubts about the soldiers of the Army of Tennessee: "We have every confidence that the men under [Bragg], if given fair play, will win a great victory, a victory so overwhelming and complete as to redeem all the disasters we have sustained in the West."[42]

Elise, in another context, had little confidence in her husband. Her concern about where to spend the winter caused her "serious uneasiness," as "your pay will not suffice to give us [herself and a slave] food & lodging." As a solution, she suggested, "You will have to consent to my becoming a *matron* of some hospital."[43]

Such were conditions on the eve of Bragg's greatest victory—his wife fretful, his soldiers deserting, and his subordinates colluding to disobey his orders. Recent events could not have been more discouraging, or less indicative of the triumph that lay just ahead. "Genl Bragg seems sick and feeble," one is not surprised to learn. "The responsibilities of his trust weigh heavily upon him."[44]

[42] Pyle to Dear Cousin, September 16, 1863, Bragg Papers, Western Reserve; Cumming, *Kate*, p. 142; Ellison Capers to his wife, September 4, 1863, Ellison Capers Papers, Duke University Library; *Daily Richmond Whig*, September 21, 1863.
[43] Elise to Bragg, September 8, 1863, Bragg Papers, Western Reserve.
[44] Brent Diary, September 15, 1863, *ibid*.

CHAPTER IV

More than he has bargin fer

September 18–23, 1863

IN AUGUST 1863 a prescient Confederate soldier confided to his diary, "If he [Rosecrans] dont watch and be vary
causishious in going through them mountains he will jump up
Bragg and his army and then he will take the back track and perhaps may git a good thrashing and that is more than he has bargin
fer I gess." This entry accurately foretold the events of September
1863. Belatedly recognizing his error in separating his army,
Rosecrans ordered his scattered corps to unite at Lee and Gordon's Mills on Chickamauga Creek. As he did so, he did indeed
"jump up Bragg and his army," and he did indeed "git a good
thrashing."[1]

Bragg decided to respond to Rosecrans's consolidation by taking
the offensive and interposing his army between Chattanooga and
the Federals. He advanced northward on the east side of Chickamauga Creek, determined to cross it north of Lee and Gordon's
Mills. Here he would occupy the road to Chattanooga and drive
back the Union left, hoping to destroy Rosecrans's army before it
could recross the Tennessee River.

On September 18 the forces on Bragg's right, instructed to
cross to the west side of Chickamauga Creek, met resistance. This
delayed them all day, and it was late before the first troops crossed
and advanced southward. Minimal movement took place on the
Confederate left, also. Here the soldiers pressed forward to a
point opposite Gordon's Mill where they found the Federals

---

[1] Seaton, *Bugle Softly Blows*, p. 37. For a full discussion of the Battle of Chickamauga, see Connelly, *Autumn of Glory*, pp. 193–229; Tucker, *Chickamauga*.

firmly established on a commanding wood-covered hill, while they themselves contended with open fields and low ground.[2]

As night fell, Bragg considered his options, and at 7:30 P.M. issued the next day's orders. Planning to pivot on his left while pressing forward with his right, he hoped to force Rosecrans back into McLemore's Cove (from which Thomas's Corps had been allowed to escape) in another attempt to destroy the Federal army. As things stood when Bragg issued these orders, he had a fair chance of achieving his objective. The Federal army, still pulling itself together, continued to be seriously overlapped by the Confederate right. During the night and early morning, however, Thomas extended the Union left far beyond the Confederate right, outflanking Bragg's army by two miles. This move secured the road to Chattanooga for the Federals, a detail Bragg had neglected in his confidence that the Federal line did not, and could not, extend beyond his own. Bragg's ignorance of this disposition of Rosecrans's forces may be partially attributed to the terrain of the area, a broken tangle of barely penetrable forest and underbrush, cutting visibility to just a few yards.[3]

Bragg spent the morning of September 19 on the field, after first moving his headquarters from Leet's Tanyard to Thedford's Ford. Preston, located near the middle of the Confederate line, sighted Bragg conferring with General John Bell Hood, newly arrived from the East, and Buckner near his position on the west side of the Chickamauga before 8:00 A.M., and by 9:00 A.M. Bragg arrived at Walker's position near the right flank of the army.

[2] *OR*, XXX (pt. 2), 46, 140, 239, 357, 451–52, 520, 524; Connelly, *Autumn of Glory*, p. 199; Richard M. McMurry, *John Bell Hood and the War for Southern Independence* (Lexington, Ky., 1982), pp. 33, 123; Brent to Walker, September 18, 1863, Bragg Papers, Western Reserve.

[3] Parks, p. 331; Herman Hattaway and Archer Jones, *How the North Won: A Military History of the Civil War* (Chicago, 1983), p. 450; Archer Anderson, "Address of Col. Archer Anderson on the Campaign and Battle of Chickamauga," *Southern Historical Society Papers*, IX (1881), 403–4; William M. Lamers, *The Edge of Glory: A Biography of General William S. Rosecrans, U.S.A.* (New York, 1961), p. 324; Stephen Z. Starr, *The Union Cavalry in the Civil War* (3 vols., Baton Rouge, 1985), III, 275.

When Forrest encountered the first fighting of the day on the extreme right, Bragg personally directed Walker to attack in support.[4]

As the day progressed, Bragg realized the Federals were not where he thought they should be, and his usual stress-induced pessimism took hold. About noon, he ordered Stewart, who formed the right of Buckner's Corps, to move to the right and rear, where firing had begun. Seeing Bragg nearby, Stewart approached him in an effort to get more specific instructions. Hardly inspiring confidence, Bragg informed Stewart that Walker, engaged on the right, "was much cut up, and the enemy threatening to turn his flank; that General Polk was [now] in command on that wing, and that I must be governed by circumstances."[5]

Following this brief conference, Stewart found himself on his own for the rest of the day. Moving in the direction indicated, Stewart searched for Polk but failed to find him—nor did anyone else seem to know where he was, including one of Polk's staff, who came searching for him. In fact, Stewart claimed, "After leaving General Bragg . . . I saw no officer whose rank was superior to my own for the rest of the day." Despite the lack of direction, Stewart pierced the Federal line near its center, and for a time held the Chattanooga Road before being pushed back across the road.[6]

This lack of direction was typical of the confusion that reigned during the battle. Until Stewart's Division moved to the right, a gap existed near the middle of the Confederate line between Cheatham and Hood which, fortunately, the Federals failed to exploit. Polk, in command on the Confederate left during the morning, later received orders to assume command on the right. Hill, too, moved to support the right flank. Adding to the con-

[4] Brent Diary, September 19, 1863, Bragg Papers, Western Reserve; *OR*, XXX (pt. 2), 413, 240.
[5] *OR*, XXX (pt. 2), 361.
[6] *Ibid*, 361, 363; Glenn Tucker, *The Battle of Chickamauga* (Harrisburg, Pa., 1981), p. 25.

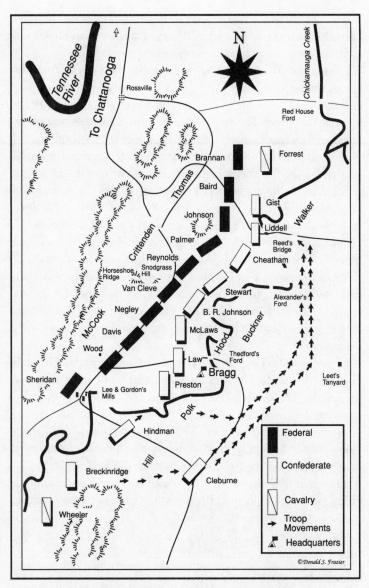

BATTLE OF CHICKAMAUGA, September 19, 1863

fusion of shifting troops, during the night General Evander McIvor Law had arrived with additional brigades from Hood's old division, prompting another reorganization of troops.[7]

During the afternoon Bragg continued to shift troops from the left to the right in an effort to gain the upper hand. Informing Hill that the right wing of the army had been driven back, Bragg ordered Cleburne's Division to the extreme right. Because of the distance they had to march, the division was not in position until after sundown, but then, Hill boasted, they advanced magnificently, driving the enemy about three-fourths of a mile.[8]

Because of Bragg's personal direction on the battlefield and his judicious shifting of units, the army not only maintained its ground but at some points had even "gained handsomely." "Night," Bragg boasted, "found us masters of the ground, after a series of very obstinate contests with largely superior numbers."[9]

Superior enemy numbers did not hold true on September 20, for during the night the long-awaited General James Longstreet arrived from Virginia with most of the remainder of the soldiers sent from the East, giving Bragg a rare superiority of forces over his opponent.[10]

In addition to Longstreet's arrival at Chickamauga, Generals Gist and Joseph B. Kershaw marched that night from Ringgold to join the battle. Kershaw, a dependable officer, commanded Lafayette McLaws's Division, a post he held until McLaws arrived on the field on September 21. Kershaw arrived on the field about 1:00 A.M. on the twentieth. Gist did not reach the battlefield until nearly sunrise on the twentieth, after marching all night.[11]

The night of September 19 witnessed another of the communication failures that plagued Bragg. At the close of the day's battle,

---

[7] *OR*, XXX (pt. 2), 32, 453.

[8] *Ibid.*, 140.

[9] Bragg, "Memorandum on the Battle of Chickamauga," n.d., Bragg Papers, Western Reserve; *OR*, XXX (pt. 2), 32.

[10] Grady McWhiney and Perry D. Jamieson, *Attack and Die: Civil War Military Tactics and the Southern Heritage* (University, Ala., 1982), p. 8.

[11] E. J. Warner, *Generals in Gray*, p. 171; *OR*, XXX (pt. 2), 503, 245.

Bragg summoned the ranking officers to his headquarters, where he issued orders for the next morning.[12] Not all of the commanders were present, however, as Longstreet did not arrive until 11:00 P.M., and Hill never did see Bragg that night.

At this meeting, Bragg reorganized and divided his army into two wings, with Forrest and Wheeler protecting the flanks. Polk continued to command on the Confederate right, with Hill and Walker under him; Longstreet, on the left, commanded the units from Virginia, as well as three of Bragg's divisions.[13] Adding to the confusion, Longstreet's orders placed him in command of an entire army wing, in the middle of a battle certain to reerupt early in the morning, on unfamiliar and difficult terrain that he had not (and, in the dark, could not have) familiarized himself with.

A further breakdown in communication occurred during the night. About midnight, Hill received the information that his corps had been placed under Polk's command and that Polk needed to see him at his headquarters at Alexander's Bridge. Hill chose to rest for three hours before making the three-mile ride to Polk's headquarters. What happened then is anyone's guess. Hill claimed he looked for Polk until nearly daylight. Polk insisted he had posted guides, but Hill never appeared. Depositions were taken, proofs were offered, and arguments have raged for more than a century, but what emerges is that neither Polk nor Hill bothered to see to the prompt and proper dissemination and discharge of Bragg's orders.[14] And Bragg's decision to place Hill under Polk's command, rather than assign him to a comparable position of authority, merely exacerbated Hill's tendency to insubordination.

Bragg's entire plan of battle hinged on Polk's attack on the Confederate right. He directed Polk "to assail the enemy on our extreme right at day-dawn"—before 6:00 A.M.—"and to take up the attack in succession rapidly to the left." He instructed Long-

[12] OR, XXX (pt. 2), 33.
[13] Ibid.; Brent Diary, September 20, 1863, Bragg Papers, Western Reserve.
[14] OR, XXX (pt. 2), 140–41. For a full discussion of this incident, see Connelly, Autumn of Glory, pp. 211–16.

street to wait for the attack on the right, and then to "take it up promptly," pushing his whole line "vigorously and persistently against the enemy throughout its extent."[15]

Subordinates' lack of attention to duty led to the usual delays on September 20. Despite all previous experience, Bragg expected the attack to take place as ordered. "Before the dawn of day," he reported, "myself and staff were ready for the saddle. . . . With increasing anxiety and disappointment I waited until after sunrise without hearing a gun, and at length dispatched a staff officer to . . . Polk to ascertain the cause of the delay and urge him to a prompt and speedy movement." The staff officer, Major Pollock B. Lee, informed Bragg that he found Polk at his headquarters two miles from his line of troops at 7:00 A.M., sitting in a rocking chair reading a newspaper. Lee contended that Polk "was much surprised" that the attack had not been made, and "he proposed to go soon and ascertain the trouble." Polk, in an explanation of the delay that morning, unintentionally implied that he was, in fact, loitering about his headquarters. "Hearing nothing of the attack," he wrote, "I sent staff officers in haste . . . to Generals Breckinridge and Cleburne, with information that . . . Hill could not be found, and with orders to attack at once." This appears to be a reference to orders Polk issued at 5:30 A.M., received by Breckinridge and Cleburne nearly two hours later, which directed them to "move upon and attack the enemy so soon as you are in position." A person of Polk's military experience knew full well there was a vast difference between "at once" and "so soon as you are in position." Since Breckinridge reported receiving only one directive from Polk early on the twentieth, and Cleburne mentioned none, it is most likely that Polk issued only this one order.[16]

---

[15] *OR*, XXX (pt. 2), 33.

[16] *Ibid.*, 47, 52, 198; Bragg, "Memorandum on the Battle of Chickamauga," Bragg Papers, Western Reserve. Although Bragg included the story of Polk in his rocking chair in his memorandum, it did not appear in his official report made in December 1863. He did, however, write of the incident to Elise in two letters, September 22 and 27, 1863, Bragg Papers, Bixby Collection; to James Seddon, September 25, 1863, James A. Seddon Papers, Duke University Library; and to

Hill also contributed to the delay on the right. Finally making his appearance at the expected line of battle about the time Cleburne and Breckinridge received their directives from Polk, Hill ordered the move delayed until the troops had their rations, and "on other accounts." He sent a communication to Polk informing him of the delay, and Polk in turn notified Bragg at 7:00 that Hill would not be ready to move for at least an hour. Around 7:30 Polk meandered his way to the line, where, according to one observer, he "seemed to acquiesce [in the decision to issue rations before the attack], and nothing was said about any orders for an advance having been given the night before." Hill also reported that Polk made no objection to the delay. When Bragg came up at 8:00, Hill learned for the first time that he should have attacked at daylight.[17]

The attack in Polk's sector, poorly organized and uncoordinated, finally began nearly four hours later than Bragg had ordered. At 9:30 A.M. Breckinridge advanced into one of the bloodiest encounters of the day. Cleburne received orders to advance at about 10:00, after Breckinridge was already in motion, and Cleburne's efforts to overtake and dress upon him created confusion in his line. Hill professed to believe that this may have been the only instance in the history of warfare where an attack was made in a single line with no reserves or support troops. Polk's poor command abilities thus caused the units of his wing to assault in unsupported details and detachments, resulting in their repulse with heavy losses.[18]

Polk's failure to move at dawn and his inadequate direction and organization of the attack shattered Bragg's plans for the battle. In later years Bragg contended, somewhat unrealistically, that but

---

E. T. Sykes, February 8, 1873 (copy), Polk Papers, University of the South. For a fuller discussion of this incident, see Connelly, *Autumn of Glory*, pp. 216–18.

[17] *OR*, XXX (pt. 2), 47, 52, 198, 53, 141; H.C. Semple to D. H. Hill, October 13, 1863, Daniel Harvey Hill Papers, North Carolina Department of Archives and History, Raleigh.

[18] *OR*, XXX (pt. 2), 199, 154, 143, 33.

for the loss of those precious hours, "our independence might have been won."[19]

Adding to the confusion in Polk's wing, Walker and Hill chose this morning to spat with one another. Between 9:00 and 10:00 A.M., Hill ordered Walker to come to his support. Upon arrival, Hill high-handedly broke up Walker's Reserve Corps and sent it piecemeal to support various units. General Liddell, one of Walker's division commanders, reported that Walker, who "disliked Hill anyway," became "highly incensed" and that the two generals "got into a high dispute" about the detachments. Walker, for good reason, "severely criticized and loudly found fault" with Hill's plans for the attack. As Polk joined them, Walker complained that he "now had no command." Meanwhile, Hill, in a snit, "walked off toward the skirmish line, apparently angry at something said by Walker." When Walker observed Hill's petulant stalk toward the front, he remarked, "'The man is mad'" and "loudly called Hill to come back, apparently much troubled." Having forced Walker into an apology of sorts, Hill soon returned but continued to sulk. After the repulse of his troops, Walker insisted on "having something to do with my own command" and made another suggestion to Hill, who, unsurprisingly, disagreed and instead followed his own erratic instincts.[20]

The inexcusable delay on the right was matched by an excusable unreadiness on the left. Longstreet reported riding out at dawn to find his command and to adjust the line, closing somewhat to the right in order to fill a gap between the Confederate wings. When the attack finally began on the right, Longstreet had not completed his arrangements, so it is probable that Bragg's plan for the fight to be taken up successively from the right to the left would not have been executed properly, even if Polk had not dawdled. In any case, Longstreet observed that "the battle [on the right] seemed to rage with considerable fury, but did not progress as had been anticipated."[21]

[19] Bragg to Sykes, February 8, 1873, Polk Papers, University of the South.
[20] *OR*, XXX (pt. 2), 241; Liddell, *Record*, pp. 144–45.
[21] *OR*, XXX (pt. 2), 288.

By the time Longstreet felt prepared, Bragg had already ordered units of the left wing to attack, thus setting in motion the
advance that broke the Federal line, long credited to Longstreet.
In his report Longstreet admitted that, hearing Bragg had already
ordered units of the left wing forward, "I at once issued orders to
attack to the troops not already in motion."[22] Bragg's timing
proved perfect: a gap had inadvertently been created in the Federal
line at the precise time and place the left wing attacked.

Although Bragg put the attack in motion, Longstreet's judicious
troop deployment aided in the success of the attack. He had arranged the brigades and divisions on a narrow front, achieving the
effect of one large column striking the center of the Union line,
totally unlike the piecemeal and uncoordinated attacks under
Polk's command. Having smashed through the enemy line, the
Confederates pursued the Federals as they raced toward Chattanooga. "When we were ordered forward," related a Confederate
captain, "we raised a yell, and went at them at a double quick, but
they went at a double quicker. I tell you they skedaddled in fine
style."[23]

Bragg surveyed the early stages of the attack from horseback on
the Chattanooga road. He looked "pale and careworn," an observer noted, "his features rendered more haggard by a white
Havelock he wears over his cap and neck."[24] After the morning he
had endured, it is no wonder Bragg looked pale and careworn.

With the Federals broken and on the run from Longstreet's
front, around 2:00 P.M. Bragg turned his attention once again to
Polk's sector. Passing along Longstreet's line on the left, Bragg
found the Confederate advance blocked by a strong, obstinately
defended enemy position. This was Snodgrass Hill and Horse-
shoe Ridge, where Thomas had established a stronghold to cover
the wild retreat of the rest of the Union army. Bragg immediately

[22] *Ibid.*, 363–64, 288.
[23] McWhiney and Jamieson, *Attack and Die*, p. 89; Joab Goodman to My dear
Niece, September 28, 1863 (copy), Chickamauga National Military Park.
[24] William Miller Owen, *In Camp and Battle with the Washington Artillery of New
Orleans* (Boston, 1885), pp. 278–84.

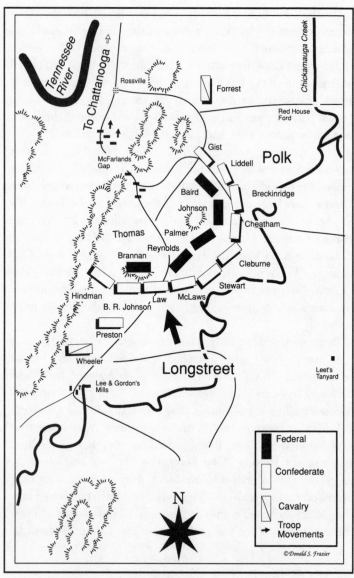

BATTLE OF CHICKAMAUGA, September 20, 1863

dispatched orders to Polk to dislodge the Federals. As he moved toward the right wing, Bragg prodded Polk again to execute the order. About 3:30, Polk belatedly ordered the advance, which, added to the pressure from Longstreet's wing, forced the enemy finally to give way around dark.[25]

The Confederates knew the day's fighting had finished when "a simultaneous and continous shout from the two wings announced our success complete." A Federal described the shouting from a different perspective. "Away to our left and rear some of Bragg's men set up the 'rebel yell.' It was taken up successively and passed round to our front, along our right and in behind us again until it seemed almost to have got to the point whence it started. It was the ugliest sound that any mortal ever heard." The cries of the wounded created another ugly sound. One soldier admitted, "The sleep of the victorious army on a field won is not very sweet when we are haunted all night long with the groans and cries of the wounded dying."[26]

Bragg expressed great pleasure with the accomplishments of his Army of Tennessee. "We captured over 8,000 prisoners, 51 pieces of artillery, 15,000 stand of small arms, and quantities of ammunition," he boasted, "with wagon ambulances, and teams, medicines, hospital stores, &c, in large quantities." Bragg lavished praise on his soldiers. "The conduct of our troops was excellent throughout the prolonged contest."[27]

The Chickamauga victory had not been cheaply won. "Our loss was in proportion to the prolonged and obstinate struggle," Bragg lamented, and "the number of general and staff officers stricken down will best show how those troops were led." In his report Bragg sang the usual Southern litany of the enemy's superior numbers, but with the reinforcements from Virginia, Bragg's army numbered 66,326, as opposed to the 58,222 Federals.[28]

[25] *OR*, XXX (pt. 2), 34.
[26] *Ibid.*, 289; quoted in Hattaway and Jones, *How the North Won*, p. 454; Coleman Diary; Joshua K. Callaway to My Dear Love, September 22, 1863, Callaway Papers.
[27] *OR*, XXX (pt. 2), 35.
[28] *Ibid.*; McWhiney and Jamieson, *Attack and Die*, p. 8.

Bragg's lamentations for the fallen were justified. Casualties were horrifying. One source discovered that "nearly half of all regimental commanders and twenty-five percent of all brigade commanders were killed or wounded." In addition, twenty-five of the thirty-three Confederate brigades engaged lost more than one-third of their strength, and many of the infantry regiments lost over 40 percent. In all, Bragg's army suffered 16,986 casualties, better than 25 percent of his force, while Rosecrans lost 11,413, more than 19 percent of his army. The combined casualties of American soldiers reached nearly 30,000.[29]

Bragg, for good reason, did not include Polk in his praise. Polk executed his responsibilities at Chickamauga poorly. On September 19, after being placed in command of the army's right, Polk could not even be found. Where was he? When Stewart briefly penetrated the Federal line, why was Polk not available to send in reinforcements? The morning of September 20 he showed no particular concern to carry out the orders issued the previous night. "The truth is," wrote Colonel Taylor Beatty, "he is a slow coach—one who cannot be depended on."[30]

A few days later Bragg accurately diagnosed the reasons for Polk's insubordination and irresponsible behavior. Polk, Bragg explained, "is luxurious in his habits, rises late, moves slowly, and always conceives his own plans the best." This behavior sounded like a man who believed his present position to be analogous to that of his civilian career as Episcopal bishop, at the top of the local hierarchy. Bragg avowed that Polk's refusal to execute orders as dictated "has proved an injury to me on every field where I have been associated with him."[31] The final rupture between the army commander and his reluctant subordinate, the bishop-general, had begun.

The rupture between Bragg and Longstreet would take longer to develop. Part of the problem proved to be Longstreet's inflated

[29] McWhiney and Jamieson, *Attack and Die*, pp. 13, 8.
[30] Beatty Diary, October 20, 1863.
[31] Bragg to Seddon, September 25, 1863, Seddon Papers.

opinion of his own abilities. The forty-two-year-old native of
Georgia had transplanted himself to Alabama in order to obtain
an appointment to West Point, where he graduated near the bottom of his class in 1842. Longstreet remained in the U.S. Army
until after the Civil War began, seeing service in the Mexican War
and on the frontier. In February 1861, while still an officer in the
U.S. Army, Longstreet offered his military services to the state of
Alabama. Belatedly tendering his resignation on May 9, 1861, his
Confederate appointment to brigadier general came on July 1,
1861. Until he joined Bragg at Chickamauga, Longstreet had
served in the East. Promoted to lieutenant general on October 9,
1862, Longstreet exercised independent command in the Department of Virginia and North Carolina from February to April
1863, after which he rejoined Lee for the Gettysburg campaign.[32]

Powerfully built, nearly six feet tall with broad shoulders, eyes
described as "glinting steel blue," and a heavy beard, Longstreet
had a grossly exaggerated opinion of his command abilities. A
letter to Senator Louis T. Wigfall in August 1863 revealed the
extent of his narcissism. Angling for an appointment in the West,
preferably an independent command, Longstreet wrote, "My
only desire in the matter is to save the country. If I remain here [in
the East] I fear that we shall go, little at a time, till all will be lost.
I hope that I may get west in time to save what there is left of us. I
dislike to ask for anything and only do it under the impression
that if I do not our days will be numbered."[33] Such an inflated
view of his abilities boded ill for Longstreet's relationship with
Bragg, and for the Army of Tennessee.

When Longstreet wrote his memoirs in 1896, he claimed that
Bragg had left the field during the crisis of battle. Bragg, Longstreet contended, refused to send reinforcements from Polk's com-

[32] Donald Bridgman Sanger and Thomas Robson Hay, *James Longstreet* (Baton
Rouge, 1952), p. 20.
[33] *Ibid.*, pp. 5, 8, 10–14, 17, 18, 63, 115, 150–51; Freeman, *Lee's Lieutenants*, I,
166, 169; II, 248, 468–69, 480; III, 40–41, 222–23; *OR*, LII (pt. 2), 549–50; James
Longstreet to Louis T. Wigfall, August 18, 1863, Wigfall Family Papers, University of Texas.

mand, exclaiming, "There is not a man in the right wing who has any fight in him," and then rode off the field to his headquarters at Reed's Bridge. These charges have been accepted and repeated by historians since Longstreet published his memoir, but Longstreet's report, made within a month of the battle, told a different tale. Although Bragg's reputed statement is similar—the troops on the right "had been beaten back so badly that they could be of no service to me"—Longstreet made no mention in the report of Bragg's leaving the field. Furthermore, Bragg's headquarters were not located at Reed's Bridge, but at Thedford's Ford, although dispatches throughout the afternoon were headed "in the field."[34]

It appears that Bragg's alleged absence from the field is, in fact, a myth, originated by Longstreet and repeated by historians who have relied upon his account. Far from leaving the field, the evidence indicates that Bragg spent the midafternoon directing activities on the right wing. Longstreet himself reported that about the time his left wing broke up the enemy in their front, "the Right Wing made a gallant dash"—the one Bragg had repeatedly urged Polk to make—"and gained the line that had been held so long and obstinately against it." Just why Longstreet even requested men from Polk's command is unclear, since Preston's Division in his own wing had not yet fought.[35]

During the night of September 20-21 the Federal army withdrew under cover of darkness from the bloody Chickamauga battlefield, stirring both further controversy among the Confederate high command and criticism of Bragg for failing to recognize his victory. Longstreet's memoir is as suspect in this matter as it is on Bragg's whereabouts during the afternoon of September 20 and

[34] James Longstreet, *From Manassas to Appomattox: Memoirs of the Civil War in America* (Bloomington, Ind., 1960; orig. ed., 1896), p. 452; Connelly, *Autumn of Glory*, p. 225; Parks, *Polk*, pp. 339–40; Francis F. McKinney, *Education in Violence: The Life of George H. Thomas and the History of the Army of the Cumberland* (Detroit, 1961), p. 264; *OR*, XXX (pt. 2), 289; Brent to B. F. Cheatham and Brent to S. B. Buckner, in the Field, 2:00 P.M., September 20, 1863, Bragg Papers, Western Reserve.

[35] *OR*, XXX (pt. 2), 289; Connelly, *Autumn of Glory*, p. 225; Tucker, *Chickamauga*, pp. 391–92.

directly contradicts not only the orders Longstreet issued on the twentieth and the twenty-first but also his official report written in October 1863. Perhaps in his dotage Longstreet truly mis-remembered, but his sorry record of veracity on other occasions leads one to believe he deliberately distorted the facts. Again, historians have accepted and spread Longstreet's fictional version of the events.

In the memoir Longstreet sarcastically contended, "The Confederate chief did not even know of his victory until the morning of the 21st," implying that he himself did know the Federals were gone. He does not explain why, if he did possess this knowledge, he did not see fit to share it with his commander. His own dispatches to Bragg disprove his contention. At 6:15 P.M. on September 20, he reported that he believed his command had been successful and that he hoped to be ready to resume the conflict early the next morning. His communication at 6:40 A.M. on the twenty-first even more explicitly revealed Longstreet's uncertainty as to the location of the Federals. "I am much occupied in sending forward my lines of sharpshooters to find and feel the enemy," he reported, and his 5:30 A.M. dispatch to Wheeler ordered the cavalry to "ascertain the position of the enemy."[36] Longstreet had no better knowledge of Rosecrans's complete withdrawal from the field than Bragg had.

Hill also implied in his memoir on Chickamauga that Bragg alone thought the enemy still nearby, but his official report made no such inference. In notes made sometime after the war, Hill even went so far as to claim that neither he nor Longstreet could locate Bragg until the afternoon of September 21, a contention repudiated by Longstreet's official report.[37]

---

[36] Longstreet, *From Manassas*, p. 458; Longstreet to Bragg, 6¼ P.M., September 20, 1863; Longstreet to Brent, 6:40 A.M., September 21, 1863, Bragg Papers, Western Reserve; *OR*, XXX (pt. 4), 682. For a discussion of Longstreet's lack of veracity, see Robert K. Krick, "'I Consider Him a Humbug . . .'—McLaws on Longstreet at Gettysburg," *Virginia Country Civil War*, V (1986), 28–30.

[37] Hill, "Chickamauga," p. 662; *OR*, XXX (pt. 2), 145; D. H. Hill, "Manuscript Notes," Hill Papers, North Carolina Department of Archives and History.

Other reports indicate a similar lack of certainty as to the enemy's whereabouts and intentions. General Patton Anderson reported that it was not until the next morning that he discovered the enemy had hastily withdrawn toward Chattanooga. Although both Kershaw and Liddell asserted that scouts informed them of the enemy's withdrawal from the field by 10 P.M., what they did with that information is questionable. Kershaw contended he immediately notified Longstreet, but Longstreet's dispatches early the following morning suggest that he did not believe Kershaw. In his official report, Liddell did not mention what he did with his information, but after the war he wrote a somewhat confused and vague account of reporting to Polk "before day" and of receiving orders from Polk to pursue. At this point, Bragg arrived, and "after delaying a little longer without getting instructions," Liddell reported, "I left him, in entire ignorance of the steps that had been determined upon." But Polk obviously had no intention of hurrying to the pursuit. When Bragg arrived at the bishop-general's headquarters "about sunrise," when others had been up and bustling for some time, he found Polk still abed.[38]

Whether Bragg knew the Federals were gone or not is a moot point, although it appears he must have had some idea of the victory, as a member of his staff dispatched a message to Wheeler at 5:00 P.M., finding "the tidings from all parts of the field cheering. Enemy has been driven back from all parts." But how far the enemy had been driven made no difference that night, given the condition of Bragg's army. Although Hill later contended that the army's organization had been little disturbed by the fierce battle, reports from other quarters showed the mendaciousness of his assertion. Johnson reported his line "entirely broken" and believed it was in no condition to advance. A colonel reported that because of the fatigue of the officers and men the regiments had become confused and mixed together.[39] Indeed, the configuration

---

[38] *OR*, XXX (pt. 2), 319, 505, 253; Liddell, *Record*, pp. 146–47; Bragg, "Memorandum on the Battle of Chickamauga," n.d., Bragg Papers, Western Reserve.
[39] *OR*, XXX (pt. 4), 675; (pt. 2), 145, 464, 347.

of the two army wings now placed them nearly in confrontation with one another.

The Confederates, even those critical of Bragg, by their own admission were in no condition for a hasty pursuit. The fighting had been hard. One Confederate who lost a brother there wrote, "The enemy poured musketry, grape & canister shell into us with powerful effect," while another tersely reported that his unit had been "fighting like tigers." Shortly after the war General Arthur M. Manigault, while criticizing Bragg's failure to pursue vigorously, admitted that the soldiers were exhausted and that there was much to be done on the battlefield. When the army did move on September 22, Hill informed Polk that thousands straggled along the road.[40]

In addition to confusion among units and the exhaustion of the soldiers, supplies needed replenishing. On the night of September 20 Longstreet reported that he ordered his line to remain where it was while the ammunition boxes were replenished. The next morning he complained to Bragg that many of his men needed provisions, and as his staff officers had not been provided with means of supplying the troops, he could do nothing. Forrest reported his men and horses suffering for want of water. His soldiers had no rations at all, and the horses had received only a partial feed for two days.[41] This hardly describes the same army Hill depicted in his memoir.

On September 21 Bragg notified Richmond of the victory but hedged his plans for the immediate future by warning that, although he held the field, the Federals still confronted him and by reporting the heavy loss of officers. Recognizing the need for his army to pull itself together before moving, Bragg gave his subordinates until 2:00 P.M. to prepare.[42]

[40] Coleman Diary; Joshua K. Callaway to My Dear Love, September 22, 1863, Callaway Papers; Manigault, *A Carolinian*, p. 101; *OR*, XXX (pt. 4), 693.

[41] *OR*, XXX (pt. 2), 289, 525; Longstreet to Bragg, 6:40 A.M., September 21, 1863, Bragg Papers, Western Reserve.

[42] *OR*, XXX (pt. 2), 23; Circular, Headquarters, Army of Tennessee, September 21, 1863, Bragg Papers, Western Reserve.

For three days the Army of Tennessee cautiously closed on Chattanooga. The night of September 21 Bragg established his headquarters near Red House Ford, remained there throughout the twenty-second, and moved on the twenty-third to the Nail House on Missionary Ridge.[43]

The Confederate march did not proceed uncontested. Cheatham ran into resistance at Missionary Ridge on September 22, and the next day Polk received orders to form a line of battle on a road crossing the ridge to block a reported Federal advance.[44]

Bragg received mixed information while he reformed his army and felt out the enemy's position. The army certainly confronted the Federals at several points during its advance, but other sources reported Rosecrans's evacuating Chattanooga. Forrest sent the first such information on September 21, advising Bragg that the army should press forward rapidly before the Federals escaped. After occupying the summit of Missionary Ridge on the afternoon of the twenty-second, General George Maney reported that heavy dust on the far side of the river indicated Rosecrans's departure from Chattanooga. The same day General Lafayette McLaws, newly arrived from Virginia, also reported that the Federals were crossing the river on pontoons.[45]

Fortunately, Bragg did not rush in headlong, for the Confederate observers were mistaken; Rosecrans had no intention of evacuating the highly prized town, gateway to the heart of the South. "We fell back in good order and commenced fortifying," a Federal wrote, "and now they can send the whole Army of Virginia here and Old Lee at their head and they cannot drive us out of there." Another Northerner informed his wife, "The way we are now fortified I do not think they can ever drive us out of Chattanooga." One Confederate reported the Federals "lost no time in making their position as secure as possible, and in restoring order and discipline amongst the rank and file," while another explained

[43] Brent Diary, September 21–23, 1863, Bragg Papers, Western Reserve.
[44] *OR*, XXX (pt. 4), 691–92, 696.
[45] *Ibid.*, 681, 691, 695.

that the enemy "fell back to his fortifications at Chattanooga . . . from which our Gen did not feel strong enough to drive him."[46]

As Bragg settled into his headquarters on Missionary Ridge, some people expressed satisfaction with his victory and predicted additional successes in the near future. General Johnston congratulated Bragg on his "glorious achievement," while a group of Atlantans sent him gifts. "We have gained a great victory," boasted a soldier, "which has had a fine effect upon the Army and the people," and he hoped Bragg would soon drive Rosecrans from Chattanooga. In Richmond, a war department clerk believed Bragg would attempt to get around Rosecrans's flanks and force him out of the city. The Federals, too, believed Bragg would try to outflank them.[47]

Others were not so pleased, nor so sanguine about the results of Bragg's victory. "Bragg will let this slip through his fingers," lamented a Southern physician. "He won't push on and make it complete." In Richmond, General Josiah Gorgas confided in his diary, "As . . . we do not hear that Rosecrans has abandoned Chattanooga the fruits of so great a victory are not yet reaped; and people are still in a state of anxious suspense, fearing that all this bloodshed may have been in vain, and that Tennessee may after all not be recovered." A Federal believed "they intended to completely anhilate [sic] Old Rosy But that is more than they can do."[48]

Elise joined those who worried the bloodshed may have been in vain. "I fear our victory is like all we are ever permitted to gain," she wrote to Braxton on September 28, "*undecisive* & with a fearful

[46] James H. Wiswell to Dear Father, September 30, 1863, James H. Wiswell Papers, Duke University Library; A. M. Ayers to Wife, September 28, 1863, Alexander M. Ayers Papers, Centenary College of Louisiana, Shreveport; Manigault, *A Carolinian*, p. 101; Thomas Butler to Aunt, September 30, 1863, Thomas Butler and Family Papers, Louisiana State University Archives.

[47] *OR*, XXX (pt. 4), 696; John W. Duncan to Bragg, September 26, 1863, Bragg Papers, Western Reserve; Butler to Aunt, September 30, 1863, Butler and Family Papers; J. B. Jones, *Rebel War Clerk's Diary*, II, 51; Hough, *Soldier in the West*, p. 145.

[48] *Confederate Veteran*, XXVIII (1920), 97; Gorgas, *Diary*, p. 63; Wiswell to Father, September 30, 1863, Wiswell Papers.

loss of men. We have the glory of some prisoners & cannon—
Rosecrans still holds the points *he* aimed at, Chattanooga, East
Tennessee, Cumberland Gap." She urged her husband on.
"When we succeed in retaking what we have just lost, I shall then
believe some substantial good is obtained." But she appeared not
to place all the blame on her husband's shoulders. "I shall never
cease to think but for the tardiness of the war dept all this might
have been easily avoided. The arrival of your reinforcements six
weeks earlier & Chattanooga & East Tennessee would not have
been lost. At what expense of noble blood," she lamented, "are we
trying to *get back* what we need never have lost?"[49]

Elise's criticisms of the War Department's ill-advised decisions
hit the mark. As usual, Richmond did too little too late. Before
the battle Elise had written: "I was not far wrong when I said our
reinforcements would come 'too late.' *If* you had had them two
months ago, Tennessee would now be free & her line our defense
instead of Georgia—but alas it ends with an *if.*" Many of Longstreet's units never did reach the battlefield for the fight but trick-
led in afterward, and no provision had been made for adequately
supplying the reinforcements. At the same time, on September
22 Bragg had to return the Mississippi reinforcements to Johnston.[50] Poor organization and a myopic, disjointed understanding
of priorities shackled the effectiveness of the support Richmond
gave to its armies in the West.

Bragg's success at Chickamauga proved a tonic to his health.
"For ten days, no symptom of any disease has appeared, and every
feeling favors bodily health," he reported to Elise a week after the
battle.[51]

With his army established on the heights overlooking Chattanooga, Bragg settled down to what he considered the important

[49] Elise to Bragg, September 28, 1863, Bragg Papers, University of Texas.
[50] Elise to Bragg, September 17, 1863, *ibid.;* Connelly, *Autumn of Glory*, p. 230.
[51] Bragg to Elise, September 27, 1863 (copy), Bragg Papers, Library of Congress.

business at hand. Virtually ignoring the enemy in his front, Bragg now waged war with the high command of his own army. Relationships that had been touchy at best now erupted into flaming feuds, complete with bickering, verbal sniping, sarcasm, backbiting, lying, and wild charges flying along with the fur.

CHAPTER V

Howling on his hind legs

September 24–October 31, 1863

"WE LOOKED [FOR] RESULTS that would pay for our losses in battles," wrote diarist Mary Boykin Chesnut, but "No! There sits Bragg—a . . . dog howling on his hind legs." And the reason for Bragg's howling? "He always stops to quarrel with his generals."[1] Chesnut, who moved among the upper political circles of Richmond, thus succinctly described Bragg's activities during the several weeks following the Battle of Chickamauga.

Early in October 1863 Bragg received hearty congratulations on his Chickamauga victory, and the compliments on his defeat of Rosecrans were matched by those on his triumph over his Confederate detractors. One correspondent expressed satisfaction that Bragg's victory had silenced "the sneers & gibes & abuse of your enemies." Senator Thomas Semmes of Louisiana congratulated Bragg on his "twofold victory—one over the enemy & the other over detractions & calumny." General Alpheus Baker declared himself "thankful that you who have been treated so ungratefully . . . have been the hero of the victory." Alabama Senator James Pugh praised Bragg for his "distinguished fidelity to duty under the pressure of hostile editors and correspondents, croakers, malcontents, worthless officers, and trashy soldiers."[2]

Uniformly, the writers urged Bragg to continue his efforts to dislodge Rosecrans from Tennessee. "I pray God you may be able

---

[1] Mary Boykin Chesnut, *Mary Chesnut's Civil War*, ed. C. Vann Woodward (New Haven, Conn., 1981), p. 469.
[2] John Forsyth to Bragg, October 2, 1863; Thomas Semmes to Bragg, October 6, 1863; Alpheus Baker to Bragg, October 10, 1863; James L. Pugh to Bragg, October 11, 1863, Bragg Papers, Western Reserve.

to give him a finishing blow—a *coup de grace* that will end him &
all Yankee hopes in the West," wrote John Forsyth, an Alabama
newspaper editor. Pugh expressed the greatest faith in Bragg's
abilities to continue where he left off. "I believe it is reserved for
you to end this war by your next great battle with Rosecranz—I
know you will do it if the President will give you the means and
let you alone."[3]

This appeared unlikely, however, as Davis conspicuously failed
to congratulate Bragg on his Chickamauga victory. "Mr. D. has
never said one word of congratulation," a staff officer complained,
"or even acknowledged the announcement of the victory. . . .
[T]he silence of the Prest. looks ominous."[4]

Ominous indeed, for by early October Bragg decided the time
had arrived to purge his army of incompetent and insubordinate
officers, a task for which he needed Davis's support. Purging began shortly after Bragg settled into his new headquarters on Missionary Ridge. The army commander first targeted Polk. On
September 25 Polk received a communication calling his attention
to the fact that an explanation of his delay in attacking on the
morning of the twentieth had not been forthcoming. Bragg now
demanded an immediate report. Polk's reply reached Bragg on the
twenty-eighth, casting blame for the delay onto Hill. Bragg returned Polk's explanation as unsatisfactory and considered placing
the bishop-general under arrest.[5]

Bragg decided to rid himself of Polk sometime that evening.
David Urquhart, one of Bragg's staff, recalled that Colonel Brent
showed him the order for Polk's removal, prompting Urquhart to
hurry to Bragg's tent to urge the general to reconsider. Bragg at
first agreed to withhold the order, but by morning he sent for
Urquhart to tell him that, although he knew he would be crit-

[3] Forsyth to Bragg, October 2, 1863; Pugh to Bragg, October 11, 1863, *ibid*.
[4] William Whann Mackall to My dearest Mimi, October 1, 1863, William
Whann Mackall Papers, Southern Historical Collection.
[5] *OR*, XXX, (pt. 2), 54; Brent Diary, September 28, 1863; Brent to Polk, September 29, 1863, Bragg Papers, Western Reserve.

icized for it, he believed that in the interest of discipline it had become necessary to arrest Polk.[6]

On September 29 Bragg suspended Polk from command, charging him with disobedience and neglect of duty. Informing Richmond of the suspension, Bragg avowed that after grave consideration he believed it necessary. The next day, Davis suggested to Bragg that the order be countermanded, but Bragg's reply left no doubt in Davis's mind as to his intention of being rid of Polk for good. After explaining the suspension constituted only a partial arrest, in order to avoid Polk's close confinement, Bragg stated his grievances against Polk even more explicitly. "The case is flagrant," Bragg insisted, "and but a repetition of the past. . . . Our cause is at stake. Without vigorous action and prompt obedience [it] cannot be saved. My personal feelings have been yielded to what I know to be the public good, and I suffer self-reproach for not having acted earlier."[7]

Davis received this letter on October 3, and replied with a lengthy but mild reprimand. Davis wrote of Polk's popularity and of the rancor his removal would surely stir against Bragg. "The opposition to you both in the army and out of it has been a public calamity in so far that it impairs your capacity for usefulness, and I had hoped the great victory which you have recently achieved would tend to harmonize the army and bring to you a more just appreciation of the country." Davis would not *order* Bragg to change his mind, but he did urge him to rethink his position. Ultimately, though, Davis relied upon Bragg's judgment. "You have a much better knowledge of the facts than myself, and I frequently pray that you may judge correctly."[8]

Meanwhile, Polk took his suspension as one would expect: he whined, he fussed, and he denigrated Bragg's character and command abilities at every opportunity. Ordered to Atlanta, he

[6] David Urquhart, "Bragg's Advance and Retreat," in *Battles and Leaders*, III, 608n.
[7] *OR*, XXX (pt. 2), 55; LII (pt. 2), 533; XXX (pt. 2), 731; LII (pt. 2), 534.
[8] *Ibid.*, LII (pt. 2), 535.

immediately began gathering evidence with which to defend himself. Hill's reply to Polk's call for help must have been most unsatisfactory to the proud bishop. To Polk's query as to why Hill
had not attacked at daylight on September 20, Hill replied, "I had
no orders to make such attack, which is a sufficient answer." Hill's
response to the question as to whether the attack was made as
soon as possible also left much to be desired. "My line was ready,
in a tactical sense, for attack; but I thought no attack ought to be
made . . . till the whole line of battle was properly arranged from
right to left." Polk could obviously look for little support from
Hill.[9]

Prior to Polk's suspension, Polk, Hill, and Longstreet had met
to discuss what they should do about the "palpable weakness and
mismanagement manifested in the conduct of the military operations of this army." The meeting resulted in letters to Davis, to
Robert E. Lee, and to Secretary of War Seddon, in which the
generals detailed Bragg's shortcomings and requested that Lee be
sent to replace him. Polk's letter had created consternation in the
capital. War Department clerk Jones believed if what Polk said
was true, "Bragg ought certainly to be relieved without delay."
But, he equivocated, although "I am reluctant to attribute the
weakness of personal pique or professional jealousy to [Polk]; yet I
still hope that events will speedily prove that Bragg's plan was the
best."[10]

Now, from his banishment in Atlanta, Polk again addressed
Davis with all the arrogance of a self-righteous bishop. Reiterating
his accusations against Bragg, he charged his commander with
"the most criminal negligence, or, rather, incapacity, for there are
positions in which weakness is wickedness." He looked forward
to a court of inquiry, not only to vindicate his own behavior, but
to establish "the truth and justice of what I have written of his lack
of capacity as a commanding general."[11]

[9] *Ibid.*, XXX (pt. 2), 56, 64.
[10] *Ibid.*, 67; Jones, *Rebel War Clerk's Diary*, II, 66.
[11] *OR*, XXX (pt. 2), 67.

Polk's personal letters sounded similar themes, although the focus turned almost exclusively to Bragg's character as perceived by the bishop-general, and on enhancing his own role in the Army of Tennessee. "I certainly feel a lofty contempt," Polk expounded to his daughter, "for [Bragg's] puny efforts to inflict injury upon a man who has nursed him for the whole period of his commission with him & has kept him from ruining the cause of the country by the sacrifice of its armies." A month later he turned even more vicious. "He is a poor, feeble . . . irresolute man of violent passion . . . uncertain of the soundness of his conclusions and therefore timid in their execution. He is . . . without elevation of character and capable of petty evasions to cover his incapacity and blunders." Polk wound up his tirade by admitting, "I [have] a contempt for his military capacity and his personal character." A biographer inaptly remarked that Polk's "forgiving spirit" underwent a "severe test" during this period.[12]

Others joined Polk in ascribing mean motives to Bragg in suspending the bishop-general from command. "The real causes date back long before the late battle," one of Polk's staff announced, "& originate in 'Envy—malice & uncharitableness.'" Another correspondent agreed. "It is believed Bragg was . . . never . . . able to forgive Genl Polk for bringing his army safely out of Ky for him last fall. . . . [V]iper like—he wishes to strike the hand that saved him."[13]

Polk positively reveled in his martyrdom. "The General is in fine health & good spirits," reported a staff member, "& meets with many evidences of sympathy & esteem from the community here." Polk himself boasted to his daughter, "I never was in better health, and am also . . . in marvelously fine spirits."[14]

Despite Polk and company's assertions to the contrary, Bragg,

[12] Leonidas Polk to My dear daughter, October 10, November 15, 1863, Polk Papers, University of the South; Parks, *Polk*, p. 385.

[13] H. C. Yeatman to Dear Fanny, October 7, 1863; Lucius B. Polk to My Dear Aunt, November 5, 1863, Polk Papers, University of the South.

[14] Yeatman to Dear Fanny, October 7, 1863; Polk to My dear daughter, October 10, 1863, Polk Papers, University of the South.

too, had supporters. Unlikely though it may seem, Breckinridge, who had become Hill's close friend, sympathized with Bragg's charges against Polk, probably because of Polk's attempts to shift the blame for the delay on September 20 onto Hill's shoulders. Colonel Taylor Beatty, also of Hill's Corps, upon hearing of Polk's suspension, opined, "If I am not mistaken he ought to be." As to Polk's insistence that his removal was due to differences between himself and Bragg, Beatty merely exclaimed, "Bah!" Furthermore, he raised other questions about Polk's conduct. If Hill had disobeyed Polk's orders, "Why did not Genl. Polk arrest him or let Genl. Bragg know of it? Why did not Genl. Polk see the order executed himself?"[15] Pertinent questions, indeed, although in all of his attempts to clear himself, Polk never addressed these issues.

John B. Sale, a loyal supporter of Bragg throughout the war, castigated the newspapers for their treatment of the quarrel between the generals. Referring to Bragg as "the great Abused," Sale accused the papers of ascribing to Bragg "impure and unworthy motives," while in "total ignorance of the facts of the case." Polk, meanwhile, "was unanimously elected a victim of tyranny and new found friends officiously garlanded him for the sacrifice with unaccustomed panegyric." Pointing out that Bragg devoted himself to the command of the Army of Tennessee to the extent of "allowing himself no pleasure, no recreation, no self-indulgence," Sale believed "that *while he is such Commander*, his hands should be held up, his authority respected, and his efforts seconded by all good citizens."[16]

Bragg also had support from other sources. The *Mobile Daily Advertiser and Register* believed the suspension of Polk "bears the stamp of high moral courage" and declared that soldiers "admire a general who . . . in the administration of military justice knows no distinction of rank, place or popularity." Nurse Kate Cum-

[15] W. C. Davis, *Breckinridge*, p. 381; Beatty Diary, October 2, 20, 1863, Southern Historical Collection.
[16] John B. Sale to Newspaper, October 15, 1863, Bragg Papers, Western Reserve.

ming related a conversation she overheard between two men. One castigated the other for making harsh statements about Bragg and told him if his remarks were in reference to Bragg's arresting Polk, "he could not but applaud him, as it showed, no matter how high the offender, he would be brought to justice."[17]

Davis visited Polk in Atlanta twice, on his way to see Bragg and on his return journey. Polk avowed that Davis "was very anxious I should have returned to my old corps after the matter was fixed up, but I told him *No* I could not do so. . . . He . . . returned to it again, but I was *unmoveable*." As a result of Polk's intransigence, Davis informed Bragg on October 23 that Polk had been relieved from duty with the Army of Tennessee, which Bragg found "entirely satisfactory." At Bragg's suggestion, General William J. Hardee replaced Polk.[18]

Bragg's requesting Hardee to replace Polk appears somewhat unreasonable. Hardee had no greater opinion of Bragg's capabilities than did Polk, and Davis felt bound to lecture Hardee on what his role in the Army of Tennessee should be. Stressing the fact that discord plagued the high command, Davis hoped Hardee would help to restore harmony. This plea went to the man who, during the retreat from Tullahoma, conspired with Polk to oust his commanding general, Braxton Bragg.[19]

Twelve days after suspending Polk, Bragg relieved Hill from duty. Requesting Davis to acquiesce in the dismissal, Bragg complained that, though Hill possessed "some high qualifications as a commander, he still fails to such an extent in others more essential that he weakens the *morale* and military tone of his command." Furthermore, "A want of prompt conformity to orders of great importance is the immediate cause of this application."[20]

---

[17] *Mobile Daily Advertiser and Register*, October 20, 1863; E. John Ellis to Dear Brother, October 4, 1863, Ellis and Family Papers; Cumming, *Kate*, pp. 159–60.

[18] Polk to My dear daughter, November 15, 1863, Polk Papers, University of the South; *OR*, LII (pt. 2), 547, 534; XXX (pt. 2), 310.

[19] *OR*, XXXI (pt. 3), 609.

[20] *Ibid.*, XXX (pt. 2), 148.

Bragg had earlier communicated his opinions on Hill's character to Seddon: he found Hill despondent, dull, slow, and nervous. "Upon the most flimsy pretexts," Bragg complained, "he makes such reports of the enemy about him as to keep up constant apprehension." Not only that, but "his open and constant croaking would demoralize any command in the world. He does not hesitate at all times and in all places to declare our cause lost."[21]

Hill reported to Richmond, where he was refused a court of inquiry. He spent the remainder of the war awaiting orders. Years later Bragg explained to an inquirer that Hill's "critical, captious, and dictatorial manner . . . and his general deportment united to the fact, *which came to my knowledge after Polk's suspension from command* . . . that Hill . . . countermanded [an order by Polk to his division commanders], induced me to ask his suspension from command." It was too late, though, as Hill had already "sacrificed thousands at Chickamauga."[22]

Hill always believed his dismissal from the Army of Tennessee came about through his expressing a want of confidence in Bragg. "There was . . . a wrong done me in relieving me alone," he complained to Davis, "and not also Longstreet Buckner & Cheatham, who had equally expressed want of confidence in Bragg." Archer Anderson supported Hill's charge in his account of a meeting between Bragg and Hill on October 16. Bragg reportedly told Hill the removal was based upon Bragg's belief that he could not expect cordial cooperation from Hill.[23]

This want of confidence referred to a petition gotten up by Bragg's high-ranking officers in early October. The petitioners complained to Davis that the fruits of the victory at Chickamauga had been lost. "The Army of Tennessee, stricken with a complete paralysis," they contended, "may deem itself fortunate if it es-

---

[21] Bragg to James Seddon, September 25, 1863, Seddon Papers.

[22] *OR*, XXX (pt. 2), 149–51, 153; XXXI (pt. 3), 701; Bragg to E. T. Sykes, February 8, 1873 (copy), Polk Papers, University of the South.

[23] D. H. Hill to Jefferson Davis, November 16, 1863 (copy); Archer Anderson, Statement, October 16, 1863 (copy), Chickamauga National Military Park.

capes from its present position without disaster." They asked Davis to replace Bragg with someone who could inspire the army and the country with confidence, but claimed they did not wish Bragg censured; Davis could justify the removal on the basis of Bragg's poor health, which made him unfit for field command. Admitting the unusual nature of their procedure, the petitioners declared, "The extraordinary condition of affairs in this army, the magnitude of the interests at stake, and a sense of the responsibilities under which they rest . . . render this . . . a matter of solemn duty, from which, as patriots, they cannot shrink."[24]

All, however, shrank from acknowledging responsibility for writing the petition. Although Longstreet, Polk, Hill, Buckner, Cleburne, and Preston, among others, signed it, no one had the courage to claim authorship after their ouster attempt failed; instead, through the years pusillanimous accusations came from the various participants. Long after Polk was dead, Hill told Davis that Polk initiated it and got Buckner to write it. The *Official Records*, also, tentatively credit Buckner with writing it. Hill's biographer claimed that if any one served as chief inciter it was Longstreet. General Mackall, Bragg's chief of staff, informed his wife that Longstreet "is talking about him [Bragg] in a way to destroy all his usefulness," and a few days later he complained to General Johnston, "I think Longstreet has done more injury to the general than all the others put together." Lafayette McLaws, a Longstreet subordinate, told Bragg in early 1864 that Longstreet had helped form the coalition against him.[25]

Hill became a favorite target of those looking for a scapegoat. At the time, Colonel Brent reported that Hill was believed to be prominent in the cabal. After Hill's death, Longstreet stated that

[24] *OR*, XXX (pt. 2), 65–66.
[25] D. H. Hill to Jefferson Davis, October 30, 1886, Jefferson Davis Papers, Louisiana Historical Association Collection, Tulane University, New Orleans; *OR*, XXX (pt. 2), 66; Bridges, *Lee's Maverick*, p. 233; Mackall to My dearest Mimi, October 10, 1863, Mackall Papers; Mackall to J. E. Johnston, October 13, 1863, Joseph E. Johnston Papers, Huntington Library; McLaws to Bragg, February 25, 1864, Bragg Papers, Western Reserve.

the document had been written by Hill ("as he informed me since the war"), although Hill had emphatically denied having written the petition in an 1888 letter to Longstreet. In that letter, Hill repeated to Longstreet what he had told Davis and then charged, "I was made the scape-goat of the whole thing, though the least prominent & active in the movement. I was the cats-paw to rake out chestnuts for others." The belief that Hill promulgated the petition, McLaws explained to him, derived from Hill's manner. "You were, as you always are, open and outspoken, made no secret of your opposition to him, and you were looked on as the head and front of the coalition."[26] This factor, perhaps, led to Longstreet's choice of Hill as a believable culprit in his fictional version of the incident.

No matter who instigated the subterfuge, they did indeed sneakily undercut their commanding general. As two of Longstreet's biographers pointed out, Bragg deserved at least the outward forms of respect and professional loyalty due an army commander. Even considering the unfortunate military situation, "it is always unbecoming in a soldier to engage in conspiracy," and these men without doubt engaged in conspiracy.[27] Even more distasteful, none of them had the courage of their convictions, as illustrated by their reluctance to admit to the authorship of the petition when their plans fell through.

Bragg learned of the petition on October 4. "It gave B much distress & mortification," noted Mackall. "I do believe he thought himself popular. . . . Bragg has the misfortune of not knowing a friend from a foe, and taking subserviency as evidence of friendship." A few days later Mackall reported that Bragg "is blind as a bat to the circumstances around him."[28]

Davis had already sent an emissary, Colonel James Chesnut, on

[26] Brent Diary, October 4, 1863, Bragg Papers, Western Reserve; Longstreet, *From Manassas*, p. 465; Hill to Longstreet, February 11, 1888, James Longstreet Papers, Duke University Library; McLaws to Hill, January 23, 1864, D. H. Hill Papers, Southern Historical Collection.
[27] Sanger and Hay, *Longstreet*, p. 213.
[28] Mackall to My dearest Mimi, October 5, 9, 1863, Mackall Papers.

a fact-finding mission to the Army of Tennessee. When Chesnut arrived in the area on October 4, Longstreet immediately accosted him to tell him "of our distressed condition, and urged him to go on to Richmond with all speed and to urge upon the President relief for us." Longstreet wanted Hill to back him up in this request and suggested that Hill and Buckner both should see Chesnut and corroborate the story.[29] Chesnut did even better than hurry to Richmond. The next day he wired the president that the Army of Tennessee urgently demanded his personal attention and that he should make the trip if at all possible.[30]

Davis came, but a Richmond diarist admitted: "I scarcely hope anything from the President's visit. He temporizes too much, takes too long to make up his mind, is as much wanting in vigor as his enemies say he is in amenability to public opinion." Mackall, on the other hand, expected Davis to make sweeping changes: to replace Bragg with Longstreet, to reinstate Polk, and to give Pemberton a corps.[31]

Mackall must have been surprised when he discovered just how wrong he had guessed. Soon after Davis arrived, he met with Bragg and the dissatisfied generals. One account of the meeting disclosed that Cleburne told Davis that Bragg's failures "had totally lost him the confidence of the army, and . . . this fact alone destroyed his usefulness." Cleburne firmly believed in the necessity of a change. The source of this account, a member of Cleburne's staff, then announced, with no apparent sense of irony, "Some others . . . did not handle the matter with the same delicacy of expression."[32]

Longstreet, in his memoirs, claimed that he was reluctant to discuss the subject of Bragg's removal. He allegedly tried to change the topic, but Davis insisted upon discussing it. When all else failed, Longstreet stated that Bragg "could be of greater ser-

[29] *OR*, XXX (pt. 4), 728.
[30] *Ibid.*, LII (pt. 2), 538.
[31] Kean, *Inside*, p. 109; Mackall to My dearest Mimi, October 9, 1863, Mackall Papers.
[32] Buck, *Cleburne*, 156.

vice elsewhere than at the head of the Army of Tennessee," and
Buckner, Cheatham, and Hill all agreed. Longstreet also implied
that Davis offered him command of the army on the following day
but that he turned it down. However, Longstreet insisted, he offered to work cheerfully in any position under General Joseph E.
Johnston, assuming Johnston received command of Bragg's
army.[33] Since Davis and Johnston had been feuding since the
early days of the war, Longstreet knew very well that Davis would
not accept this suggestion.

Whatever passed at the meeting, or between Davis and Longstreet, the president upheld Bragg as commander of the Army of
Tennessee. In 1872 Davis told Bragg that the decision to retain
him in command came about because "the conference satisfied me
that no change for the better could be made in the commander of
the army."[34]

Here was the nub of Davis's dilemma—if not Bragg, then who?
Both Johnston and Beauregard were disagreeable to Davis on personal grounds, he would not send Lee from Virginia, and as General Liddell conceded, "Indifferent as Bragg was, I did not know
of any better general to take his place." When a nephew of Polk
said that "anyone would do better," Liddell challenged him "to
name one, which he declined doing."[35] And so, by default, Bragg
remained in command.

Bragg did not use his new authority graciously. His normally
even-tempered chief of staff believed that Bragg "ought not to
command this army unless his enemies are taken away, for he is
vindictive and cannot do justice." William Gale, of Polk's staff,
gloated "to learn that so far from having harmony and confidence
restored among his Genl. officers . . . the discord is on the increase." Liddell found Bragg willing "to let the disaffected generals grumble to their hearts' content, since he himself was secure

[33] Longstreet, *From Manassas*, pp. 465–66.
[34] Davis to Bragg, June 29, 1872, Braxton Bragg Papers, Lincoln National Life
Foundation Archives, Fort Wayne, Indiana.
[35] Liddell, *Record*, p. 151.

beyond peradventure in his position with the President." Nothing had been solved. "Here, all this trouble ended to the satisfaction of nobody," acknowledged Liddell. "Everything remained just as in the beginning. Nobody was pleased but Bragg."[36]

Bragg may have been pleased with Davis's support of his position, but his troubles had only begun. Two of his remaining senior officers, Forrest and Mackall, now sought reassignment. Bragg's problems with Forrest began before Davis's visit and, in fact, had much earlier roots. In August, Forrest had requested an independent command to foray through North Mississippi and West Tennessee, a request denied because of Bragg's insistence that he needed Forrest. Now Bragg changed his mind. Shortly after the army settled in on Missionary Ridge, Liddell heard Bragg complaining of Forrest's behavior. "Instead of attending to . . . [orders]," Bragg grumbled, Forrest "has allowed himself to be drawn off toward Knoxville on a general *rampage*, capturing villages and towns that are of no use whatever to me in the result. . . . The man is ignorant and does not know anything of *cooperation*. He is nothing more than a good raider."[37]

On September 25 Bragg ordered Forrest to turn over to Wheeler all but two of his brigades. The next day Forrest strongly protested this order, but on the twenty-eighth Bragg repeated the order, insisting that he turn the troops over to Wheeler without delay.[38]

It is difficult to reconstruct the events of the next several days. Forrest's earliest biographers wrote that Forrest believed the order unjust and disparaging and that in both writing and a personal interview he let Bragg know how he felt. The writers related that a few days later Forrest had a conversation with Bragg, at which time Bragg assured him he would have his old command again at

[36] Mackall to My dearest Mimi, October 9, 1863, Mackall Papers; William D. Gale to W. E. Huger, October 31, 1863, Polk Papers, University of the South; Liddell, *Record*, p. 154.

[37] *OR*, XXX (pt. 4), 507–10; Liddell, *Record*, p. 150.

[38] Brent Diary, September 25, 1863, Bragg Papers, Western Reserve; *OR*, XXX (pt. 4), 710.

the conclusion of Wheeler's expedition. On October 5, however, Forrest received an order placing him permanently under Wheeler's command, causing Forrest to be "extremely dissatisfied."[39]

This version, written in 1868, is mild when compared with the 1899 account related by John Allan Wyeth. Wyeth contended that the letter Forrest sent to Bragg accused the commanding general of lying and duplicity and that Forrest boasted, "Bragg never got such a letter as that before from a brigadier." Furthermore, when Forrest arrived at Bragg's headquarters, what ensued was not a conversation but a confrontation. In a statement undoubtedly made long after the war, Dr. J. B. Cowan disclosed that he accompanied Forrest on his visit to Bragg, where Forrest allegedly verbally assaulted Bragg, accusing him of cowardice and shouting, "If you were any part of a man I would slap your jaws and force you to resent it." Bragg supposedly sat in a chair and "did not utter a word or move a muscle of his face during this shower of invective."[40]

None of Forrest's biographers thought to mention the dates on which these incidents allegedly took place. The "absolutely reliable" Dr. Cowan apparently gave his tale to Wyeth four decades after the war, and it may have been nothing more than the maudlin meanderings of an old man. His story placed the confrontation in early October, but Colonel Brent, the indefatigable diarist on Bragg's staff who missed little, did not mention Forrest's appearance at Bragg's headquarters until three weeks later, recording in his journal on October 20: "Forrest is here and is much dissatisfied. Troubles are brewing in the command"—a rather laconic description if the dramatic confrontation described by Cowan actually took place. Another biographer, Andrew Lytle, admittedly primarily a creative writer, placed the incident during

[39] Thomas Jordan and J. P. Pryor, *The Campaigns of Lieut.-Gen. N. B. Forrest, and of Forrest's Cavalry* (New Orleans, 1868), p. 357; John Harvey Mathes, *General Forrest* (New York, 1902), pp. 154–57.
[40] Wyeth, *That Devil Forrest*, pp. 241–43.

the time Davis visited the Army of Tennessee—in other words, sometime between October 9 and 14. Lytle also, however, placed Forrest home on leave on October 3, not reporting back to Bragg until after he met with Davis in Montgomery.[41]

Whatever the sequence of events and however dramatic the meeting between Forrest and Bragg, on October 13 Bragg proceeded to have Forrest transferred by withdrawing his disapproval of Forrest's August request. In doing so, Bragg undoubtedly acquiesced to a request by Davis to settle this matter in such a way that Forrest's services would not be lost to the Confederacy. On October 29 Davis notified Forrest that his application had been granted and that he should proceed to his new field of duty.[42]

At least one of Bragg's staff was sorry to see Forrest go. "This change is I think injudicious," remarked Brent. "Coupled with the existing discontents in the Cavalry it will tend materially to still further impair its usefulness. Forrest," he continued, "with many objections, is however the best Cavalry commander in the Army."[43] There were indeed many objections to Forrest's services. He turned out to be, as Bragg had said, a good raider, but for the day-to-day screening and surveillance duties of the Army of Tennessee, Forrest had proven unreliable.

Brent also lamented Mackall's reassignment. "I part with him with great regret," Brent mourned. "An invaluable and faithful officer. A courteous soldier, an affable gentleman and a true friend."[44] This assessment of Mackall's character is confirmed by letters written to his wife, Mimi, during this period of strain in the Army of Tennessee. Always loving and filled with concern for her well-being in her state of late pregnancy, Mackall nevertheless shared with her the dissatisfactions and anxieties of his position.

Mackall, a forty-six-year-old former classmate of Bragg's at West Point and a career soldier, had joined the Confederacy at the

[41] Brent Diary, October 20, 1863, Bragg Papers, Western Reserve; Andrew Lytle, *Bedford Forrest and His Critter Company* (New York, 1931), p. 243.

[42] *OR*, XXXI (pt. 3), 603–4.

[43] Brent Diary, October 30, 1863, Bragg Papers, Western Reserve.

[44] *Ibid.*, October 16, 1863.

outbreak of war, receiving his promotion to brigadier general on February 17, 1862. A few months later he was captured at Island No. 10, and after his exchange he was assigned on April 17, 1863, as Bragg's chief of staff. This proved to be an unofficial position with no clearly defined guidelines to delineate its responsibilities. Before Mackall's arrival, Brent had performed many of the duties now assigned to Mackall.[45]

Bragg and Mackall established a satisfactory working relationship, with Mackall acting as the medium through which communications passed between Bragg and his immediate subordinates. June I. Gow, the historian of the army's staff, explained that at this point the chief of staff became far more involved in tactical matters, and possibly also in strategy, than ever before. General Johnston believed Mackall "absolutely necessary" to the effective organization of Bragg's army, his importance probably enhanced by Bragg's frequent ill health.[46]

But now Mackall was thoroughly disenchanted with Bragg and with his own position. Although he conceded that Bragg "is very earnest at his work, his whole soul is in it," Mackall found that Bragg's "manner is repulsive and he has no social life—Is easily flattered and fond of a seeming reverence for his high position. . . . If he don't want news to be true, he will listen to nothing—'It can't be so' is his reasoning, and if it prove true he is not prepared to meet it." Regarding the relief of Polk and Hindman, Mackall asserted he warned Bragg of the dissatisfaction to follow, "but he is hard to persuade when in prosperity and I do not think my warning will be heeded until too late." Bragg, Mackall complained, "is as much influenced by his enemies as by his friends—and does not know how to control the one or preserve the other."[47]

---

[45] E. J. Warner, *Generals in Gray*, pp. 203–4; Boatner, *Dictionary*, pp. 498–99; Mackall to My darling, October 1[?], 1862, Mackall Papers; Brent Diary, April 17, 1863, Bragg Papers, Western Reserve.

[46] June I. Gow, "Chiefs of Staff in the Army of Tennessee under Braxton Bragg," *Tennessee Historical Quarterly*, XXVII (1968), 355, 356.

[47] Mackall to My dearest Mimi, September 29, 1863, Mackall Papers.

Mackall seems to have been dissatisfied with more than just Bragg. Brent returned to the staff of the Army of Tennessee on July 26, and although Mackall later wrote, "He was a most excellent and intelligent officer and we had served without anything unpleasant ever occurring," Gow found the parameters of authority blurred with Brent's return. Mackall expressed dissatisfaction with the loose arrangements Bragg employed in assigning staff duties and even complained that Bragg himself did too much of what Mackall regarded as his own administrative domain. His remark on October 9 that "If B[ragg] goes I still propose to go & not stay long if he remains" indicates that his dissatisfaction was not entirely with Bragg, but also with the situation in which he found himself.[48]

Regardless of his motivations, by early October Mackall wrestled with the idea of leaving Bragg. On the tenth he wrote, "I am satisfied that Bragg cannot usefully command this army and that I can do no good for if Mr. D[avis] sustains him he will be too elated to listen to reason." Two days later he unburdened himself to his wife, explaining that although he feared his leaving would exacerbate Bragg's troubles, to stay was disagreeable. On October 13 Mackall expressed the same ambivalency to Johnston. "I think I ought to go," he wrote, "& at the same time—I feel that if I left now I would be looked upon as trying to add to the discontent."[49]

On October 16 Mackall finally decided to leave Bragg. Bragg thanked Mackall for his services and wished him well. He did not appoint another chief of staff during the brief remainder of his tenure with the Army of Tennessee.[50]

The reassignment of Forrest and Mackall and the removal of Polk and Hill did not end Bragg's conflicts with his subordinates. On October 20 Bragg asked Davis to relieve both Preston and Buckner from command, and on October 31 Cheatham requested

[48] Mackall to Wife, March 4, 1864, *ibid.*; Gow, "Chiefs," p. 357; Mackall to My dearest Mimi, October 9, 1863, Mackall Papers.
[49] Mackall to My dearest Mimi, October 10, 12, 1863; Mackall to Johnston, October 13, 1863, Mackall Papers.
[50] *OR*, XXX (pt. 4), 757; Liddell, *Record*, p. 155; Gow, "Chiefs," p. 359.

that he be relieved from duty with Bragg. Bragg merely forwarded Cheatham's request, but Cooper did not know of another command to which he could be assigned consistent with his rank. Cheatham, choosing rank over settlement of his grievance (which seemed to be because his "whim for the removal of Bragg is not gratified"), remained at his post.[51]

The Buckner-Preston conflict with Bragg proved more complicated than that of Cheatham and was, in fact, a continuation of the controversy regarding Buckner's authority, or lack thereof, to administer military affairs in East Tennessee after he joined Bragg's army with his troops. On October 22 Buckner wrote Bragg "quite a severe letter," complaining "in bold terms of the injustice which has been done him."[52]

Bragg had pointed out that most of Buckner's former department suffered enemy occupation. Buckner used the same argument to criticize Bragg's performance in his own department. "Even if all of it were so occupied, such occupancy would not in itself extinguish the command; as is evidenced by the fact that the General Commanding exercised the full rights of a Department Commander even when the enemy's forces occupied almost his entire Department." He then gave an even deeper dig: Bragg "continued the exercise of that authority until the arrival of the forces of Generals Hood and Longstreet reinstated him in a territorial fraction of his Department." He pointed out that "every foot of that territory [Buckner's old department] which was relinquished was under peremptory orders of the General Commanding; and that the propositions I made for its defense and which I have every reason to think would have been successful were entirely disregarded."[53]

Bragg naturally took umbrage. He returned the letter as "unfit

[51] Brent Diary, October 20, 1863, Bragg Papers, Western Reserve; Cheatham to Brent, October 31, 1863, Benjamin Franklin Cheatham Papers, Tennessee State Library and Archives, Nashville; E. John Ellis to Thomas C. W. Ellis, November 22, 1863, Ellis and Family Papers.
[52] Brent Diary, October 22, 1863, Bragg Papers, Western Reserve.
[53] Buckner to Brent, October 20, 1863, Buckner Papers.

to put on file in his office," to which Buckner replied by demanding again an explanation of his status as department commander, stating that it was in his capacity as department commander that he had sent Preston to western Virginia.[54]

Bragg now took the case to Davis. "General Buckner continues to give me great trouble about his . . . command in Southwestern Virginia," he complained to the president. "He gives orders and sends officers from here [to] there without consulting me." Davis assured Bragg that Buckner and Preston were indeed subject to Bragg's orders and that Buckner had no authority to give orders that contradicted or interfered with Bragg's. He would not, however, grant Bragg's request to relieve the two generals from duty with the Army of Tennessee, pointing out that "restlessness is not a sufficient reason for removal."[55]

By October 29 Bragg decided to stage a showdown. He asked Davis to return to the army, intending to demand either that some of his subordinates be removed or that he be relieved himself. Davis's reply cooled Bragg down somewhat when he declared that "he thoroughly sustained him, but was disinclined to make any removals, & declined relieving Gen Bragg." Fearing he had overplayed his hand, Bragg hastened to assure Davis that he understood his duty, but he continued to be troubled by Buckner.[56]

Bragg's problems with military personnel extended beyond his immediate command. Commissary General Lucius B. Northrop "took in high dudgeon" Bragg's suggestion that his subsistence problems needed immediate attention. Northrop's endorsement left no doubt as to who deserved blame for this situation. He explained that the subsistence of Bragg's army had been a subject of solicitude since it withdrew from Kentucky. He pointed out that much effort had been expended in getting the railroad functioning so as to supply the army, and this, along with other actions, should have made Bragg aware that the problem did receive constant attention. "The present call for early attention," Nor-

54 Buckner to Brent, October 24, 1863, ibid.
55 OR, LII (pt. 2), 548, 552.
56 Brent Diary, October 29–30, 1863, Bragg Papers, Western Reserve; OR, LII (pt. 2), 557; Buckner to Bragg, November 3, 1863, Buckner Papers.

throp snapped, "is superfluous." The commissary general then turned his attention to Bragg's generalship, commenting, "Every move in Tennessee by General Bragg has intensified my anxiety." Northrop reluctantly agreed to aid Bragg from Mississippi but reminded the War Department that Bragg must recover East Tennessee in order to subsist his army.[57]

Of all Bragg's troubles the most serious and far-reaching revolved around Longstreet. There is little doubt that Longstreet hoped, even expected, to replace Bragg, an expectation shared by his former chief, Robert E. Lee. "I think you can do better than I could," Lee wrote Longstreet in response to Longstreet's suggestion that Lee come to Tennessee to take command of the army. "It was with that view I urged your going."[58] This indicates Lee conspired with his subordinate in an effort to remove Bragg from command of the army.

Longstreet wasted no time opening his campaign. After only six days with the western army, he detailed Bragg's failings to Seddon. Longstreet charged: "This army has neither organization nor mobility, and I have doubts if its commander can give it them. . . . It seems he cannot adopt and adhere to any plan or course, whether of his own or of some one else." Furthermore, he asserted, far from exaggerating, "I have failed to express my convictions to the fullest extent." His sole concern, he insisted, was for the country. "In an ordinary war I could serve without complaint under any one whom the Government might place in authority, but we have too much at stake in this to remain quiet. . . . I am convinced that nothing but the hand of God can save us or help us as long as we have our present commander." An apparently gullible clerk in Seddon's department believed Longstreet's letter "to be written without feeling and purely from a sense of duty."[59]

[57] J. B. Jones, *Rebel War Clerk's Diary*, II, 62; *OR*, XXX (pt. 4), 713–14.
[58] *OR*, LII (pt. 2), 549–50.
[59] *Ibid.*, XXX (pt. 4), 706; Kean, *Inside*, p. 109. William Garrett Piston, *Lee's Tarnished Lieutenant: James Longstreet and His Place in Southern History* (Athens, Ga., 1987), pp. 65–75, contended that Longstreet did not actively seek, or expect, to replace Bragg, but he offers no concrete evidence for this conclusion.

Longstreet stopped at nothing in his efforts to dislodge Bragg. A subordinate declared Longstreet "has no scruples,"[60] a charge abundantly borne out by his activities during this period, and by his memoirs, a virtual fantasy of his role in the war. Longstreet's intransigence, his incompetence, his subversive activities, and his refusal to serve Bragg as a trustworthy lieutenant boded ill for the future of the Army of Tennessee and, indeed, for the entire Confederate States of America.

[60] McLaws to Hill, January 23, 1864, Hill Papers, Southern Historical Collection.

CHAPTER VI

An unhappy course of conduct

September 24–October 31, 1863

"BRAGG IS SO MUCH AFRAID of doing something which would look like taking advantage of an enemy that he does nothing," complained a Confederate in early October. "He would not strike Rosecrans another blow until he has recovered his strength and announces himself ready. Our great victory has been turned to ashes."[1] And so it seemed as Bragg quarreled with his subordinates while the Federal army firmly established itself in Chattanooga. For two months the opposing forces lived and worked within view of each other while they bit at one another's flanks and heels, each hoping to gain an advantage. Finally, at the end of November, the Federals seized the initiative provided by Confederate blundering and neglect to establish themselves in stronger positions from which to assault the Army of Tennessee.

In late September Bragg posted his army in a thin semicircle along six miles of heights and valleys southeast of Chattanooga. They occupied a range of high hills about two and a half miles from, and overlooking, Chattanooga. The right flank rested on the Tennessee River above the town, and the left on the river below, holding Lookout Mountain.[2] When Bragg established this line, Longstreet held the left, Hill the center, and Polk the right, but by November Bragg had dismissed Hill and Polk, replacing them with Breckinridge and Hardee.

From his headquarters perched atop Missionary Ridge, Bragg "looked directly upon the swarms of Yankees behind and in the

---

[1] Susan Leigh Blackford, *Letters from Lee's Army; or, Memoirs of Life in and out of the Army in Virginia during the War between the States* (New York, 1947), p. 219.
[2] Thomas Butler to Aunt, September 30, 1863, Butler and Family Papers.

stone entrenchments," and Joshua K. Callaway of the Twenty-eighth Alabama described the grand scene created by the thickly massed Federal tents. In places, the lines of the opposing armies were so close that a Union soldier "got all most onto one of their batteries thinking it was our own."[3]

Having a good view of the Federals' works did not inspire confidence, as the experienced Confederate soldiers knew what awaited them. Many of the Southern soldiers were familiar with the fortifications, as the Union troops simply reinforced forts that the Southerners had constructed around Chattanooga with their own hands. One veteran accused Bragg of "sending out sounders to find out what the rank and file thought of charging the works around Chattanooga, a clear indication of his weakness, and old Granny methods of thought." It is highly unlikely, however, that Bragg seriously entertained the notion of a frontal assault on the Federals. "Bragg knows [the works around Chattanooga] and he knows that his men know them," wrote one of his soldiers. "And I fear it would be hard to get men to storm such places." Indeed, Bragg explained to Elise, "To assault in front would be destructive to my whole army," and in the same week he told Davis, "It would be murderous."[4]

Bragg intended to starve the Federals out of Chattanooga by cutting Rosecrans's communications. Given the state of his own infantry—short on rations, supplies, and transportation, with thousands of wounded to be cared for and protected—Bragg had no choice but to rely on his cavalry. Soon after the Battle of Chickamauga he ordered a three-pronged cavalry raid led by Wheeler on the right, Roddey in the center, and General Stephen D. Lee, on loan from General Johnston, on the left.[5]

[3] Bragg to Elise, September 27, 1863 (copy), Bragg Papers, Library of Congress; Joshua K. Callaway to My Darling Wife, October 26, 1863, Callaway Papers; A. M. Ayers to his wife, September 22, October 5, 1863, Ayers Papers.
[4] Connelly, *Autumn of Glory*, p. 233; Collins, *Chapters*, pp. 164, 165; Callaway to My Dear Love, September 24, 1863, Callaway Papers; Bragg to Elise, September 27, 1863, Bragg Papers, Library of Congress; *OR*, LII (pt. 2), 534.
[5] *OR*, XXX (pt. 4), 695; Starr, *Union Cavalry*, III, 300.

As usual with Bragg's cavalry, plans went awry. On September 29 Bragg assigned Wheeler to command all of the army's cavalry, the action that soon resulted in Forrest's transfer to Mississippi. Bad feelings in Forrest's former command surfaced. General F. C. Armstrong informed Wheeler that his command was unfit for an expedition, and himself "too unwell to start on an expedition across the mountain," although not too ill to serve under Forrest.[6] From there on in, the expedition suffered a lack of cooperation exceeded only by the lack of accomplishment.

On the night of September 29 Wheeler crossed the Tennessee River with orders to disrupt the wagon trains traveling through the Sequatchie Valley and Walden's Ridge area. Within a few days his force had captured and ransacked a large Union wagon train, but that proved to be the outstanding success of his entire jaunt. After raiding some towns and destroying negligible and easily repaired sections of the railroad, Wheeler recrossed the Tennessee on October 9 in a panic. "During the last day's march," reported a Federal, "Wheeler's retreat was a rout, and his command were running all day for the river, every man for himself, and hats, caps, coats, guns, and broken-down horses were strewn along the whole route." Brent reported rumors that the command began plundering shortly after it reached Middle Tennessee, much of the loot being "appropriated to private use."[7]

Wheeler's performance was disappointing, but at least he penetrated his assigned area; Roddey and Lee did not even manage that much. From October 2 until he returned to Mississippi, Lee attempted to make contact with Roddey, attempts repeatedly frustrated by Roddey's erratic movements. Roddey crossed the river by October 8 and spent a couple of days skirmishing with Federal cavalry. On the tenth, however, he learned of Wheeler's repulse and decided to countermarch in order either to join with Wheeler or to relieve some of the pressure on him. He failed to reach him,

[6] *OR*, XXX (pt. 4), 718.
[7] *Ibid.*, 370–71; (pt. 2), 724–25; Brent Diary, October 26, 29, 1863, Bragg Papers, Western Reserve.

since Wheeler had already fled across the Tennessee. On October 13, Wheeler informed Lee that he believed Roddey to be across the river and that his position might be critical. Suggesting that Lee go to his aid, Wheeler declared, "I would give anything if I could cross the river immediately" but excused himself from doing so because of the condition of his troopers and their mounts. Shortly before Lee returned to Mississippi, Roddey finally joined him for some inconclusive skirmishing with General William T. Sherman's advancing forces.[8]

Lee's attempts to cooperate with Wheeler proved as elusive as his efforts with Roddey. By the time Lee contacted Wheeler's forces, they had fled the Federals and, believing them still pursuing, were "disinterested in joining Lee for any more fighting." For a week, Lee remained near Wheeler, the two generals exchanging mutually flattering, supportive communications resulting in much talk but no activity. On October 17 Bragg directed Wheeler to move ninety miles southeast to Guntersville, Alabama, effectively ending any hope of a joint venture with Lee.[9] On November 10, Lee decided to return to Mississippi, having accomplished little more than slightly delaying Sherman's arrival in Chattanooga.[10]

In addition to the lack of organization and cooperation among the cavalry leaders, Bragg had to chastise the troopers for the abuses and irregularities that had injured the morale of the army as well as that of civilians in the area. He forbade straggling and pillaging, promising those found doing so the harshest punishment possible—to be dismounted and assigned to infantry.[11]

While Bragg depended upon the cavalry to cut the Federal communications at a distance, he relied upon the equally inept Longstreet to disrupt the short line of supply closer to Chattanooga. All of Rosecrans's supply lines—the railroad, the river, and the wagon road—merged at the foot of Lookout Mountain,

---

[8] *OR*, XXX (pt. 4), 729, 743.

[9] Herman Hattaway, *General Stephen D. Lee* (Jackson, Miss., 1976), p. 103; *OR*, XXX (pt. 4), 743, 746–48, 752, 757–58, 762–65, 766–67; XXXI (pt. 1), 27–28.

[10] *OR*, XXXI (pt. 3), 676, 700.

[11] *Ibid.*, p. 622.

held by Longstreet's Corps. Bragg ordered the artillery to cut this route of supply and directed Longstreet to post sharpshooters along the river road on the north bank of the Tennessee in order to close that route to the enemy. He granted Longstreet discretionary powers to "take any other measure which you may deem proper to effect this object."[12]

Despite his sarcastic remarks that implied the artillery and the sharpshooters merely got some target practice from their activities, Longstreet admitted it put the Federals on shorter rations until they could open another route. Shorter rations became mighty short indeed—by late September the Union army and its animals received only half rations. But Union morale remained high, despite the hardships. "We are all in good health and spirits," wrote a Federal cavalryman, "excepting that 'grub' is a little short at present but that will come right in the end."[13]

The Federals were no more uncomfortable than their beseigers. Rain fell equally on both armies. "There is a tradition amongst these flats that there has been a time in the past when it wasn't raining," reported one recent arrival, "but saving and excepting one or two days I have seen nothing to make me give credence to such a belief." Mackall told his wife that a cold rain was falling, and as the soldiers were without tents, he feared it would cause much sickness. Walker, however, rather than worrying about illness, believed that since the army had no tents, "the hard rain of last night will give them a good washing." General Lafayette McLaws, whose men lacked tents, blankets, and shoes, was disgusted with the area. "This seems to be a most detestable climate and the men are suffering by the change from Virginia." When a bridge across the Chickamauga washed away, a Georgia battalion of sharpshooters went without rations for two days. A British

[12] Larry J. Daniel, *Cannoneers in Gray: The Field Artillery of the Army of Tennessee, 1861–1865* (University, Ala., 1984), p. 106; Brent to Longstreet, Headquarters, Army of Tennessee, October 9, 1863, Bragg Papers, Western Reserve.

[13] Longstreet, *From Manassas*, pp. 463–64; Ayers to his wife, September 28, October 5, 1863, Ayers Papers; James H. Wiswell to Cousin Will, October 20, 1863, Wiswell Papers.

observer described Bragg's army as being "in a bad way. Insufficiently sheltered, and continually drenched with rain, the men were seldom able to dry their clothes; and a great deal of sickness was the natural consequence. . . . [M]oreover, the nights were bitterly cold, and the blankets were almost as scarce as tents. There was a great deal of discontent."[14]

The men continued to complain. "The prospects for rations are not flattering," wrote an Alabama volunteer. "We have nothing here to protect us but the starry heavens. . . . [W]e are bound to have hard times here." "Bragg is as badly off for provisions as Rosecrans," admitted a diarist, while a soldier on picket duty summed up all the miseries of his position. Soldiers would grumble about "the corn bread which is familiarly yecleped [sic] 'ole Bragg's bread,'" he wrote. Moreover, they were "very tired of the present 'situation,' and desire a 'change of base' from the hill side as we have to prop ourselves up with rocks and stumps when sleeping." In late November Elise reprimanded her husband, "Are you going to let your poor army make their beds of stones, & lay exposed to the bleak mountain air, without a sufficiency of tents, blankets or clothes?"[15]

Poor conditions took their toll on morale. Following the battle at Chickamauga, Bragg had informed Elise that, although the army had suffered severe losses, "still we are in fine tone, and my troops will respond promptly and cheerfully to any demand made on them." Mary Chesnut's husband, Davis's aide-de-camp, had agreed; after reviewing the Army of Tennessee, he told her, "It was a splendid cavalcade." But as the foul weather and the in-

---

[14] S. L. Blackford, *Letters*, p. 220; Mackall to My dearest Mimi, October 1, 1863, Mackall Papers; William H. T. Walker to his wife, October 1, 1863, William H. T. Walker Papers, Duke University Library; Lafayette McLaws to his wife, October 10, 1863, Lafayette McLaws Papers, Southern Historical Collection; W. R. Montgomery to My Dear Aunt Frank, October 16, 1863, Chickamauga National Military Park; Fitzgerald Ross, *Cities and Camps of the Confederate States*, ed. Richard Barksdale Harwell (Urbana, Ill., 1958), pp. 138–39.

[15] Robert J. Thigpen to W. J. Melton Thigpen, November 15, 1863, Chickamauga National Military Park; *OR*, XXXI (pt. 3), 700; Kean, *Inside*, p. 110; *Mobile Daily Advertiser and Register*, October 29, 1863, "Letter from Claude," October 20, 1863; Elise to Bragg, November 23, 1863, Bragg Papers, University of Texas.

adequacies of rations and supplies continued, Bragg instituted stricter measures to keep his army fit and content. In mid-November he ordered daily parade inspections and required weekly written reports covering all areas affecting the soldiers.[16]

The perennial problem of desertion led to Bragg's insistence on daily counts of effectives present. "Desertions are frequent," noted Brent. "A Lieutenant of the Guard deserted, last night." One man recounted a story of deserting with some companions. After laying their plans, they "bid adieu to Braxton B," and walked 736 miles in forty-five days before arriving home. Meanwhile, Bragg told General Johnston, "The deserters are an incumbrance to me and must be shot or they run off again," and he directed Brent to inform General Pillow, who had requested amnesty for deserters in Tennessee, that "the only promise he could give deserters was to shoot them if caught." Before sending the dispatch, however, Brent modified the order to read, "No conditions could be promised."[17]

Soldiers' preying upon the civilian population, an "unhappy course of conduct so common," continued to be a problem. "Defenseless women, peaceable and loyal citizens, and the families of soldiers . . . have been deprived of their subsistence," Bragg chastised his army. The commander enjoined his officers to suppress this pastime and to arrest offenders. Bragg instructed civilians who were able to identify the offenders to report the facts to him so the soldiers could be punished and reparation could be made. Bragg took his promise of reparation seriously. According to one newspaper account, a woman appeared at his headquarters complaining of damage done to her property when "Forrest with his crittur company" made a "line of fight rite through my yard." Bragg, sitting within earshot, ordered Brent to see the woman's claim settled immediately.[18]

[16] Bragg to Elise, September 27, 1863, Bragg Papers, Library of Congress; Chesnut, *Civil War*, p. 482; *OR*, XXXI (pt. 3), 694.

[17] Brent Diary, November 18, 11, 1863, Bragg Papers, Western Reserve; Heartsill, *Journal*; *OR*, XXXI (pt. 3), 716.

[18] Brent Diary, November 21, 1863, Bragg Papers, Western Reserve; *OR*, XXXI (pt. 3), 710–11; *Mobile Daily Advertiser and Register*, October 10, 1863.

In an effort to boost morale, Bragg offered a furlough of forty days to any man who secured a recruit for his company, providing the recruit had been mustered in and reported for duty before forwarding the furlough application. One soldier, recognizing the difficulty of meeting these requirements, declared it "a perfect humbug!" Bragg later specified that the granting of furloughs depended upon an increase in the number of men present for duty, and he directed those furloughed to bring back both stragglers and recruits.[19]

In November Bragg issued a curious statement to his army dealing with the Federal refusal to exchange prisoners. Bragg appeared to believe that many of his soldiers preferred prisoner-of-war status to serving in his army, and he may have been right. He warned his soldiers that "if taken prisoners those who survive their cruel treatment will . . . languish in Northern dungeons . . . subjected to the taunts and barbarity of a merciless foe." He closed his peroration by generously assuming, "Death on the field of battle . . . will be accepted by brave and patriotic Southern soldiers" rather than imprisonment. "This squints at the black flag," remarked Brent.[20]

Even as Bragg warned his troops of Yankee craft, cunning, and general perfidiousness, considerable fraternizing took place. "After a week or two, our pickets ceased firing at each other," a Confederate officer remembered. "The understanding between them was that as the siege . . . promised to be a long one . . . there was no use to make themselves uncomfortable, and it would be more agreeable to watch each other without trying to kill, than to be incessantly engaged in that disagreeable duty."[21]

At times it appeared the opposing armies were more kindly disposed toward one another than were the eastern and western elements within each army. Historian Bell Wiley believed Long-

[19] OR, XXX (pt.4), 757; Edwin H. Rennolds Diary, October 18, 1863 (copy), Chickamauga National Military Park; OR, XXXI (pt. 3), 647–48.
[20] OR, XXXI (pt. 3), 701; Brent Diary, November 16, 1863, Bragg Papers, Western Reserve.
[21] Manigault, A Carolinian, p. 125.

street's command had a condescending attitude toward the Army of Tennessee. One eastern soldier, while homesick for Virginia, professed himself "willing to help Bragg out of the mud before we go" and another snorted, "These Western troops dont know how to fight Yankees." E. P. Alexander, Longstreet's chief of artillery, observed, "This army is far inferior to the Army of Va." The westerners proved equally contemptuous of the Virginians. After Longstreet's Corps suffered a defeat at the end of October, Liddell wrote, "They had learned how to respect the valor of these Western men, whom with overwhelming confidence they had previously underestimated." Even the Federals knew of this rivalry. One Union soldier reported trouble between the eastern and western factions in Bragg's army, and another attributed it to mutual disparagement. "Some of the rebels that we took belonging to Longstreet's Corps said that they expected that when they gave a yell and made a charge that we would break and run like the Army of the Potomac," he reported, "but in the place of that our men received them on the point of the Bayonet and it rather cooled their military ardor. Now they have got a holy horror of the Army of the Cumberland and want to get back into Virginia."[22]

Although the soldiers fraternized peaceably, the same could not be said for the commanders. In late September Rosecrans sent a flag of truce for the purpose of collecting his wounded, which Bragg granted. Within a week, however, the truce failed because of Bragg's demanding "man for man in exhange of prisoners, sound men for wounded." Not surprisingly, Rosecrans deemed this an extravagant demand and put an end to the agreement. Bragg also enraged Federal general George Thomas by refusing to forward a letter Thomas sent to him by a flag of truce, endorsing

[22] Bell Irvin Wiley, *The Life of Johnny Reb: The Common Soldier of the Confederacy* (Baton Rouge, 1982), p. 340; Maury Klein, *Edward Porter Alexander* (Athens, Ga., 1971), p. 97; Liddell, *Record*, p. 157; Chesley A. Mosman, *The Rough Side of War: The Civil War Journal of Chesley A. Mosman, 1st Lieutenant, Company D, 59th Illinois Volunteer Infantry Regiment*, ed. Arnold Gates (Garden City, N.Y., 1987), p. 100; James H. Wiswell to Dear Father, September 30, 1863, Wiswell Papers.

it, "Genl. Bragg declines to have any intercourse with a man who has betrayed his state." The usually phlegmatic Thomas "warmly uttered many threats." An observer commented, "Few knew that he could flare up in that way."[23]

During October and November Bragg indulged himself in his great passion for reorganizing the army, primarily to dissolve the anti-Bragg cliques. He began by breaking up Walker's Reserve Corps, most of which he transferred to Longstreet's command, thus reducing Walker from corps to division commander. Liddell, too, lost troops and was transferred to Cleburne's Division in Hill's Corps. Requesting an explanation from Bragg, the commander merely told him that "Polk complained so much . . . and Walker had annoyed him so greatly, that he had no other course to pursue."[24]

These changes signaled the beginning of wholesale shuffling. Buckner's Division moved to Polk's Corps, and Bragg exchanged a brigade and two regiments between Breckinridge's and Buckner's divisions. Bragg then really got carried away, ordering a total of twenty-seven transfers of units from one organization to another, often simply swapping units; for example, Bate's Brigade moved from Stewart's to Breckinridge's Division, exchanging with Adams's Brigade, which moved from Breckinridge to Stewart. "All the divisions are being turned Topsy-turvy," complained a soldier, "and soon no one but Gen. Bragg will know anything of the organizations of other troops than those directly around him." This disruption, according to historian Richard McMurry, had much to do with the army's poor conduct under attack a few weeks later.[25]

---

[23] Brent Diary, September 27, October 2, 1863, Bragg Papers, Western Reserve; Freeman Cleaves, *Rock of Chickamauga: The Life of General George H. Thomas* (Norman, Okla., 1948), p. 192.

[24] McMurry, *Two Great Rebel Armies*, pp. 135–36; *OR*, XXX (pt. 4), 704–5; Liddell, *Record*, p. 149.

[25] *OR*, LII (pt. 2), 546; XXXI (pt. 3), 628, 685–86; Rennolds Diary, November 13, 1863, Chickamauga National Military Park; General Orders No. 206, Headquarters, Army of Tennessee, November 15, 1863, Bragg Papers, Western Reserve; McMurry, *Two Great Rebel Armies*, p. 136.

The army also remained sadly depleted. When Bragg informed
Davis by cipher that the effective force of his infantry totaled
41,972, the president was surprised and hoped "there is an error
in the cipher." "There was probably no mistake in the cipher,"
Bragg assured him. "Heavy losses resulting from a desperate and
prolonged fight have depleted us." Elise wrote, "I am filled with
amazement at the small force you had—at the most modest com-
putation I supposed you had 70,000." So reduced were his numbers that Bragg had to disappoint an old supporter, General
Lovell, in his hopes for an appointment in the Army of Tennessee. Bragg explained that he had so few rank-and-file soldiers
that his army already had a glut of officers, "especially Generals,
such as they are."[26]

Bragg tried to secure more soldiers for the Army of Tennessee.
An appeal to Robert E. Lee to send troops from Virginia unsurprisingly met with a denial, but General Howell Cobb offered
a few Georgia state troops, and General Johnston grudgingly forwarded some soldiers at Davis's direction. Just prior to the Federal
advance at Chattanooga in late November, Johnston complained to
Davis that Bragg gave him no information upon which he could
compare their relative needs but hastened to assure the president
that he would help Bragg whenever he decided to attack Rosecrans. At the same time, Johnston informed Bragg that he had
ordered troops to Tennessee with the stipulation that they be used
only for a battle and should then return to him at once. Even
when reinforcements were sent, Bragg had difficulties getting
them forwarded from Atlanta, a situation the quartermaster in
Atlanta happily attributed to Bragg's removing much of their roll-
ing stock to another railroad for transporting Longstreet's Corps
to East Tennessee.[27]

In addition to reinforcements from other departments, Bragg

[26] Bragg to Davis, September 29, 1863 (telegram), Davis Papers, Duke University Library; OR, LII (pt. 2), 534; Elise to Bragg, September 28, 1863, Bragg
Papers, University of Texas; Bragg to Mansfield Lovell, October 20, 1863, Mansfield Lovell Papers, Huntington Library.
[27] OR, LII (pt. 2), 536–37; XXXI (pt. 3), 639, 738–39, 684, 698–99.

assigned Colonel H. W. Walter to gather up all absentees from the Army of Tennessee. Walter's instructions directed him to visit all the places where malingerers might gather—the "quartermasters, commissaries, commandants of post, provost-marshals, and hospitals in the rear"—and to return to the army all those improperly or unnecessarily detailed. Bragg's efforts succeeded to some extent. He soon requested additional infantry accoutrements from the arsenal in Atlanta, explaining that the army was increasing rapidly. It was, in fact, larger than before the Battle at Chickamauga. On October 18 he reported an increase of 5,000 effectives, giving him a total of 46,875.[28]

Bragg, however, had no specific plans for the use of these troops, although Davis prodded him to make some movement. In early October Bragg explained to Cooper that he hoped soon to cross the river in an effort to cut Rosecrans's communications and force him out of Chattanooga. But Bragg equivocated, citing both inadequate transportation and general disorganization. Two weeks later, Bragg used the heavy rains as the reason for not moving forward, compelling Davis to remind his general, "The period most favorable for active operations is rapidly passing away." Echoing Northrop's complaint that Bragg's retreating from Tennessee caused the shortage of supplies, Davis insisted that this situation made it imperative that Bragg recover as much of the lost territory as possible. Later Davis again insisted on a move before all the Federal reinforcements arrived.[29]

Bragg, perhaps influenced by Davis, believed an expedition into East Tennessee against General Ambrose Burnside would draw off some of the Union troops from around Chattanooga. Neither Bragg nor Davis recognized the Union's determination to gain the heart of the South through Chattanooga and Atlanta. Bragg decided to send Longstreet against Burnside, a decision prompted by Longstreet's ludicrous and irresponsible behavior

[28] *Ibid.*, XXXI (pt. 3), 717; XXX (pt. 4), 738, 765.
[29] *Ibid.*, XXX (pt. 4), 726; LII (pt. 2), 545, 555, 561.

during the previous month, which had culminated in the loss of Confederate control of the Union lines of supply.[30]

Longstreet's conduct illustrated his opinion of his own magnificence, as revealed in a series of letters to Senator Louis T. Wigfall in 1863. Longstreet told Wigfall, "In the far west there appears to be opportunities for all kinds of moves to great advantages. Hence my reasons for wishing to go there." However, he warned, only under certain circumstances would General Lee permit him to go: "He will not object to my going anywhere when I can have a separate command. But he will not be likely to consent to my going under any one else. Nor do I desire it." Seeking Wigfall's support for a western command, Longstreet had boasted in February that he could save the Confederacy if he commanded in the West, disingenuously declaring, "I have no personal motives in this."[31]

Wigfall and other powerful figures supported Longstreet's ambition. "I have been pressing Seddon to remove Bragg & send Longstreet to his Army," Wigfall admitted to General Johnston, who believed the president intended to remove Bragg. "If so," he acknowledged, "Longstreet is the man, undoubtedly, especially as [Senator James M.] Mason tells me that he would like it." Seddon also seemed supportive. One of Longstreet's staff officers reported that just before leaving to join Bragg, Seddon's brother told him, "When you get to the Army of Tenn you will find Longstreet in command of the army."[32]

Even as Longstreet traveled toward the Army of Tennessee, he complained to Wigfall, "I don't think that I should be under Bragg." But Longstreet worried, "If I should make any decided

<hr/>

[30] Connelly and Jones, *Politics of Command*, p. 137; *OR*, XXXI (pt. 3), 576–640.
[31] James Longstreet to Louis T. Wigfall, February 4, August 18, 1863, Wigfall Family Papers, University of Texas.
[32] Wigfall to Joseph E. Johnston, February 28, 1863, Joseph E. Johnston Papers; Johnston to Wigfall, March 4, 1863, Wigfall Family Papers, University of Texas; John Walter Fairfax to Joseph Bryan, August 1, 1902, John Walter Fairfax Papers, Virginia Historical Society, Richmond.

opposition the world might say, that I was desirous of a position which would give me fame."[33]

The frustration Longstreet felt at failing to replace Bragg explains, but does not excuse, his behavior throughout October. Assigned to the Lookout Mountain sector, a position allowing the Confederates control of the Federal supply lines, Longstreet displayed a highly cavalier attitude toward his area of command. In later years he even denied that Bragg had entrusted him with the responsibility for this important position.[34]

While Longstreet nonchalantly ignored Bragg's directives and his own responsibilities, the Federals received 20,000 reinforcements under General Joseph Hooker, and a new commander. On October 19 Rosecrans turned his command over to General George Thomas, and on the twenty-third General Ulysses S. Grant arrived to take overall command. Three days later Grant put into motion plans laid by Rosecrans before his departure.[35]

The Federals received full cooperation from Longstreet. Learning of a probable Federal movement in the vicinity of Bridgeport on October 25, Bragg immediately ordered Longstreet to make a reconnaisance, an order Longstreet ignored. Early on the morning of October 27 Hooker's troops crossed the river with no opposition and established a strong position near Brown's Ferry. Once again Bragg ordered Longstreet to dislodge the enemy, and again Longstreet simply did not obey.[36]

On the morning of October 28 Bragg went to Lookout Mountain to observe the execution of his orders, but upon his arrival he discovered nothing to observe, and Longstreet nowhere to be seen. He sent a staff officer to find Longstreet. The officer discovered him "at his camp, two or three miles from his line, at 9 oclk at breakfast." Liddell, joining Bragg in his vigil, reported

[33] Longstreet to Wigfall, September 12, 1863, Wigfall Family Papers, University of Texas.
[34] Longstreet, *From Manassas*, p. 471.
[35] Long and Long, *Civil War*, p. 416; Lamers, *Edge of Glory*, pp. 392, 395.
[36] George W. Brent, "Notes on the investment and operations around Chattanooga," dated September 23, 1863, but obviously written at a later date; Brent Diary, October 27, 1863, Bragg Papers, Western Reserve.

Longstreet eventually "came hastily up on foot," just as an artillery shell exploded close by. Unwilling to witness hot words between his superiors, Liddell wandered off a short distance, where he soon spotted Federal soldiers moving through Raccoon Mountain to join those previously established on the south side of the river. When Bragg learned of these developments, he became "very restless and complained with bitterness of Longstreet's inactivity and lack of ability, asserting him to be greatly overrated." Even though Longstreet had been amply forewarned of the enemy movements, Bragg found he had made no dispositions to attack. The Federals simply moved up an united unmolested.[37]

That afternoon Longstreet decided to try to save face with a night attack on the Federal rear guard. When he presented his plan, Bragg directed Longstreet to use his entire corps as he wished. In addition, he could take a division of Breckinridge's Corps under his command if he needed them. Longstreet, who later denied he had access to these troops, employed only one brigade of 1,700 men to attack the 12,000 Federals.[38]

Exactly what occurred during this night attack, the Battle of Wauhatchie, is unknown. The ill-conceived, ill-planned, and poorly coordinated attack resulted in a shambles. In his report, Longstreet blamed General Evander M. Law, who commanded the attacking brigade, for withdrawing his troops too soon. Law explained that he withdrew on the basis of his understanding of Longstreet's plan of operations. Longstreet would have none of that, accusing Law of abandoning his position because of jealousy among the brigadier generals. However it happened, a soldier succinctly explained, "Longstreet's forces . . . allowed themselves to be surprised and we . . . lost a great advantage we had over the enemy."[39]

[37] Bragg to Chesnut, November 9, 1863, Bragg Papers, Western Reserve; Liddell, *Record*, pp. 156–57.
[38] Brent to Longstreet, 6:00 P.M., 7½ P.M., October 28, 1863, Bragg Papers, Western Reserve; Longstreet, *From Manassas*, p. 475.
[39] *OR*, XXXI (pt. 1), 218, 228; Clement Stanford Watson to My dear Mary, October 19, 23, November 2, 1863, Clement Stanford Watson Family Papers, Louisiana Historical Association Collection.

Longstreet also tried to blame the cavalry forces assigned to cooperate with him. He claimed that Colonel Warren Grigsby failed to report to him as ordered, but Grigsby denied the allegations, stating that Longstreet sent him no instructions for a reconnaisance and that he had indeed reported the enemy's movements to Longstreet.[40]

On the morning following the debacle, Longstreet penned an amazing letter to Bragg in which he stated, "I did not contemplate any such move as your note would indicate." What he intended to do, he claimed, was merely to seize a commanding hill over the enemy's road and hold it. To what purpose he did not say. However, he went on in some confusion, "if time and circumstances favored," he had planned to attack the Federals with an entire division in an attempt to crowd them into the river. When it became too late, in his opinion, to begin a forward movement, he left the field believing nothing could be done. Soon thereafter, however, he received word from General Micah Jenkins that a brigade was indeed heavily engaged with Union troops. "I presume," he wrote hours after the engagement, "that little or nothing was accomplished."[41]

Bragg's first communication to Davis on the Wauhatchie affair strongly insinuated "disobedience of orders & slowness of movements." In another message to Davis, Bragg described Longstreet's performance as "a gross neglect resulting in a most serious disaster." Davis expressed dismay. "Such disastrous failure as you describe cannot consistently be overlooked," he wrote. "I suppose you have received the explanation due to the Government, and I shall be pleased if one satisfactory has been given."[42] It was not.

The closest Longstreet came to taking responsibility for the failure appeared in his fairy-tale version of the war. "It was an oversight of mine," he humbly confessed, "not to give definite

[40] J. R. B. Burtwell to J. P. Jones, November 3, 1863, Bragg Papers, Western Reserve.

[41] Longstreet to Brent, Headquarters, October 29, 1863, *ibid.*

[42] Brent Diary, October 30, 1863; Bragg to Chesnut, November 9, 1863, *ibid.*; *OR*, LII (pt. 2), 558.

orders for the troops to return to their camps before leaving them." Others have not been so gentle. "If anyone should bear the blame it is General Longstreet," concluded an article on the affair. Connelly described the battle as blundering and a disaster. One set of biographers decided Longstreet "was careless and handled matters poorly," while perhaps the kindest words came from a pair of biographers who reported with fine understatement, "The Longstreet of this period is not one to whom great deeds can be credited." E. P. Alexander declared Longstreet guilty of "contributory negligence." The most generous and ingenious treatment of all came from Longstreet's chief of staff, Moxley Sorrel. In his recollections, Sorrel virtually ignored all military activities during the entire month spent in Chattanooga, neatly jumping in his narrative from the Battle at Chickamauga to Longstreet's East Tennessee campaign.[43]

Longstreet's failure to hold his assigned position on the Confederate left resulted in his separation from the Army of Tennessee. On October 29 Davis suggested to Bragg that Longstreet might be assigned to rout Burnside from East Tennessee. After the war, Grant wondered why these troops were sent away during the critical period at Chattanooga, since Knoxville was of no use to the Confederates as long as the Federals held Chattanooga. Pointing out that if Chattanooga fell to the Confederates, Knoxville would follow suit, he wrote, "I have never been able to see the wisdom of this move." Grant failed to understand the workings of the mind of Jefferson Davis, who feared the real Federal thrust would be through East Tennessee and then into Virginia. Grant read Davis well enough, though, to conclude that Longstreet was sent to Knoxville "because Mr. Davis had an exalted opinion of his own

[43] Longstreet, *From Manassas*, p. 447; Guy R. Swanson and Timothy D. Johnson, "Conflict in East Tennessee: General Law, Jenkins, and Longstreet," *Civil War History*, XXXI (1985), 106; Connelly, *Autumn of Glory*, p. 260; H. J. Eckenrode and Bryan Conrad, *James Longstreet, Lee's War Horse* (Chapel Hill, N.C., 1936), p. 249; Sanger and Hay, *Longstreet*, p. 219; E. P. Alexander, "Manuscript," vol. 41, Edward Porter Alexander Papers, Southern Historical Collection; G. Moxley Sorrel, *Recollections of a Confederate Staff Officer* (Dayton, Ohio, 1978; orig. ed., 1905), pp. 199–215.

military genius. . . . On several occasions during the war he came to the relief of the Union army by means of his *superior military genius*."[44]

Bragg later claimed he preferred to send Breckinridge on the expedition to Knoxville, but because of Longstreet's "disobedience of orders . . . I yielded my convictions to the President's policy and sent Longstreet instead." This statement, made ten years after the incident, does not jibe with statements Bragg made at the time. On October 31 Bragg told Davis that the movement of the Virginia troops would be a great relief. He remarked to Liddell that he sent Longstreet "to get rid of him and see what he could do on his own resources." Liddell believed this decision foolish, but "Bragg was headstrong and too often unreasonable." Artillery chief Alexander held that sending Longstreet to Knoxville "cannot be excused or palliated. It was a monumental failure [of Bragg] to appreciate the glaring weakness of his position."[45]

Bragg was, however, fully versed on the folly of depending upon Longstreet to carry out assignments in a reasonable and responsible manner. He probably did not injure his chances at Chattanooga any more by sending him than by keeping him. Meanwhile Longstreet proved what he could do with independent command—he failed completely.

[44] *OR*, LII (pt. 2), 554; Ulysses S. Grant, *Personal Memoirs of U. S. Grant* (2 vols., New York, 1885), II, 96–97, 87.

[45] Bragg to E. T. Sykes, February 8, 1873 (copy), Polk Papers, University of the South; *OR*, LII (pt. 2), 556; Liddell, *Record*, p. 157; E. P. Alexander, *Military Memoirs of a Confederate: A Critical Narrative* (New York, 1907), p. 480.

CHAPTER VII

No satisfactory excuse

November, 1863

"I AM INFINITELY STRONGER than ever with my Army," Bragg boasted to Elise in mid-November 1863. "It will be seen my friends are aroused, and even the soldiers and inferior officers are coming out."[1] It is no wonder he felt a sense of accomplishment and triumph. In the past six weeks, while besieging the Federals in Chattanooga, he had rid himself of the more irascible and recalcitrant of his subordinates, and in the process had received the blessing of President Davis. But his good fortune would not last much longer. Bragg had allowed the Federals to strengthen their position, and they were now ready to push the Army of Tennessee off of the heights and out of the Chattanooga area.

Those six weeks had been difficult. Shortly after the battle at Chickamauga he complained to Elise, "In mind I am greatly harrassed and distressed." Two weeks later he unburdened himself to the brother of General Beauregard. Bragg, fearing that his responsibilities had become too heavy for him to carry without assistance and support, appeared "dejected and nearly despondent." Bragg's despondency and care showed in his face and manner. "His countenance shows marks of deep and long continued study," wrote an infantry captain. "He has a wild abstracted look, and pays little attention to what is passing around him; his mind seems to be in a continued strain."[2]

---

[1] Bragg to Elise, November 14 [1863] (photostat), Bragg Papers, Library of Congress.

[2] Bragg to Elise, September 27, 1863 (photostat), *ibid.*; *OR*, XXX (pt. 4), 735; Joab Goodman to My dear Niece, September 28, 1863 (copy), Chickamauga National Military Park.

Despite the strains on him, Bragg elicited admiration from observers. A correspondent on duty at Lookout Mountain found Bragg's face "more expressive of goodness than of greatness." Although he seemed "careworn," his face "quite wrinkled" and his beard "quite gray," the reporter declared Bragg resembled an "amiable pastor." Bragg also received accolades from Tennessee's congressional representative William G. Swan, who believed Bragg's qualities had so endeared him to his soldiers "that those who have served with him longest love him most." An officer declared, "No army ever had more confidence in its leader and . . . followed . . . more enthusiastically than this ragged army has & will follow the lead of its gaunt grim chieftain."[3]

Bragg also provoked sympathy, tempered with doubts. "I do not think that justice is done to Bragg," Josiah Gorgas wrote. "I think what he has done is not entirely appreciated, tho' it must be confessed what he has lost is most apparent." Kate Cumming admitted that she was losing confidence in Bragg but believed "we must not judge, as we can not tell with what General Bragg has to contend."[4]

In the midst of these mixed reviews, Bragg's good spirits put him in a playful mood as he wrote to Elise. "To avoid trouble," he explained, "and enable me to get along with only a small pocket comb," he had had his hair "cropped almost as close as poor Morgan's in the penitentiary. Even you," he teased, "would not get a hold on that or my beard were you at my side." But now he found himself in a quandary. A woman in Virginia had requested locks of his and of Elise's hair. Having none to spare, and not having access to the hair Elise had had cut and sent to him in the spring, he told her, "You will now have to make it good from what is left [of yours]. How to gratify her about my own is a difficulty." Elise did not feel she could part with any of hers, either. "My hair is far

[3] *Richmond Sentinel*, November 14, 1863; William G. Swan to *Atlanta Constitutionalist*, quoted in *Mobile Daily Advertiser and Register*, November 24, 1863; E. John Ellis to Thomas C. W. Ellis, September 27, 1863, Ellis and Family Papers.
[4] Gorgas, *Diary*, p. 69; Cumming, *Kate*, p. 171.

too short & too little of it, to send to an entire stranger," she remonstrated. Besides, she had other requests to tend to. "A young lady . . . neither pretty[,] amiable or interesting, has been boring me to send a kiss," she teased, but she confessed, "perhaps if she had been *pretty* I might not have sent it."[5]

In the same letter, taking advantage of her husband's good humor, Elise broached the subject of joining him at his winter quarters. "I scarcely hope you will be chivalrous enough to let me visit you," she complained. Having heard of several Union wives who spent time with their general-husbands, she believed "the northern ladies cannot be so *demoralizing* to an army as we southern ones. . . . Yet," she challenged, "their husbands successes were not the less great." But then, she conceded, "Perhaps as they are *strong minded* women, they may assist their husbands mentally." Fortunately for Bragg, military events intervened before he had an opportunity to respond to Elise's goad regarding his chivalry.[6]

Bragg's good spirits and health, never experienced during periods of stress, indicate that he did not recognize the dangerous position of his army, although it was obvious to others. Liddell reported that Bragg "hesitated, delayed, and finally sat down on the ridge overlooking the place, apparently undecided what to do." When Longstreet and his troops left for East Tennessee, Colonel Brent voiced doubts on the wisdom of dispersing the army, noting that it was now in a dangerous position. Two days before the Federals attacked, Brent remained anxious: "This distribution of forces seems hazardous."[7]

While Bragg dispersed his forces, frequent reports reached his headquarters of Federal movements and reinforcements. On November 11 Brent noted that Sherman approached Chattanooga with 25,000 soldiers, and on the eighteenth Bragg ordered Gen-

---

[5] Bragg to Elise, November 14, 1863, Bragg Papers, Library of Congress; Elise to Bragg, November 23, 1863, Bragg Papers, University of Texas.

[6] Elise to Bragg, November 23, 1863, Bragg Papers, University of Texas.

[7] Liddell, *Record*, p. 148; Brent Diary, November 5, 8, 21, 1863, Bragg Papers, Western Reserve.

eral Liddell to reconnoiter Wills Valley, where enemy troops were reported to be accumulating. Soldier Joshua K. Callaway, on picket at the foot of Missionary Ridge, told his wife on November 19 that the Federals had driven in the Confederate pickets, and warned, "You need not be at all surprised to hear of some demonstration at any moment."[8]

Still, Bragg virtually ignored the situation. On November 21, as Grant began deploying his army for an attack, Bragg believed that his left flank, anchored on Lookout Mountain, faced little danger, but that the enemy would probably attempt a move on the right in an effort to get between Longstreet and himself. Just hours before his left bore the brunt of the first Federal advance, Bragg continued to believe the movement only a feint. He felt so secure in his army's position that, on his invitation, fourteen ladies were expected to visit the army on November 22. On the same day Bragg further dispersed his army by ordering Buckner's division to Longstreet's aid.[9]

In this somewhat euphoric state, with all of his attention focused on his backyard enemies, Bragg simply failed to recognize the danger in his front yard. Buckner reported that his commander "seems blind to the state of affairs," and Liddell found Bragg "singularly indifferent. . . . I thought he was infatuated with the hopeless anxiety to take Chattanooga. This caused him to overlook the gathering storm."[10]

While Bragg thus dallied, played, and depleted his army, Grant reinforced the Federal army and carefully planned his strategy. Having amassed 56,359 effectives as opposed to Bragg's 46,165, and having opened the lines of supply, Grant turned his attention

[8] Brent Diary, November 11, 18, 1863, Bragg Papers, Western Reserve; Joshua K. Callaway to Dear Lolly, November 19, 1863, Callaway Papers.

[9] Brent Diary, November 21, 23, 1863, Bragg Papers, Western Reserve; *Richmond Daily Dispatch*, November 28, 1863 (item reported by Missionary Ridge correspondent on November 22, 1863).

[10] Simon B. Buckner to Victor von Sheliha, November 5, 1863, Buckner Papers; Liddell, *Record*, p. 148. For full discussion of the battles on Lookout Mountain and Missionary Ridge, see Connelly, *Autumn of Glory*, pp. 270–71, 273–76; Foote, *Civil War*, II, 845–59.

to forcing the Confederates out of Chattanooga. On November 21 he moved, deploying Sherman on his left, Thomas in the center, and Hooker on the right. His plan called for Sherman and Hooker to attack on Bragg's flanks, while Thomas threatened the center and formed a reserve to aid either of the others as necessary. Because of rain and wind, the deployment took longer than planned, so the Federals did not make final preparations for the attack until the next day.[11]

On November 23 Grant finally managed to grab Bragg's attention. In the afternoon, his army advanced, drove in the pickets all along the greatly extended Confederate line, and took possession of Orchard Knob and another prominent point, both of which he promptly fortified with rifled guns.[12]

Bragg's primary concern continued to be for his right, and in this he read Grant correctly. Grant expected Sherman to spearhead the attack. Bragg's attention was so focused on his right, however, that in order to strengthen it he seriously weakened the left. In late afternoon of November 23, Bragg ordered Hardee, in command on the left, to move to the extreme right, taking Walker's Division with him. This left General Carter L. Stevenson in command on Lookout Mountain with a total of 8,726 troops to cover an extended line of defense. Because of the length of the line (more than a mile) and the small force allocated to protect it, the position was extremely vulnerable. So thin was the defense that along parts of the line there were no soldiers for yards at a time.[13]

With this small force, strung out along a lengthy line and

[11] Thomas L. Livermore, *Numbers and Losses in the Civil War in America, 1861–1865* (Dayton, Ohio, 1986), pp. 106–8.

[12] John Hoffmann, *The Confederate Collapse at the Battle of Missionary Ridge: The Reports of James Patton Anderson and His Brigade Commanders* (Dayton, Ohio, 1985), p. 60.

[13] *OR*, XXXI (pt. 2), 668, 674, 718, 734, 720, 721, 686, 687; Kinloch Falconer, "Statement of the Strength of the Army of Tennessee in the Engagement before Chattanooga, Losses in These Engagements, Strength of the Army on Its arrival at Dalton, Its Strength on the 20th Inst., and the Increase of Effective Strength since the Retreat and to 20th December," December 20, 1863, Joseph E. Johnston Papers.

poorly situated and entrenched, Stevenson tried to hold the Confederate left against attack by Hooker's three divisions. About 1:00 P.M. on November 23 Stevenson heard heavy firing in the valley, and after spending the afternoon observing the enemy's movements, he notified Bragg that the Federals intended to attack his sector. Nevertheless, at 8:45 P.M., Hardee ordered Stevenson to send the Parrot guns from Lookout Point to the right of the Confederate line and to replace them with two Napoleons. Stevenson did so, but the Napoleons could not be depressed sufficiently to reach the base of the mountain, where their fire would be most effective against the advancing foe.[14]

At nine the next morning the Federals began a concerted assault on Lookout Mountain, easily taking the overstretched Confederate picket line in the left flank and rear. Despite the pickets' ferocious fighting, the Federals, after a brief setback, advanced steadily and irresistibly. As the Confederates fell back, they used rocks and irregularities of the ground to provide some protection. The troops held so tenaciously that many waited too long to retreat and found themselves prisoners. Reinforcements allowed the Confederates to hold until darkness covered their retreat.[15]

Bragg seemed to have little understanding of the events taking place on his left. Sometime during the morning he notified Stevenson that he must "defend obstinately" any attempt by the enemy to cross Chattanooga Creek, under no circumstances allowing himself to be cut off from the rest of the army. In the afternoon Stevenson made several requests for reinforcements. At 2:00 P.M. on November 24 he reported the enemy had the Craven House and was massing a large force there, but if he received strong reinforcement immediately, he thought he could drive them away. These appeals proved useless, and Stevenson finally received verbal notification that no reinforcements would be sent. Instead, Bragg wanted him to withdraw as best he could under cover of the dense fog that proved both a help and a hindrance

[14] OR, XXXI (pt. 2), 718, 728, 675, 726; L. J. Daniel, Cannoneers, p. 110.
[15] OR, XXXI (pt. 2), 694; J. W. Ward to Dear Mother, December 2, 1863, J. W. Ward Family Correspondence, University of Texas.

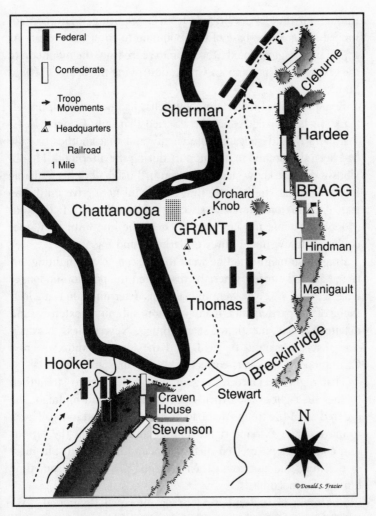

BATTLES OF LOOKOUT MOUNTAIN & MISSIONARY RIDGE

throughout the day. A brigade from Breckinridge's Division advanced as far as the base of the mountain to cover the retreat. At 2:30 P.M., Bragg ordered Stevenson to retire from the mountain to the east side of Chattanooga Creek, destroying the bridges behind him.[16]

Bragg remained uncertain about what had occurred on his left flank. In his official report, he asserted that only General E. C. Walthall's Brigade engaged the enemy and that another brigade had been dispatched to his support during the afternoon. He obviously did not know that Stevenson had used all of his available forces and that the brigade Bragg sent did not arrive until 8:00 P.M. At that time Stevenson's weary soldiers finally left Lookout Mountain, while the new arrivals held the line until they, too, could withdraw under cover of darkness and fog.[17]

Bragg also maintained he went to the scene of the fighting, arriving around sunset, where he discovered the position no longer tenable. Just where he went to make this determination is unclear. None of the participants, many of whom submitted extensive and detailed reports, mentioned seeing Bragg. Nevertheless, his decision that the ground be held until the forces withdrew across Chattanooga Creek was correct in the circumstances.[18]

That night, at Hardee's urging, Bragg decided to strengthen further his right at the expense of the left. Around midnight, he ordered all of the troops that had been west of Chattanooga Creek to move to the extreme right. Throughout the night the various unit commanders received their orders and moved out, but most of the units did not reach their assigned places until sometime during the morning.[19]

The night of November 24 Bragg informed Richmond, "We have had a prolonged struggle for Lookout Mountain to-day and sustained considerable loss in one division. Elsewhere the enemy

[16] Stevenson to Brent, 2:00 P.M., [November] 24, 1863, Bragg Papers, Western Reserve; OR, XXXI (pt. 2), 721, 678.
[17] OR, XXXI (pt. 2), 664, 721.
[18] Ibid., 664.
[19] Ibid., 722.

has only maneuvered for position." A clerk in the war department called the dispatch unintelligible, complaining that the report gave no indication of the probable result. Although Bragg's dispatch made no mention of the heavy fog which hung over Lookout all day, the diarist aptly remarked, "To us it *seems* as if Bragg has been in a fog ever since the battle of the 20th of September."[20]

Bragg still did not appear to comprehend that his army could be dislodged from their position of seeming impregnability, although some of his subordinates seriously doubted the wisdom of remaining to fight. Cleburne, who had been recalled from Chickamauga Station on November 23 while preparing to take his division to Longstreet's aid, moved to the far right, where he checked Sherman's advance. Bragg also expected Cleburne to protect the railroad bridge to his rear. Having learned of the loss of Lookout Mountain and recognizing the vulnerability of the position on Missionary Ridge, Cleburne assumed the army would retreat beyond the Chickamauga and, in preparation, sent his ordnance and artillery across that river. In the meantime he sent Captain Irving A. Buck to Bragg's headquarters, expecting to receive orders to fall back. At midnight Buck returned with astounding news: Bragg had decided to remain on Missionary Ridge to await the enemy's attack.[21]

Cleburne had made his assumption of a withdrawal upon his knowledge of the situation on the right. General Arthur Manigault, posted in the center of the Confederate line, also believed the army would retreat the night of November 24–25. He came to that conclusion from the movements of the wagon trains and the tenor of several orders he received from army headquarters. Based on these movements and orders, Manigault later thought the retreat must have been called off for some reason unknown to him. He also believed that if Grant had not attacked on the twenty-fifth, Bragg would have retreated that night.[22]

[20] *Ibid.*, 677; J. B. Jones, *Rebel War Clerk's Diary*, II, 104.
[21] *OR*, XXXI (pt. 2), 746–48.
[22] Manigault, *A Carolinian*, p. 136.

Both of these experienced soldiers knew their business. Bragg did question the advisability of remaining in position on the ridge and held a conference with Hardee and Breckinridge to decide what action should be taken. Hardee opted for an immediate withdrawal to Chickamauga, but Breckinridge disagreed. According to one account, Breckinridge stated that "if they couldn't fight here with such advantage of position, they couldn't fight anywhere." Brent, however, noted in his journal at the time that Breckinridge and Bragg both agreed that there simply was not enough time to organize an orderly retreat. When Hardee realized he had been outvoted, he insisted upon reinforcements to hold the right; hence the movement of the troops who had unsuccessfully defended Lookout Mountain to the far end of the Confederate line throughout the night.[23]

Despite the seeming impregnability of Missionary Ridge, the position lacked real security. Manigault wrote after the war that Bragg was overconfident in the strength of his position and had underrated the number and the fighting qualities of his adversaries. In justification it must be noted that during the war neither Bragg nor his army had ever prepared for a defensive battle; consequently they lacked experience in selecting and preparing a position to repulse a determined foe.[24] Believing Missionary Ridge secure against frontal assault, Bragg focused his concern on the flanks, particularly the right.

The lack of preparation for the center's defense indicates just how secure Bragg believed it to be. Until the night of November 23, Hindman's entire division, commanded by General Patton Anderson, held a line at the foot of Missionary Ridge. That night, Breckinridge ordered the line be divided, General Zachariah Deas taking command of the troops at the foot, and Anderson commanding those moved to the crest. Not until these troops reached the top of Missionary Ridge did the construction of protective works begin.[25]

[23] Hughes, *Hardee*, p. 171; Brent Diary, November 24, 1863, Bragg Papers, Western Reserve.

[24] Manigault, *A Carolinian*, p. 142; W. C. Davis, *Breckinridge*, p. 387.

[25] Manigault, *A Carolinian*, pp. 134–35; Hoffmann, *Collapse*, pp. 36–37, 59.

Manigault's frustrations in carrying out his assignment atop the ridge exemplified the problems faced by all of the brigade commanders. The line hurriedly determined by an engineer officer did not meet with Manigault's approval. Manigault's proposal that he lay out the line himself seemed to please the engineer, who informed Manigault that the line was to be established on the highest point of the ridge, rather than on the military crest. This was exactly what Manigault did not want to do, as this would make much of the slope inaccessible to Confederate fire. In addition to poor engineering, the troops lacked the necessary tools to accomplish their mission. To start, the men had about forty entrenching tools, but shortly these were taken away by someone in higher authority, leaving them with only four axes. Consequently, the work progressed very slowly and in the end provided little protection. Because of his own intervention in the laying of the line, Manigault at least succeeded in firing on the approaching Federals with some effect. This proved not to be the case in other units of Breckinridge's Corps.[26]

Bragg's placement of artillery also lacked perception of the problems of holding a position such as Missionary Ridge. Larry Daniel, historian of the artillery of the Army of Tennessee, charged that Bragg had distributed the guns poorly, sprinkling them all along the overstretched line, often widely separated from each other, and some with no infantry support whatsoever. On the morning of November 25, much of the artillery had not even been positioned, and some did not arrive until the Federals began their advance. Because of this tardiness, many of the batteries lacked protective works. "Despite the army's presence at Chattanooga for two months," Daniel asserted, "it soon became evident that much of the artillery's defense would be a hurried, last-minute affair."[27]

On the far right of Bragg's extended line, Cleburne's command had already blocked one Federal attempt to capture a Confederate retreat route, and the battle would begin here the next morning.

[26] Manigault, *A Carolinian*, pp. 134–35.
[27] L. J. Daniel, *Cannoneers*, pp. 112–13; *OR*, LII (pt. 1), 97.

Albert Jernigan, destined to lose his arm on the morrow, reported his position as poorly prepared for defense as the rest of Bragg's line. "We had slept but little," he wrote, "having been engaged in felling trees, entrenching and erecting breastworks. But the morning found our works but frail, and along portions of the line none at all on account of the scarcity of implements with which to work."[28]

Bragg, however, believed the extreme right to be well protected and soldiered during his two visits there on the morning of November 25. One soldier who saw him early in the morning feared that "his presence with us indicates hot work at our point today." Hot work, indeed, but when Bragg returned to this point about 11:00 A.M., he himself felt confident. "Though greatly outnumbered," he later wrote, "such was the strength of our position that no doubt was entertained of our ability to hold it."[29]

Bragg's confidence in the defense of his right flank proved correct. Despite fierce assaults by the Federals, Cleburne managed to hold firmly. He held, in fact, until dark, at which time the order came to retire, "on account," declared a soldier, "of the disgraceful conduct of troops of other parts of the field." But the units to Cleburne's left had little to do for most of the day. A soldier posted in Walthall's Brigade described the battle as "the grandest and most sublime scene I ever witnessed," but his own unit's participation was so tame he believed that "ladies could have witnessed [it]."[30]

Such was not the case in other sections of the line. During the morning, while listening to the fight raging on the far right, the troops in Breckinridge's Corps watched the Federals prepare for an advance against the army's left and center. The sight inspired one Confederate to describe it as "a huge serpent, uncoil[ing] his massive folds into shapely lines." Although a cavalryman believed

[28] Albert Jernigan to Dear Parents, May 18, 1872, Jernigan Letter, University of Texas.
[29] Coleman Diary, November 25, 1863; OR, XXXI (pt. 2), 664–65.
[30] Coleman Diary, November 25, 1863; Ward to Dear Mother, December 2, 1863, Ward Family Correspondence.

it "appalling to behold," Manigault had no doubt the Army of Tennessee could repulse the enemy.[31] He was wrong.

Posted in two lines, one at the foot of Missionary Ridge, and the other at the crest, Breckinridge's troops proved poorly prepared for the battle. When Deas was assigned command at the foot of the ridge, his orders instructed him to hold the position to the last. Protesting that the position offered no advantages for a stubborn resistance, Deas sought a change in orders, which did not come until mid-morning of November 25. The tardiness of the new instructions—to fall back skirmishing as the enemy advanced and to form up at the crest of the ridge—caused confusion in the first line of defense as the battle opened. The lower-echelon officers and the soldiers had not been informed of the change in orders. As the Federals advanced, those who did not hear the order to retire up the ridge believed their comrades were simply fleeing. Refusing to follow suit, many were captured or killed.[32]

Those who did hear the order to retreat to the crest fared little better. One soldier believed they should never have left the entrenchments at the foot of the ridge. "Our first position . . . was infinitely better than the elevated position at its top," he wrote. "I do not believe any troops would have reached our line of works, had we remained at them." Another described the difficulties encountered in retreating up the ridge under battle conditions. "The hill was dreadful steep and the enemy kept up a continual fire. . . . Many a poor fellow fell exhausted and was taken prisoner. I did not think that I should be able to reach the top for I had on a heavy knapsack. . . . When I reached the top of the ridge I . . . lay there for several minutes to recover breath." This example bears out Manigault's complaint that "many failed to reach the summit at all . . . & those who at last gained the crest, reached it in a broken down, exhausted & demoralized condition." Many

[31] OR, XXXI (pt. 2), 739; Manigault, A Carolinian, p. 137; Howell Carter, A Cavalryman's Reminiscences of the Civil War (New Orleans, n.d.), p. 98.
[32] Hoffmann, Collapse, pp. 53–54, 61.

arrived with no arms or accoutrements, leaving them behind in an effort to save their lives.[33]

With hardly a pause, the Federals clambered up the ridge behind the fleeing Confederates. The positioning of the lines along the crest prevented the defenders from effectively reaching the attackers with their fire. Before long the center began to crumble as Union soldiers seized point after point, in some cases firing captured Confederate artillery into those still holding on. Many individuals and units panicked, while others maintained their composure and organization. Enough fled, however, to make the position of those who remained untenable. "Resistance," Deas remarked, "now had ceased to be a virtue."[34]

At about the same time, the extreme left, commanded by Stewart, also gave way. This position, too, had been poorly prepared for defense. Since falling back from Chattanooga Valley (between Lookout Mountain and Missionary Ridge) early on November 25, there had been little time to construct protective works. One soldier described the line as having "long intervales [sic] between brigades which the Federals soon discovered." The Union's second assault "came up in a collum through our intervales and got over the Brest works . . . in a few minutes the whole left give way and [a] regular run commenced . . . it appeared a marical how any of us got out of such a shower of bulletts." Troops sent to their aid discovered them surrounded on three sides. As the Southerners retreated in disorder, the enemy overran the entire ridge; great numbers of unfortunate Confederates did not escape.[35]

With such pressures on the left and the center, it is no wonder the Southern soldiers broke and ran. "We made . . . a perfect stampede," one soldier confessed. "It was a disgraceful affair our men did not half fight," he complained, blaming their behavior on

[33] R. M. Gray, "Reminiscences," Southern Historical Collection; Hoffmann, *Collapse*, pp. 60–61.

[34] Hoffmann, *Collapse*, p. 55.

[35] Bailey Diary, November 25, 1863, Louisiana Historical Association Collection; William W. Mackall to J. E. Johnston, December 9, 1863, Mackall Papers; *OR*, XXXI (pt. 2), 665, 319.

the discouragement caused by the fall of Lookout Mountain. "If we could not hold such a place as this," he believed, "we could not hold anything." Another recalled, "Such Confusion and disorder I never beheld before amongst 'Rebels.' . . . [F]right was in the ascendant and no entreaty or threat could stem the current." As they fled, the various units became separated and mixed with others. Adding to the confusion, a Federal shell made a lucky hit, exploding the limber chests of a battery.[36]

Bragg still seemed enveloped in a fog, with no understanding of the desperate plight of his soldiers. His army had suffered most of the classic symptoms of defeat—the loss of batteries, the involuntary retreat of his firing line, useless efforts to regain certain positions, an abnormally rapid thinning out of his troops, units cut off and captured because of disruption of the battle line—and yet he futilely attempted to stem the tide of retreat. Taylor Beatty reported, "General Bragg exposed himself very much—but uselessly—the men would not rally." Others described Bragg's efforts more colorfully. "He got down off his horse," one soldier wrote, "and as the men ran past him, he called out to them not [to] disgrace themselves, but stop and [save] their country—fight for your families &c and says I (your General) am here." During Bragg's harangue, a large soldier "stepped up behind Genl Bragg and carr[ied] him around the waist and says 'And Heres your mule' and went on." Unsurprisingly, the commander lost his temper. "Bragg had joined the church at Shelbyville," a soldier testified, "but he had back-slid at Missionary Ridge. He was cursing like a sailor."[37]

Bragg's predicament elicited sympathy. One of his soldiers testified that now Bragg discovered how little his soldiers respected

[36] Bailey Dairy, November 25, 1863; Gray, "Reminiscences"; Robert Watson, Confederate War Diary, part II, p. 20, November 25, 1863 (typescript), Chickamauga National Military Park; *OR*, LII (pt. 1), 97.

[37] Michael Howard, *Clausewitz* (Oxford, 1983), p. 45; Beatty Diary, November 25, 1863; Samuel T. Foster, *One of Cleburne's Command: The Civil War Reminiscences and Dairy of Capt. Samuel T. Foster, Granbury's Texas Brigade, C.S.A.*, ed. Norman D. Brown (Austin, Tex., 1980), p. 66; Sam R. Watkins, *"Co. Aytch": A Side Show of the Big Show* (New York, 1979), pp. 117–18.

him, as they "execrated and denounced him as the author of all
their misfortunes." "I felt sorry for General Bragg," wrote another observer. "The army was routed, and Bragg looked so
scared. Poor fellow, he looked so hacked and whipped and mortified and chagrined at defeat, and all along the line, when Bragg
would pass, the soldiers would raise the yell, 'Here is your mule';
'Bully for Bragg, he's h——l on retreat.'"[38]

Fortunately, not all of the army had been routed. The left and
center had collapsed, but some of the units maintained integrity.
General A. W. Reynolds reported his brigade "acted with the gallantry & coolness of veterans. . . . [They] obeyed every order
promptly & without the slightest confusion or disorder." Bate's
Division also held together. Admitting that "there was much difficulty in stopping the debris which had sloughed off from the first
line," Bate praised the personal exertions of Bragg and his staff,
which helped to establish a new line about 1,000 yards to the rear.
Bragg ordered Bate to hold as long as possible before retiring to
Chickamauga Station behind the rest of the army. Bate did so,
buying enough time for the army to cross Chickamauga Creek.[39]

Hardee's Corps, on the right flank, did not break at all. As the
Federals swept along the crest of Missionary Ridge, units to
Hardee's left, led by Walthall, changed front so their lines lay
perpendicular to the ridge, holding the enemy in check until after
dark, while the army retreated across the river and gathered at
Chickamauga Station. Many who fought on the right heard the
order for a retreat with amazement. When Albert Jernigan, hospitalized in the rear of the line, heard the order to evacuate, he
remarked, "This was the first intimation I had of a defeat. . . .
Until now I was under the impression that we had gained a
glorious victory. I knew we had beaten them on the right."[40]

One rear-guard observer reported the sad condition of many of
the soldiers. "They were gunless, cartridge-boxless, knapsackless,

[38] *Southern Historical Society Papers*, XII (1884), 36; Watkins, *"Co. Aytch"*, p. 118.
[39] Hoffmann, *Collapse*, p. 77; *OR*, LII (pt. 2), 578; XXXI (pt. 2), 742–43.
[40] *OR*, XXXI (pt. 2), 697, 706, 738; Jernigan to Dear Parents, May 18, 1872,
Jernigan Letter.

canteenless, and all other military accoutermentsless, and sword-less, and officerless, and they all seemed to have the 'possum grins, like Bragg looked."[41] They must, indeed, have felt as sheepish as their commander: Bragg because of the disaster to his army, the soldiers because of the sad spectacle they presented to those lucky enough not to have been pursued up Missionary Ridge.

The troops displayed varying attitudes to their predicament. "Some were mad, others cowed, and many were laughing," reported a soldier. "Some were cursing Bragg, some the Yankees, and some were rejoicing at the defeat." Bragg "was so much depressed that I had not an unkind word at hand to reproach him for his unmitigated follies," stated Liddell. Even under these distressing circumstances, though, one soldier still admired his commander. "If Bragg did not display superior Generalship," he declared, "he did show unusual courage and presence of mind."[42]

Bragg attempted to regroup the army at Chickamauga Station during the night of November 25-26. "Everything is confusion," declared one soldier. "Stragglers innumerable hunting their command." Others apparently did not care to join their units. Cleburne charged that by 9:00 P.M. "everything was across [the Chickamauga] except the dead and a few stragglers lingering . . . for the purpose of being captured, faint-hearted patriots succumbing to the hardships of the war and the imagined hopelessness of the hour."[43]

Desertions continued heavy for a time after the loss of Missionary Ridge. On November 29 Bragg informed General Howell Cobb that many stragglers had left the army and directed him to arrest and return all who reached Atlanta. A week after the defeat, a soldier still complained of "a great deal of straglin . . . and goin home." A statement of strength on December 20 bears out the charges of desertion and straggling. Although the army's loss in killed and wounded totaled 2,521, upon its arrival in Dalton,

[41] Watkins, "Co. Aytch", p. 119.
[42] Ibid., pp. 127-28; Liddell, Record, p. 160; Gray, "Reminiscences."
[43] Coleman Diary, November 25, 1863; OR, XXXI (pt. 2), 753.

7,238 soldiers could not be accounted for. A Tennessee woman reported that many deserters came home with tales of starvation, nakedness, and demoralization; but, she charged, their appearance "gives the *lie*, to their assertions."[44]

Bragg's presence of mind noted by the admiring soldier stood him in good stead during the night of November 25. After determining the condition of the army at Chickamauga Station, Bragg decided to withdraw even farther from Grant's powerful and victorious army. Early the next day his forces continued southward, marching seventeen miles before stopping for the night at Catoosa.[45]

Bragg assigned Cleburne's Division as the rear guard. On November 27, as the rest of Bragg's straggling and undisciplined army continued the thirteen-mile retreat to Dalton, Federal pursuers under Hooker's command attacked. At 3:00 A.M. Bragg directed Cleburne to check the enemy's pursuit at Taylor's Ridge until the rest of the army was well advanced. Fighting began about 8:00 A.M. and by noon had sufficiently delayed the Federals for Cleburne to begin carefully withdrawing his troops to another defense line. At 2:00 P.M., feeling secure in the new position, he withdrew the last of his soldiers and burned the bridges. The enemy abandoned their pursuit.[46]

Although Grant declared that on November 27 Bragg's retreat was "most earnest" and "seemed to be moving like a disorganized mob," he declined to force another battle. He later remarked he would have destroyed Bragg's army, had he been familiar with the

[44] Bragg to Howell Cobb, November 29, 1863, Braxton Bragg Papers, Huntington Library; Bailey Diary, December 2, 1863 (mistakenly dated October 2, 1863); Kinloch Falconer, "Statement of Strength," December 20, 1863, Joseph E. Johnston Papers; Livermore, *Numbers and Losses*, p. 108; Bettie Ridley Blackmore, "Behind the Lines in Middle Tennessee, 1863–1865; The Journal of Bettie Ridley Blackmore," ed. Sarah Ridley Trimble, *Tennessee Historical Quarterly*, XII (1953), 67.
[45] *OR*, XXXI (pt. 2), 666; Brent Diary, November 26, 1863, Bragg Papers, Western Reserve.
[46] Brent Diary, November 27, 1863, Bragg Papers, Western Reserve; Beatty Diary, November 27, 1863; *OR*, XXXI (pt. 2), 754, 757.

NO SATISFACTORY EXCUSE 145

NO SATISFACTORY EXCUSE 145

terrain. That may well be, but after being handsomely repulsed by Cleburne, Grant decided to leave Bragg to his retreat.[47]

Bragg, of course, did not know of Grant's decision. Resting at Dalton on November 28, he took stock of his army's condition. In addition to the loss of stragglers, deserters, and discipline, Bragg had lost one-third of his artillery and its accoutrements, as well as a huge number of small arms.[48]

As usual after a battle, Bragg reorganized his army, moving units here and there. Breckinridge's performance at Missionary Ridge caused Bragg to change his mind about Hindman, still under arrest in Atlanta for his failures at McLemore's Cove. On November 30 Bragg asked Howell Cobb to send Hindman at once to take command of Breckinridge's Corps. At the same time, Bragg requested the corps commanders to forward the names of all officers who had left the battlefield without authority that they might be "dropped from the rolls."[49]

The battle with the Federals finished, the time had come to find scapegoats for the loss of Chattanooga. "The enemy attacked us & in *our chosen* position—*drove us back* & *took the position*," one Confederate declared. "This looks badly. There must have been some bad management on our part." After complaining of the "bitter humiliation of this disastrous day," a soldier asserted, "There was bad conduct somewhere—I don't know where."[50] Although no one seemed quite sure who was responsible, everyone received a share of the blame.

Charges that the soldiers fled without real cause circulated throughout the Confederacy. "For the first time," reported a news correspondent on the scene, "our defeat is chargeable to the

[47] U. S. Grant, *Personal Memoirs*, II, 90; John Russell Young, *Around the World with General Grant* (2 vols., New York, 1879), II, 626; Brent Diary, November 27, 1863, Bragg Papers, Western Reserve.
[48] Rennolds Diary, November 27, 1863, Chickamauga National Military Park.
[49] *OR*, XXXI (pt. 3), 767; Bragg to Howell Cobb, November 30, 1863, Bragg Papers, Western Reserve.
[50] I. [or J.] O. Harrison to W. C. P. Breckinridge, November 28, 1863, Breckinridge Family Papers, Library of Congress; Coleman Diary, November 25, 1863.

troops themselves and not to the blunder or incompetency of their leaders." Edwin Rennolds, absent from the army to purchase supplies in Atlanta, could not believe the stories he heard. "Oh! what a situation," he cried. "Southern troops running from such a position as that. I await to see for myself." The following day he saw for himself. Arriving in Dalton in time to see the army straggle in, he had to admit that some of the soldiers had acted shamefully.[51]

Even their own officers condemned the behavior of the soldiers. Bate accused some of his men of abandoning their arms on the field, thus leaving them to the Federals, who would use them to lay "waste their country" and "desolate their homes." Bate accused those who had lost their weapons of being cowardly traitors. He ordered that all who had behaved so basely were to be reported to his headquarters "that they may be promptly and summarily punished, in addition to being charged . . . with the value of the guns."[52] Bate apparently failed to understand that for many of the soldiers the retreat up Missionary Ridge entailed a choice between saving one's possessions or one's life.

In his first report on the defeat, written on November 30, Bragg could find "no satisfactory excuse . . . for the shameful conduct of our troops on the left. . . . The position . . . ought to have been held by a line of skirmishers." In their defense Bragg offered the excuse that for two days his army had witnessed the marshaling of a great host before them. This "may have intimidated weak-minded and untried soldiers," Bragg admitted, but his "veterans had so often encountered similar hosts . . . with perfect success, that not a doubt crossed my mind."[53]

The soldiers, in turn, along with others, blamed President Davis. In a backhanded compliment, the *Daily Richmond Whig* found little fault with Bragg, stating, "Doubtless he did the best

[51] *Richmond Daily Dispatch*, December 4, 1863; Rennolds Diary, November 27, 1863, Chickamauga National Military Park.
[52] *OR*, XXXI (pt. 2), 744.
[53] *Ibid.*, 666.

he could. It is no fault of his that he has held a command for which he was incompetent." The writer believed, rather, that "responsibility for . . . this crowning disaster must rest with those who . . . have required him to remain in command," despite requests for his replacement. Johnston blamed the defeat on "presidential generalship," while another highly placed Confederate called Davis a fool. Still another asked, "Why on earth does Prest. Davis persist on keeping this man Bragg at the head of the army?" A diarist tersely noted, "So much for an incapable general & an obstinate President."[54]

While he blamed his soldiers for the debacle, Bragg also turned on his subordinate generals. He accused Breckinridge of "*Drunkeness most flagrant*, during the whole three days of our trials," a charge he repeated to Davis and to others through the years, and he demoted Breckinridge from corps to division command. A Breckinridge biographer offered a long and convoluted, although unconvincing, argument that Breckinridge was possibly not drunk during the battle.[55] If the charge was true, Bragg used poor judgment, to say the least, when he relied on Breckinridge's assessment of his troops' ability to hold fast on Missionary Ridge.

Even former subordinates, no longer with the army, received their share of blame from Bragg. Although Hill had been removed before the battle, Bragg charged, "He had . . . greatly demoralized the troops he commanded," those under Breckinridge at Missionary Ridge. In later years, Bragg accused Hill, along with

[54] *Daily Richmond Whig*, November 27, 1863; Joseph E. Johnston to L. T. Wigfall, n.d., Louis Trezevant Wigfall Family Papers, Library of Congress; Thomas Ruffin, *The Papers of Thomas Ruffin*, ed. J. G. de Roulhac Hamilton (4 vols., Raleigh, N.C., 1920), III, 348, 346; Catherine Ann Devereux Edmonston, "*Journal of a Secesh Lady*": The Diary of Catherine Ann Devereux Edmonston, 1860–1866, ed. Beth G. Crabtree and James W. Patton (Raleigh, N.C., 1979), p. 502. Edmonston was married to a prominent North Carolina planter and slaveholder; she spent most of the war on her plantation, making occasional visits to Richmond. An avid newspaper reader, she kept herself informed of current events.
[55] Bragg to Davis, November 30, December 1, 1863, Bragg Papers, Western Reserve; Bragg to Marcus J. Wright, December 14, 29, 1863 (typescripts), Marcus J. Wright Papers, Southern Historical Collection; Bragg to E. T. Sykes, February 5, 1873 (copy), Polk Papers, University of the South; W. C. Davis, *Breckinridge*, pp. 393–98.

Longstreet and Buckner, of "treasonable act[s] . . . in sacrificing the army in their effort to degrade me for personal ends."[56]

On December 1 Bragg admitted to Davis that perhaps it had been a mistake to retain him in command. "The warfare [conducted by his subordinates] has been carried on successfully and the fruits are bitter," he lamented. Others agreed. One soldier recalled that Bragg had received "more abuse from the rear than any other General connected with our heroic struggle. . . . The entire army was aware of this want of confidence," he asserted, "and in this [the division commanders] were much to blame." Another Confederate told his sister that it had been Bragg's "misfortune . . . to have under him a set of high officers . . . who either had not, or affected not to have, confidence in him, & had no hesitation in making it known to those under them." Rather than trying to prevent demoralization, "they omitted nothing that could produce it." He even went so far as to aver that "*some* amongst them . . . preferred our defeat rather than to see Genl Bragg have the credit of a victory." Tennessee's Governor Isham Harris, declaring Bragg "a much abler and better man than the world is willing to believe," nevertheless admitted that the general had "lost the Confidence of the officers and men of the army." The resulting "discentions [*sic*] proved an element of weakness."[57]

Harris did not explicitly blame Bragg for the loss of confidence or for the loss of Chattanooga, but others did. A Confederate captain reported that Cleburne made severe remarks on Bragg's mismanagement. Liddell wailed, "If only he had not been so infatuated with his projects," while another soldier reported, "From all I can learn Bragg as usual blundered in having too long a line and putting the bulk of his forces just where the mass of the enemy *was not*." Manigault simply commented that Bragg "was

56 Bragg to Sykes, February 8, 1873, Polk Papers, University of the South.

57 Bragg to Davis, December 1, 1863, Bragg Papers, Western Reserve; Gray, "Reminiscences"; Thomas Ruffin, Jr., to My dear Sister, December 15, 1863, Cameron Family Papers; S. L. Blackford, *Letters from Lee's Army*, p. 224; Isham Harris to Mrs. General Ewell, March 7, 1863, George Washington Campbell Papers, Library of Congress.

completely outgeneraled by the Yankee commander," and a Richmond newspaper inelegantly editorialized, "An army of asses led by a lion is better than an army of lions led by an ass."[58]

Some who blamed Bragg also felt sympathetic toward him. One soldier believed that if Bragg had "cultivated the love and respect of his troops . . . the result would have been different." Former chief of staff Mackall felt sorry for Bragg, and he predicted that Davis would now have no choice but to send someone else to command the Army of Tennessee.[59]

Bragg, too, realized a storm would be raised against him. On November 29 he informed Cooper of the position of the army, suggested means of reinforcing it, and requested a formal investigation into the causes of the disaster. Almost as an afterthought, perhaps one he hoped would not be noticed, he stated, "I deem it due to the cause and to myself to ask for relief from command."[60] Davis, to Bragg's utter consternation and chagrin, snatched up this half-hearted offer of resignation with unseemly haste.

[58] Thomas J. Key and Robert J. Campbell, *Two Soldiers: The Campaign Diaries of Thomas J. Key, C.S.A., December 7, 1863–May 17, 1865, and Robert J. Campbell, U.S.A., January 1, 1864–July 21, 1864*, ed. Wirt Armistead Cate (Chapel Hill, N.C., 1938), p. 9; Liddell, *Record*, p. 163; Eugene E. McLean to D. M. Hayden, November 28, 1863, C.S.A. Army Archives, Miscellany, Officers' and Soldiers' Miscellaneous Letters, Duke University Library; Manigault, *A Carolinian*, p. 142; *Daily Richmond Whig*, November 30, 1863.

[59] Watkins, *"Co. Aytch"*, p. 126; William Whann Mackall to My dearest Minie, November 27, 1863, Mackall Papers.

[60] *OR*, XXXI (pt. 2), 682.

CHAPTER VIII

Have a little charity for Bragg

December 1, 1863–February 23, 1864

THE RAPIDITY with which President Davis accepted Bragg's offer to resign stunned the general. Using the same ploy after Chickamauga, his offer then had been declined. Now, with apparently just a moment's reflection, Davis peremptorily notified Bragg, "You are relieved from command."[1] For the next three months Bragg languished in uneasy retirement.

The curtness of the order may have revealed Davis's feelings on the matter. "It is said the President wept when he heard of General Bragg's misfortunes at Lookout Mountain and Missionary Ridge," reported a newspaper. "Certainly the President was very much attached to the General." Despite his attachment, Davis had already faced the possibility of Bragg's relief. In late November John B. Jones, the ubiquitous war clerk gossip, reported rumors of dissent in Davis's cabinet, the majority favoring Bragg's removal.[2]

Bragg's dismay at his relief from command prompted him to write two conciliatory letters to Davis in as many days, both clearly attempts to change Davis's mind. On December 1 he explained that, although "the disaster admits of no palliation, and is justly disparaging to me as a commander," he believed that "you may find upon full investigation that the fault is not entirely mine." Charging Breckinridge and Cheatham with inebriation during the battle, Bragg avowed, "I can bear to be sacrificed myself, but not to see my country and my friends ruined by the vices

---

[1] *OR*, XXXI (pt. 2), 682.
[2] *Mobile Daily Advertiser and Register*, December 13, 1863; J. B. Jones, *Rebel War Clerk's Diary*, II, 106.

of a few profligate men who happen to have an undue popularity." But he did not really wish to be sacrificed. "I shall ever be ready to do all in my power for our common cause," he declared, but first "some rest will render me more efficient than I am now."[3]

The following day Bragg did not mention his weariness; instead he asked what "our policy" should be. Apologizing for reiterating his views on the military situation, he trusted to Davis's "appreciation of my zeal and sincerity in the cause to excuse any seeming indelicacy." The responsibility for the recent disaster, he admitted, should "rest on my humble head. But we can redeem the past." His plan for redemption called for a concentration of all available troops with "this gallant little army," which should be led, he suggested, stooping to overt flattery, by "our greatest and best leader . . . yourself."[4]

When Davis declined to command the Army of Tennessee and refused to reinstate Bragg, the general surely agreed with General William Bate, who declared in late January, "I thought at the time and think now you erred in asking to be relieved from command."[5] But it was too late. The deed had been done, the decision made, and Bragg had no choice but to comply.

On December 2, 1863, Bragg bade his "gallant little army" farewell. The separation, he announced, "is made with unfeigned regret." He spoke of the "common cause and dangers shared on the many hard-fought fields from Pensacola to Chickamauga," generously forgetting to mention Lookout Mountain and Missionary Ridge. He appealed to the soldiers to "give to his successor that cordial and generous support so essential to the success of our arms," implicitly chiding them for not giving him that same generous support. In conclusion, Bragg bid his army and its officers "an affectionate farewell," assuring them they "have the blessing and the prayers of a grateful friend."[6]

On the night before he departed, the soldiers serenaded Bragg.

[3] *OR*, LII (pt. 2), 745.
[4] *Ibid.*, 567–68.
[5] William B. Bate to Bragg, January 25, 1864, Bragg Papers, Western Reserve.
[6] *OR*, XXXI (pt. 3), 774–76.

Called upon to speak, he "took a long and sad farewell of them." The soldiers "vociferously cheered" him, and "the greatest enthusiasm prevailed."[7]

Bragg now turned to Elise for solace. Shortly after the disaster at Missionary Ridge, Elise had pleaded with her brother, Towson Ellis, to "comfort the General—it is a terrible blow to him." She made this appeal before her husband's resignation, and at that time she did not "think the President will remove him for he knows *he* alone can repair this great disaster." Her fear, as usual, was that "his health will give way." If that happened, "I must go to him. . . . I am so well now," she assured her brother, "I can stand any privations."[8] As it turned out, Braxton spared her the trip and the privations. He came to her, seeking the comfort only a loyal and loving wife can provide.

Bragg had great need for expressions of devotion. Missionary Ridge, asserted one historian, dealt a hard blow to Bragg's ego and prestige. Some indeed rejoiced at Bragg's relief from command. "This rumor [of Bragg's relief]," crowed a newspaper, "was received with as much, or more, satisfaction by the public yesterday, than would the official news of a victory over the Yankees." The editor of the *Richmond Examiner* believed only Davis's "pitiful perversity" had kept Bragg in command of the Army of Tennessee for so long.[9]

Some military figures also expressed delight at Bragg's discomfiture. General Lucius Polk regarded the debacle at Chattanooga as a blessing, since it got rid of Bragg. Another soldier declared, "While I have every faith in his loyalty and courage, still there is

---

[7] *Daily Richmond Whig*, December 4, 1863; Watson, Confederate War Diary, part II, p. 21, Chickamauga National Military Park; Charles E. Leverich Diary, December 4, 1863, pp. 50–51, Louisiana State University Archives.

[8] Elise to Towson Ellis, n.d., Braxton Bragg Papers, Rosenberg Library, Galveston, Texas.

[9] Stanley F. Horn, *The Army of Tennessee* (Norman, Okla., 1941), p. 303; *Daily Richmond Whig*, December 2, 1863; Frederick S. Daniel, *The Richmond Examiner during the War; or, The Writings of John M. Daniel. With a Memoir of His Life* (New York, 1868), p. 146.

not a feature in his military character that makes him the man to command our largest army in a crisis like this."[10]

Civilians, too, expressed satisfaction. Mary Chesnut, Richmond diarist, declared, "The army will be relieved to get rid of him. He has a winning way of earning everybody's detestation." Kate Cumming, usually sympathetic to Bragg, remarked, "For his own sake and ours, I am heartily glad."[11]

Despite assertions that Bragg's relief from command prompted universal accolades, the evidence indicates that many regretted Davis's action. From representatives of all sides of the Southern population, Bragg received letters expressing confidence in his leadership. Dr. Carlisle Terry told Bragg, "No man yet has gained the confidence & love of *this* Division to the extent that you have." General Roddey announced: "We Can Never be as well satisfied with a Commander as we have been heretofor. Nor do we believe that any officer on the Continent could have done more or better with the Army of Tennessee than has been done." "I find but one sentiment," reported H. W. Walter, "that of deep respect, amounting to affection for you, & but one wish, that you will again be placed in command." An army inspector told Bragg that he found "a general regret at your leaving. . . . The people throughout the country are disappointed and depressed." Colonel Brent assured his old commander, "I can safely say that you possess the confidence & affection of the Army of Tennessee."[12]

Civilians, too, expressed dismay at Bragg's removal. The people of Warren County, North Carolina, "proud of the services you have rendered your country," believed Bragg had "done all that

---

[10] Ruffin, *Papers*, III, 360; Eugene Verdery to Dear Sister, December 4, 1863, Eugene, Jr., and James Paul Verdery Papers, Duke University Library.

[11] Chesnut, *Civil War*, p. 496; Cumming, *Kate*, p. 182.

[12] Carlisle Terry to Bragg, March 7, 1864; P. D. Roddey to Bragg, December 13, 1863; H. W. Walter to Bragg, December 30, 1863; Joseph Wheeler to Bragg, December 15, 1863; Joseph P. Jones to Bragg, December 10, 1863; J. H. Fraser to Bragg, December 2, 1863; Edward C. Walthall to Bragg, March 11, 1864; Officers and men of the Second Georgia Battalion of Sharpshooters to Bragg, March 5, 1864; George W. Brent to Bragg, April 16, 1864, Bragg Papers, Western Reserve. See also S. H. Stout to Bragg, December 5, 1863; William J. Holt to Bragg, December 4, 1863, *ibid.*

mortal man could do." Citizens of Eufaula, Alabama, asked Bragg to pay them a visit, as they wished to "testify their admiration for the man who achieved so much . . . [and] who displayed such gallantry."[13]

In addition to invitations, Bragg received gifts. Some newspaper proprietors sent him "a handsome pair of spurs," the men of Bate's and Finley's brigades presented him with an inscribed sword, and Walthall's gave him a horse appropriately named Chickamauga.[14]

Perhaps one of the most comforting letters came from Francis Parker, the father of an aide on Bragg's staff. Parker assured Bragg that his name would not be forgotten by future generations. "A redeemed Country," Parker believed, "will at some future day enroll many names entitled to grateful recollection. Among those to whom a full measure will be due & surely accorded, will be yours."[15]

Given Bragg's wretched reputation today, one might question the motives of these warm supporters and wonder if perhaps each sought something from the general. However, the same regret at his removal is found in sources not intended for Bragg's eyes. Mackall, Bragg's former chief of staff, informed General Johnston that a correspondent from the Army of Tennessee had told him "there was no manifestation of gratification at Bragg's relief," and Taylor Beatty more positively stated that he found "an almost universal feeling of regret." A soldier told his father that his company "considered it a dark hour for Bragg's army" when Davis removed the commander and averred they would not have let Bragg go "for a Lee or Johnston or a Beauregard," while another avowed, "The army was loathe to give him up." A Mississippi soldier declared that Bragg's place, "neither in the Army . . . nor in the affections

[13] Joseph S. Jones to Bragg, March 18, 1864; Thirty-nine Citizens to Bragg, January 20, 1864, *ibid*.
[14] L. J. Dupree, J. A. Sperry, James McCulla, and M. W. Hutcheson to Bragg, January 18, 1864; I. J. Finley and Joseph T. Smith to Bragg, March 15, 1864; Officers and Men of Walthall's Brigade to Bragg, March 19, 1864, *ibid*.
[15] Francis S. Parker to Bragg, December 25, 1863, *ibid*.

of his troops, can ever be filled." Another Southerner declared, "No one ever questioned his patriotism or his courage."[16]

Patriotism and courage notwithstanding, Bragg's career as an army commander virtually ended with the disaster at Missionary Ridge. He spent the next several weeks at Warm Springs, where, with Elise's help, he nursed his wounded pride, rested his tired body, and reveled in the many sincere expressions of regret at his retirement.

Bragg's place of retirement, a popular summer resort owned by an old family friend, was quiet when Bragg arrived in December. Twenty-eight miles from La Grange, the nearest railroad station, the atmosphere seemed "completely out of the world." Bragg had a few of his staff with him—Surgeon T. G. Richardson, Towson Ellis (Elise's brother), Thomas Butler (Elise's cousin), Lieutenant F. Parker, and Colonel David Urquhart. The peaceful surroundings proved salubrious to Braxton and Elise. "The relief from hard work which Genl Bragg is now enjoying has improved his health very much," reported Butler, "and Cousin Elise is looking as well as I ever saw her."[17]

Bragg apparently regained his health quickly, once again indicating that stress induced his illnesses. "In very feeble health," Bragg later wrote (in third-person narrative), "and with energies both mental and physical greatly overtaxed by his incessant labors, he . . . [found that] a quiet and perfectly retired life soon restored him to his usual health." He also wrote of his continued popularity at this time. "During this period he was frequently importuned to accept public dinners and other honors," he

[16] William W. Mackall to J. E. Johnston, December 9, 1863, Mackall Papers; Beatty Diary, December 1, 1863; C. T. Jones, "Five Confederates," p. 190; W. J. Worsham, *The Old Nineteenth Tennessee Regiment, C.S.A.* (Knoxville, 1902), p. 104; Simon Mayer, Note, c. December 1863, owned by Harold S. Mayer, New Orleans; Joseph Jones, "Manuscript," c. 1887–1892, Joseph Jones Collection, Louisiana Historical Association Collection; J. N. Hale, "Typescript," Confederate Sketches Collection, Southern Historical Collection.
[17] Thomas Butler to Sarah Butler, December 26, 1863, Butler and Family Papers.

boasted, "but declined anything more than a social meeting with friends at points he visited."[18]

Letters to friends indicate Bragg did not feel comfortable in retirement. He also gave differing accounts of his reasons for resigning, the most common being his health, but his explanation to General Marcus Wright cited another reason. By mid-December Bragg heard of problems with the new command of the army. "It is now apparent to all, and it is what I desired to establish by the change," he claimed, "that the whole clamor against me was by a few individuals of rank and their immediate partisans, who were actuated by one of two motives, *Ambition* and *Revenge*." He also suggested he intended his resignation to be temporary. Complaining that his health had been poor, he stated, "I saw a chance for a respite, knowing the enemy would not advance on us for a long time."[19]

Bragg's ambivalence shows clearly in several of his letters. "The quiet of this delightful retired spot so fully accords with my present feelings and wishes, that I feel no disposition to seek a change," he declared—"tho' active service would be my choice." To another, after complaining about the impossibility of commanding an army such as that he just left, Bragg declared himself "ready for *any* duty they may assign me."[20]

While Bragg rested and reflected at Warm Springs, Davis tried to find a new commander for the Army of Tennessee. Bragg had turned the command over to General William J. Hardee, his senior subordinate, who immediately declined to accept it as a permanent position, believing he could not successfully carry out the duties of an army commander. Actually, Hardee had more interesting things on his mind than commanding the Army of Tennessee. Encountering Liddell during the retreat from Missionary

[18] Bragg, "Notes of Gen'l Bragg's services in the cause of the Confederacy after leaving the Army of Tennessee in Dec. 1863," Bragg Papers, Western Reserve.
[19] Bragg to Marcus Wright, December 14, 1863, Wright Papers.
[20] Bragg to My dear Judge, January 4, 1864, H. W. Walter Papers, Southern Historical Collection; Bragg to Marcus Wright, December 29, 1863, Wright Papers.

Ridge, Hardee took time to boast to his friend, "I am engaged to be married to a most estimable young lady." The lady in question was very young indeed, being little older than widower Hardee's own daughter. As the wedding took place in January 1864, one can well understand his lack of concentration on his martial, as opposed to his marital, duties.[21]

In the search for a new commander for the Army of Tennessee, Davis had few from whom to choose. Only three generals received serious consideration: Beauregard, Lee, and Johnston. Davis considered Beauregard only briefly before offering the position to Lee, a sure indication of the president's desperation. But on December 7 Lee told Davis he failed to see any advantage in his going to the western army. Lee assured Davis he did not intend to obstruct the president's wishes but rather to "give you the opportunity to form your opinion after a full consideration of the subject." But Lee told Davis only what he wished to hear. It is unlikely that Davis would willingly send Lee out of Virginia, any more than Lee would willingly go. Which left Joseph E. Johnston, the obvious choice, but one that rankled Davis because of their long-standing feud. However, on December 27, 1863, Davis yielded, appointing Johnston commander of the Army of Tennessee.[22]

On December 10 Johnston had written to Bragg expressing dismay over Bragg's retirement, and hoped he would return to a field command as soon as his health improved. A month later Bragg responded, congratulating his successor. "I shall follow you and your noble comrades with prayers as fervent and hopes as strong as when I shared the toil and honors of the field, and no one of you will rejoice more than myself at the success which I trust awaits you."[23]

[21] Hardee to Samuel Cooper, November 30, 1863, Bragg Papers, Western Reserve; Liddell, *Record*, pp. 170, 160.

[22] J. B. Jones, *Rebel War Clerk's Diary*, II, 110–11; William Porcher Miles to G. T. Beauregard, December 12, 1863, Miles Letter, University of Texas; *OR*, XXXI (pt. 3), 775, 792, 801; Long and Long, *Civil War*, pp. 447, 449.

[23] J. E. Johnston to Bragg, December 10, 1863; Bragg to Johnston, January 10, 1864, Bragg Papers, Western Reserve.

Johnston found his new command a difficult one, the problems greatly exacerbated by the characteristics of its subordinate officers. In refusing the offer to command the western army, Lee had said he feared that he would not receive cooperation. In addition, he recognized the tremendous burden involved in commanding that army. "I have not that confidence either in my strength or ability as would lead me of my own option to undertake the command in question." Bragg himself had told Liddell, "I am disgusted with politicians for generals and executive officers." Shortly after he left the army, Bragg announced that "some have found the bed of roses [command of the army] well set with *thorns*, and that it is easier to condemn than remedy." Pointing out that no one could successfully command an army without the support of subordinates, Bragg complained that too many of his generals were "so ambitious or venal as to forget their country in such a struggle as this, and turn their energies to malignant detraction or personal advancement." Some years later Bragg again complained of his subordinates, declaring, "No man could do his duty and sustain himself against the combined power of imbeciles, traitors, rogues and intriguing politicians."[24]

Others supported Bragg's contention that too many of his generals used politics and political connections to advance themselves at the expense of the army. Mackall, a native of Maryland, explained his failure to secure promotions by telling his wife, "I am an Exile [and] have the influence of no men in the south to push my interests either from family or political motives." "You were always impatient at the pains I took to acquire some political influence," another Confederate scolded his wife. "I think now you must regret it as I do, that I had not devoted myself to it more thoroughly, for it is unquestionably true, that political influence has much to do with all appointments in the Army Com[mand]." In December 1863, Wheeler complained to Bragg of someone at-

[24] *OR*, XXXI (pt. 3), 792; Liddell, *Record*, p. 164; Bragg to Wright, December 14, 1863, Wright Papers; Bragg to E. T. Sykes, February 8, 1873 (copy), Polk Papers, University of the South.

tempting to take over command of his cavalry through lies to the War Department. "It is very hard," he lamented, "that such men should find it necessary to use such ungenerous means to injure the character of another for their own elevation." However, he believed "these troubles are necessary to the more correct forma- tion of character. They certainly teach me a good lesson."[25]

In January, Johnston warned Senator Wigfall, his friend and supporter, of the severity of politicking in the Army of Tennessee. "If you have doubts of the merits of an officer . . . don't seek information from those of his class whom you find in Richmond, where few of those who depend upon service for advancement are ever seen. This rule," Johnston declared, "applies especially to this army, which has the reputation, here in itself, of having the only general officers in the Confederacy who practice here against each other, the arts to which they were accustomed to resort in electioneering before the war.—Hence," he concluded, "its pres- ent condition." Bragg, Johnston admitted, had had much to con- tend with. "When you see me overcome by the simultaneous efforts of the enemy's numbers & faction here," he advised Wig- fall, "have a little charity for Bragg." Johnston could see only one solution to the command problems. "If I were president I'd dis- tribute the generals of this army over the confederacy."[26]

Besides problems in the command structure, the Army of Ten- nessee under Bragg had had other disadvantages. His tenure as commander illustrated a primary defect in the South's conduct of the war: the authorities ensconced in the East simply failed to recognize the importance of the Western theater, although many expressed anxiety about it. A historian of Confederate supply concluded that deficiencies hampered Bragg's campaigning, re- sulting in a disastrous blow to the Confederacy when he was forced to give up the heartland of the nation. Part of the problem

[25] Mackall to My dearest wife, January 7, 1864, Mackall Papers; Henry C. Semple to My dear Wife, June 8, 1863, Semple Papers; Joseph Wheeler to Bragg, December 20, 1863, Bragg Letters, Duke University Library.

[26] Johnston to L. T. Wigfall, January 9, 1864, Wigfall Family Papers, Library of Congress.

arose from the Confederate commissaries stripping the region to maintain the Army of Northern Virginia and other Eastern troops. One agent appeared to believe that the Army of Tennessee was actually an alien army, serving in a foreign state. In notifying Northrop of Bragg's seizure of collected subsistence in 1862, he complained, "I understand my mission to be to collect supplies for the Armies of the C[onfederate] S[tates] & not for Genl Braggs [sic] Army."[27] In part this agent reflected the views of those in Richmond—the West at times seemed so remote and unimportant as to not constitute a part of the Confederacy at all.

Richmond thus largely ignored the West, where the war would be won or lost, to focus on the holding actions taking place in the East, ineffectually squandering their staying power in an untenable position. Davis's reliance upon Lee fostered and fed his shortsightedness and narrow vision regarding military decisions affecting the West, seeing only the supposed importance of Virginia. Two historians have contended that Davis imposed too much of his own thinking on the army and that its disasters came about through Davis's efforts to conduct offensives in the West from his office in Richmond. A Confederate congressional representative put it more succinctly. "With the President paralysing the brains and Northrop pinching with hunger the bellies of the Army the prospect is discouraging indeed."[28]

The eastern armies not only drained off supplies, they also drew away many of the western soldiers. Richard McMurry discovered that in mid-1862, 18.5 percent of the units in the Army of Northern Virginia were from the West. At the same time, only

[27] Joseph E. Johnston to B. F. Cheatham, November 14, 1867, Benjamin Franklin Cheatham Papers, Southern Historical Collection; see also McMurry, *Two Great Rebel Armies*, pp. 11, 55, 58, 60, 64–65, 149, 154–55; Richard D. Goff, *Confederate Supply* (Durham, N.C., 1969), pp. 188–93; Edward Hagerman, *The American Civil War and the Origins of Modern Warfare: Ideas, Organization, and Field Command* (Bloomington, Ind., 1988), pp. 179–82; McWhiney, *Bragg*, pp. 321–23; John F. Cummings to Lucius Northrop, November 10, December 5, 1862, Francis Gildart Ruffin Papers, Virginia Historical Society.

[28] J. F. C. Fuller, *The Conduct of War, 1789–1961* (n.p., 1961), p. 102; Hagerman, *Origins*, p. 68; Connelly and Jones, *Politics of Command*, p. 137; Miles to Beauregard, December 12, 1863, Miles Letter.

1.2 percent of the Army of Tennessee came from the East. And, he maintains, this pattern did not change significantly throughout the war. Although the imbalance was largely due to demographics,[29] it still indicates what Richmond considered of paramount importance. It also appears that the West was used as a dumping ground for generals who annoyed their superiors. Davis sent two of his particular thorns (J. E. Johnston and Beauregard), as did Lee (Longstreet and D. H. Hill). There were no corresponding transfers of difficult high-echelon officers from west to east.

The cavalry, too, had always been a liability to Bragg. Manigault described this branch as so undisciplined and demoralized that they failed to perform their primary purpose of providing Bragg with the intelligence necessary to carry out his duties successfully. One soldier saw the cavalry as a judgment on the South. Describing the debacle of Wheeler's October raid, he told his wife, "It seems that a just Providence still thinks we have not suffered enough." Isham Harris, totaling up the number of reinforcements needed for a successful campaign by the Army of Tennessee, listed only infantry and artillery. "I dont [sic] count Cavalry," he explained, "though it is an admirable arm of the service to get up sensational paragraphs."[30]

Bragg, on the other hand, seldom saw sensational paragraphs on his own behalf. Many, including Bragg, believed his unpopularity stemmed from his treatment by the press. From Warm Springs, Bragg blamed the discontent in his army on "a venial press reacting thro the public on the Army." Wheeler wrote to Bragg that the troops believed "the only enemies you had were a few bad Generals and some newspaper editors," and an editor admitted to Bragg that "I was influenced . . . by the whispered slanders of your enemies." Furthermore, this editor had found it impossible to ignore this influence, as "it filled the very atmosphere of all newspaperdom." Manigault charged, "The press

[29] McMurry, *Two Great Rebel Armies*, pp. 88–89.

[30] Manigault, *A Carolinian*, p. 130; Clement Stanford Watson to My dear Mary, October 19, 23, November 2, 1863, Watson Papers; Isham Harris to Mrs. General Ewell, March 7, 1864, Campbell Papers.

of the country did him great injustice . . . chiefly owing to the fact that he did not like newspaper correspondents, and these gentlemen . . . turned their letter-writing abilities against him in a spirit of spite and pique."[31]

In defense of the press, it must be said Bragg did little to court its favor. The diary of reporter Samuel Chester Reid, Jr., does much to explain Bragg's relationship with the press. In August 1862, while in Chattanooga, Reid requested permission to accompany the army. Bragg not only denied the request but also told Reid to leave. Moving to Knoxville, Reid began composing an "expose [sic] of Braggs persecution & tyranny," an epic he worked on for a week before sending it to the *Charleston Mercury*. In October, still in Knoxville, he recorded, "Wrote out account of retreat. Bragg universally anathamatized." Reid rejoined the army sometime after it settled in at Tullahoma, but not for long. "At night O'Hara informed me Bragg intended to arrest me tomorrow—concluded safe to leave started at 9 P.M. dark & rainy—for Winchester—14 m distance on horseback." Reid, however, was persistent, and returned in May. This time he persuaded Wheeler to intervene for him, and Bragg granted Reid permission to stay. A few days later, he "met Gen B. Bragg who bowed to me!" But his troubles with the general continued. In October, during the miserably heavy rains, Reid disgustedly reported, "Bragg took my qrs in house & gave me up his tent."[32]

Bragg's treatment of Reid differed little from his treatment of others. Manigault characterized Bragg as "one of the most honest . . . officers of our army," and this honesty often made Bragg too outspoken. Writing to Davis on the battles at Chattanooga, Bragg accused General Stevenson of "utter imbecility" at Lookout Mountain and believed General John K. Jackson "is equally as unreliable." Yet, Bragg insisted, both of these men "are my

[31] Bragg to Wright, December 29, 1863, Wright Papers; Wheeler to Bragg, December 26, 1863; L. J. Dupree to Bragg, February 25, 1864, Bragg Papers, Western Reserve; Manigault, *A Carolinian*, pp. 158–59.
[32] *Richmond Sentinel*, October 1, 1863; Samuel Chester Reid, Jr., Diary, Samuel Chester Reid Family Papers, Library of Congress.

strongest personal friends," and he declared, "They will both acknowledge the justice of this criticism."[33] It is difficult to believe, however, that these men would continue a warm friendship with a man who labeled them imbecilic and unreliable.

Davis needed Bragg, despite his outspokenness—the only problem being where Bragg would be most useful. Some expected he might return to the Army of Tennessee as its commander or as Johnston's chief of staff. Liddell, who had been transferred to the Trans-Mississippi Department, wanted Bragg to come there to take charge. Rumors circulated that, rather than a field command, Bragg might receive a position in Richmond. One rumor suggested that Bragg would replace Seddon as Secretary of War, while another alleged that he might get Cooper's job.[34]

But Bragg did not get either of these positions. Instead, after being summoned to Richmond on February 5, Davis appointed him military adviser to the president. Bragg accepted the post, and on February 24 Cooper's office issued the necessary orders, charging Bragg with "the conduct of military operations in the Armies of the Confederacy." Just how independent he would be remained to be seen, as the order made clear that Bragg would work "under the direction of the President."[35]

Wigfall contended Davis placed Bragg in this high position "in contempt" of public opinion. A woman expressed even greater outrage. "So the deed is done!" she wrote on reading of the appointment. "What we last week laughed at as idle and wild . . . is 'un fait accompli.' Gen Bragg, Bragg the incapable, the unfortunate, is Commander in Chief! Unhappy man . . . and now

---

[33] Manigault, *A Carolinian*, p. 158; Bragg to Davis, Warm Springs, Georgia, December 8, 1863, Davis Papers, Duke University Library.

[34] Liddell to Bragg, January 7, 1864, Bragg Papers, Huntington Library; Bragg to Wright, December 14, 1863, Wright Papers; Wheeler to Bragg, December 15, 1863, Bragg Papers, Western Reserve; Gorgas, *Diary*, pp. 73–74; T. G. Richardson to Bragg, January 5, 1864; Bate to Bragg, January 25, 1864; Liddell to Bragg, December 10, 1863, Bragg Papers, Western Reserve; Warren Akin, *Letters of Warren Akin, Confederate Congressman*, ed. Bell Irvin Wiley (Athens, Ga., 1959), p. 92; *OR*, LIII, 307.

[35] Bragg to Wright, February 6, 1864, Wright Papers; Bragg, "Notes," Bragg Papers, Western Reserve; *OR*, XXXII (pt. 2), 799.

164 CHAPTER VIII DECEMBER 1, 1863-FEBRUARY 23, 1864

doubly unhappy in being elevated to a post for which he is unfit."[36]

Dismay, however, was not universal. Congratulations and expressions of faith in Bragg poured in. General Daniel W. Adams believed Bragg would prove valuable in the South's fight for independence. Soldiers in his former command assured Bragg "of the great satisfaction which is felt in this Army, at the present important relation . . . which so enlarges the sphere of your usefulness." The *Montgomery Weekly Mail* ran out of superlatives while reporting Bragg's new position. "His high order of talent . . . , his shrewdness and tact . . . , his indomitable perserverance . . . , his rigid sense of justice . . . , his elevated moral courage, his personal bravery, his untiring industry, his zeal, his devotion, his patriotism . . . are to be brought to bear upon our military situation from a higher stand point than he has heretofore occupied."[37]

And so Bragg's brief respite from the toils and cares of military service ended. As he wended his way toward Richmond, an observer met him on the train. "I saw a very stern looking old man with gray hair and I knew that it must be Gen. Bragg," he wrote. "After repeated calls he made his apperance [*sic*] and was introduced to some of the citizens. He has a gray eye and seems to be very restless. He wears his beard very neatly trimmed. He had on no uniform except a cap."[38]

Bragg had good cause to feel restless. He had given up his peaceful refuge, where he was "beyond the reach of that opprobrium which has so long pursued him," once again to allow himself to become a target of abuse for all and sundry.[39]

---

[36] Wigfall to Johnston, March 19, 1864, Joseph E. Johnston Papers; Katherine Ann Devereux Edmonston Diary, February 28, 1864, North Carolina Department of Archives and History.
[37] Daniel W. Adams to Bragg, March 26, 1864, Bragg Papers, Huntington Library; Finley and Smith to Bragg, March 15, 1864, Bragg Papers, Western Reserve; *Montgomery Weekly Mail*, March 29, 1864. See also W. H. T. Walker to Bragg, March 8, 1864; Wheeler to Bragg, March 3, 1864; States R. Gist to Bragg, February 27, 1864; Alexander P. Stewart to Bragg, March 19, 1864; Jones M. Withers to Bragg, February 26, 1864; H. B. Shepard to Bragg, March 4, 1864, Bragg Papers, Western Reserve.
[38] Walter Bullock to His Mother, February 18, 1864, John Bullock Papers, Duke University Library.
[39] *Mobile Daily Advertiser and Register*, December 10, 1863.

CHAPTER IX

When a man has power

February 24–October 14, 1864

"I THINK BRAGG—between ourselves is humbugged by the Prest.—and is in 'honorable exile,'" Mackall wrote to his wife.[1] He was not the first, nor the last, to belittle the position and the achievements of Bragg while he served as Jefferson Davis's military adviser. Bragg apparently enjoyed the assignment—his health remained good during most of the period—but, more than ever, he became the center of controversy.

Bragg found himself in an ambiguous position on February 24, 1864. A contemporary complained that the post was anomalous, and there were differences of opinion on what it entailed.[2] General Robert E. Lee had briefly held the post in 1862, but since that time Davis had chosen not to fill the position. After Bragg's resignation from command of the Army of Tennessee, however, Davis decided to use his friend's talents in this unofficial capacity.

Bragg and Davis together defined the job. Bragg quickly made it clear that he viewed it as chief of staff, heading his correspondence "Head Quarters Armies Confederate States." The historian of Confederate supply problems contended that the areas of authority of Bragg and Secretary of War Seddon often overlapped. It appeared that Davis gave Bragg authority to command the lower echelons of bureau officials as well as field officers. Before long, Bragg managed to assume many of the duties and some of the authority of Seddon, which also had never been clearly delineated. Bragg soon pushed the secretary of war into the uncertain position Bragg had occupied.[3]

---

[1] William W. Mackall to Darling Minnie, July 15, 1864, Mackall Papers.
[2] William P. Snow, *Lee and His Generals* (New York, 1982; orig. ed., 1867), p. 360.
[3] Goff, *Confederate Supply*, p. 128; Dowdey, *Lee's Last Campaign*, pp. 302, 331.

Bragg diffused his considerable energies among a variety of responsibilities, primarily bureaucratic. He inaugurated inspections of field armies and their supply systems and investigated the prisoner-of-war system, the quartermaster department, and the conscription bureau. These inspections created turmoil, prompting the head of the Bureau of War to comment: "Bragg gets worse and worse, more and more mischievous. He resembles a chimpanzee as much in character as he does in appearance. . . . Prying, indirection, vindictiveness, and insincerity are the repulsive traits which mark Bragg's character, and of which together or separately I see evidences almost daily."[4]

Such criticism may have been useful to Davis. Diarist Mary Boykin Chesnut, moving among Richmond's political circles, wrote, "Mr. [John S.] Preston says Bragg is acting as lightning rod: drawing off some of the hatred of Jeff Davis to himself."[5]

To do his job Bragg needed the help of a competent staff. On March 4 he appointed Colonel John B. Sale, a former lawyer, as his military secretary. Sale was, as described by Senator James Phelan, a man to Bragg's liking: systematic, rigid, exact, truthful, and impartial in administering justice. After the war, praising both Sale and himself, Bragg boasted that his secretary "proved himself no less devoted, laborious, and thorough than his chief had ever been." Bragg made another wise choice in reappointing Colonel George Brent to his staff.[6] These two men, around whom Bragg built his staff, proved faithful supporters.

Bragg barely had his staff assembled before he received a deluge of favor-seeking letters. "Pardon me for troubling you with these matters," one correspondent apologized, "but the fact is when a man has power he must expect his friends to call on him for favors."[7] And call on him they did.

[4] Bragg, "Notes," Bragg Papers, Western Reserve; Kean, *Inside*, p. 175.
[5] Chesnut, *Civil War*, p. 643.
[6] James Phelan to Bragg, December 4, 1862; Bragg, "Notes," Bragg Papers, Western Reserve; William W. Mackall to My darling, March 4, 1864, Mackall Papers.
[7] James L. Pugh to Bragg, July 5, 1864, Bragg Papers, Western Reserve.

Bragg's handling of one set of petitions revealed something of the contradictions in his personality—his vituperative nature, as well as his military acumen. In January General John Hunt Morgan, following his escape from an Ohio State penitentiary, arrived in Richmond to press for the reorganization of his cavalry. Numerous requests from soldiers formerly serving under him, and longing to return to his command, landed on Bragg's desk. Bragg, to whom Davis had referred the whole matter, appeared accommodating. Kentuckian congressional representative E. M. Bruce, after an interview with Bragg, wrote: "Gen. B. talked very kindly . . . and said that Gen. Morgan should have all the men raised by him. But he made several qualifications." One of these was that Morgan had not personally raised all of the men who had served under him; many of them had been raised by Bragg during the Kentucky campaign in 1862, and others by General E. Kirby Smith. However, Bruce assured his correspondent, Bragg disavowed any intent to do Morgan injustice, and he believed Bragg would give Morgan all that he requested. But Bruce had been taken in. Ever since Morgan had deceived Bragg regarding his intentions in June and July of 1863, when Morgan took off on the joyride that ended with his capture, Bragg had never forgiven or trusted him. In the end, Bragg allowed him only one of his old battalions. Within a few months, Morgan launched an ill-conceived and unauthorized foray into Kentucky, where he was killed. One Confederate charged that this raid had proved Morgan nothing more than an outlaw who neglected his command in favor of plundering.[8] Morgan had demonstrated himself irresponsible, impulsive, careless in command, and, on the whole, untrustworthy—exactly Bragg's estimate of him.

Many besides Morgan made requests of Bragg. Some sought promotion for themselves or for friends or relatives. Alpheus

---

[8] Ramage, *Rebel Raider*, pp. 201, 160, 206, 237; J. R. Butler to S. Cooper, March 19, 1864; John Hunt Morgan to Cooper, March 19, 1864, Bragg Papers, Western Reserve; E. M. Bruce to W. C. P. Breckinridge, March 30, 1864, Breckinridge Family Papers; *OR*, XXXIX (pt. 1), 66, 76; Ruffin, III, 416.

Baker asked for and got promotion to brigade command, and when a former subordinate requested transfer to Baker's new brigade, Bragg again accommodated his friend. General H. H. Chalmers wrote on behalf of his brother, a steadfast friend of the administration, whom he considered deserving of promotion. Bragg agreed, and Chalmers was promoted. Sometimes parents requested that their sons be transferred to more favorable positions.[9]

Many requests came from officers who desired active field command. R. H. Anderson begged to be ordered into active service, blatantly flattering Bragg to achieve his ends. H. D. Capers asserted that his command itched for combat, and Patton Anderson wished to be reassigned to one of the two most active armies. One request came from a man who wanted to transfer from one hospital to another. "I hav got some surtificates from difrent surgents and was advised . . . to git some of my frends to assist me in gitting me a . . . trans fur," he explained. "I ask you as a frend to assist me."[10]

Some communicants sought appointments. William Bate, who announced that he had properly provided for Bragg's nephew Yancey, asked Bragg to do something for Colonel John G. Coltart. Benjamin S. Ewell wrote on behalf of Colonel E. J. Harvie, enumerating all of Harvie's positive qualities and then clinching the matter by pointing out that Harvie was also endowed with a large, influential Virginia family. Senator G. A. Henry sought a staff position for his son. Among other requests that poured in: Winchester Hall wanted his old regiment back, D. C. Govan asked that some troops be returned to his command, and L. P.

[9] Baker to Bragg, March 2, 1864; John A. Minter et al. to Alpheus Baker, April 13, 1864, Bragg Papers, Western Reserve; OR, XXXIII, 1317; H. H. Chalmers to Bragg, August 29, 1864; John Forsyth to Bragg, February 25, 1864; W. W. Garrard to Bragg, July 15, 1864; Mary Baldwin to Bragg, August 18, 1864; Daniel Wheeler to Bragg, August 16, 1864, Bragg Papers, Western Reserve.

[10] R. H. Anderson to Bragg, May 21, 1864, Bragg Papers, Western Reserve; H. D. Capers to Bragg, May 20, 1864, Davis Papers, Duke University Library; Patton Anderson to Bragg, June 17, 1864; A. M. Higgins to Bragg, July 4, 1864, Bragg Papers, Western Reserve.

Walker requested that S. L. Harris be appointed judge advocate of Walker's military court. One man asked only for a letter of recommendation, "which may assist me with those I do not know."[11]

One correspondent clearly revealed the power contemporaries believed Bragg wielded. Newspaper editor L. J. Dupree requested an amendment to, and extension of, a government contract. Explaining that he had not been an original party to the contract, Dupree directed that his name be inserted with that of G. H. Monsarrat of Montgomery, Alabama. Monsarrat and Dupree obviously believed they needed Bragg's influence to obtain the necessary extension.[12]

As a body, this correspondence indicates that Bragg's contemporaries recognized his power and influence. Virtually all of these requests came from people with whom Bragg had had contact while he commanded the Army of Tennessee, either as part of his military family or as civilians who had met him or felt they knew him through their geographical proximity to his areas of activity. While some fawned and flattered, others merely wished him well in his new position, or simply stated their business and hoped he would do what he could for them. These letters gave a much-needed boost to Bragg's morale. That people viewed him as influential and powerful worked as a salve for his wounded spirit, still recovering from the disgrace surrounding his retirement from field command.

Records reveal that in important instances, such as those of

[11] William B. Bate to Bragg, March 17, 1864; B. S. Ewell to Bragg, July 16, 1864; G. A. Henry to Bragg, September 7, 1864, Bragg Papers, Western Reserve; Winchester Hall to Bragg, June 13, 1864, Davis Papers, Duke University Library; D. C. Govan to Bragg, July 16, 1864; L. P. Walker to Bragg, June 14, 1864; L. J. Murphy to Bragg, July 20, 1864, Bragg Papers, Western Reserve. See also Arthur Shaaff to John Forsyth, April 27, 1864; Warren Stone to Bragg, July 18, 1864; Francis H. Smith to Bragg, February 27, 1864; C. J. Pope to Bragg, March 12, 1864; B. H. Magruder to Bragg, July 18, 1864; William Lovell to Bragg, March 27, 1864; Charles S. Shorter to Bragg, April 14, 1864, Bragg Papers, Western Reserve.

[12] L. J. Dupree to Bragg, Montgomery, Alabama, May 16, 1864, Bragg Papers, Western Reserve.

Baker and Chalmers, Bragg granted the requests. Those of lesser importance fail to appear in official records or correspondence, but it is certain that if Bragg had the power to dispose of cases of greater consequence, he surely could influence the less important.

More pressing business demanded Bragg's attention, however, beginning with the infamous Kilpatrick-Dahlgren raid into the Richmond locale. In mid-February Federal general Judson Kilpatrick devised a plan to distribute President Lincoln's amnesty proclamation, to destroy the enemy's communications, and to release Federal prisoners held in Richmond. On February 28 Kilpatrick led 3,500 cavalry troops toward Richmond from the north, while his co-commander, one-legged Colonel Ulric Dahlgren, led an additional 500 troopers to attack the city from the west. Faced with an unexpected defense, as well as bad weather, Dahlgren retreated, but not soon enough. On March 2 the Confederates killed him in an ambush and took about 100 of his troopers prisoner. Papers found on Dahlgren's body urged released Union prisoners to destroy Richmond and to kill "Davis and his traitorous crew."[13]

This incident, coming only one week after Bragg assumed office, quickly thrust him into sharing responsibility for determining government policy. Confederate officials were uncertain how to respond. On March 5 Davis met with his cabinet for several hours, trying to determine how best to use the situation for propaganda purposes. On March 4 Bragg had recommended executing the captured raiders and publishing the papers as justification. Seddon appeared to agree, but in a letter to Lee the following day he hinted at concern about the possibility of Federal retaliation against Confederate prisoners of war.[14] This was a sly move on Seddon's part, as he knew Lee had good reason to fear retaliation—his own son was imprisoned in the North.

Lee, to Seddon's relief, favored caution, pointing out that Confederate troops had also engaged in unauthorized and discredit-

13 *OR*, XXXIII, 172, 178.
14 J. B. Jones, *Rebel War Clerk's Diary*, II, 166; *OR*, XXXIII, 217–18.

able behavior. When a Washington investigation concluded that
Dahlgren held sole responsibility for the orders, Lee's cautionary
views prevailed.[15] Thus in his first attempt to influence Confederate policy Bragg found himself overruled, an inauspicious beginning for a proud man trying to regain his self-respect and sense of
importance.

The question of retaliatory executions of prisoners of war persisted. In July Confederates accused Union soldiers of killing two
citizens. The circumstances in each incident indicated the "citizens" were in reality bushwhackers, thereby justifying (to the
Federals) their execution. As before, Bragg favored stern retaliation, but Davis again wanted Lee's views. Lee counseled modera-
tion, and once again, Lee's counsel prevailed over Bragg's.[16]

While Bragg advocated severe retaliations against prisoners,
he also assumed responsibility for improving the entire prison
system. Reports crossed his desk describing the overcrowded, un-
sanitary conditions in the prison hospitals, as well as in the prisons themselves. An inspection of the hospitals serving the
Richmond prisons prompted Colonel Brent, along with Surgeon
T. G. Richardson, to conclude it was imperative that the hospital
be enlarged. Bragg sent a copy to the officer in charge of prisons,
who responded that "the ratio of mortality does not exceed that of
our own prisoners in the hands of the enemy," an untrue statement that he apparently believed excused him from laxity in the
execution of his duties.[17]

Prison conditions outside the hospitals were even worse. The
appalling conditions and the treatment of prisoners at Anderson-
ville, Georgia, moved a Confederate guard to complain to Davis:
"We have many thoughtless boys here who think the killing of a
Yankee will make them great men. As a consequence, every day
or two there are prisioners shot." To alleviate some of the pressure

[15] *OR*, XXXIII, 222–23, 175–76.
[16] *Ibid.*, Series 2, VII, 430–32, 463–64, 473.
[17] *Ibid.*, Series 2, VI, 1049–51, 1084–89; Series 2, VII, 39.

Bragg ordered two additional prisons established, one near Millen, Georgia, and the other in Alabama.[18]

Problems also arose in the exchange of prisoners, exacerbated by General John H. Winder, the man in charge. The Confederates did not always know just how many or what sort of prisoners they held. An investigation in May characterized the whole system, as directed by Winder and his band of "rogues and cut-throats," as "makeshift." General W. M. Gardner, post commander at Richmond, complained that, when called upon to account for individual prisoners, he had to write to prison posts scattered all over the South, usually to discover, after much delay, that the person in question was in Winder's jurisdiction. Gardner called for a separate and independent bureau under a single officer with authority to enforce the necessary measures. Bragg strongly concurred, and on May 25 alleviated some of the problems by replacing Winder with General Robert Ransom.[19]

The prison system was just one of the military institutions to which Bragg devoted attention. Supply and subsistence had also been long-standing problems, as Bragg knew from his experience while commanding the Army of Tennessee. Now he held partial responsibility, and the situation had reached crisis proportions. In mid-January Lee informed Davis of his army's great need for food. He pointed to laxity in the handling of subsistence by the railroads, suggesting that government agents accompany each train of provisions. This report crossed Bragg's desk several weeks later, at which time he agreed with Lee that the whole system was fraudulent. He recommended Colonel William M. Wadley as a railroad expert who might do good service. Seddon, however, replied that Wadley was unavailable, and that seemed to end the matter.[20]

Transportation problems were indeed to blame for many of the Confederacy's supply problems. One historian believed Bragg exacerbated these already severe problems simply by being there,

[18] *Ibid.*, Series 2, VII, 392, 403, 550, 589.
[19] J. B. Jones, *Rebel War Clerk's Diary*, II, 219; *OR*, Series 2, VII, 986–87.
[20] *OR*, XXXIII, 1076–77.

charging that the already obscure decision-making processes in
the War Department became "absolutely enigmatic" when Bragg
arrived. This is an overstatement. Bragg and others did attempt to
remedy the situation, only to be overruled by Davis. On April 7
Commissary General Lucius B. Northrop submitted a litany on
the abuses of the railroads, warning that if they continued, they
might "result in the . . . pillaging of our own country by a soldi-
ery disorganized and demoralized by hunger." To ameliorate conditions, Bragg recommended military supervision of the railroads,
and Seddon concurred. But Davis disagreed. Instead, he sought
again to secure the cooperation of the railroad companies. Davis's
reluctance to act seemed related to his doubts about the competence of the military to manage the railroads, although one historian believes Davis allowed the business elites to influence his
decision. Indeed, they enjoyed complete freedom throughout the
war to run the railroads at a maximum profit.[21]

Although the problems did not disappear, with the arrival of
spring things improved, for which Bragg received credit. In mid-
March a Richmond war clerk noted that after Bragg took measures to see that meat and grain moved more quickly along the
supply line, much food had arrived for Lee's army. Another vote
of confidence came from Bragg's old army, as testified to by Kate
Cumming, whose brother reported the army had plenty to eat,
including coffee and sugar, and that they all credited this improvement to Bragg. Bragg patted his own back for the turn of affairs.
"By an active supervision of the different lines of rail road, by . . .
securing the early completion of [another route] . . . , by check-
ing sources of unofficial . . . consumption, and by opening other
sources of supply," he boasted, "these difficulties were not only
removed, but our means became sufficient to sustain [Lee's] army
when more than doubled in strength."[22]

But shortages persisted, and even Bragg felt the pinch. In Sep-

[21] Goff, *Confederate Supply*, p. 198; *OR*, LI (pt. 2), 851–52; Hagerman, *Origins*,
p. 68.
[22] J. B. Jones, *Rebel War Clerk's Diary*, II, 172–73; Cumming, *Kate*, p. 207;
Bragg, "Notes," Bragg Papers, Western Reserve.

tember he inquired about obtaining forage for his horses. "I have but one very valuable animal and two others are getting on their last legs from starvation," he complained. "All this time I find, daily, large loads of fine Hay & Oats passing in public wagons through the streets. . . . All I ask is to be put on an equal with others." And finally, in a swipe at one of the departments inviting his inspection, "I see the Quartermaster riding and driving fine, fat Horses." This comment, along with a negative report Bragg filed on the same day regarding the Richmond quartermaster department, prompted the quartermaster to reply in such a manner that Bragg turned to Davis for satisfaction. "As these records are to constitute a part of the future history of the country," he complained, "I feel sure you will appreciate my appeal to be relieved from an attitude so mortifying to my self-respect and so humiliating to my professional pride." Just what Bragg expected Davis to do remains unclear. Davis solved it by dumping it into Seddon's lap.[23]

In April Bragg proposed a desperate measure to alleviate the supply problems; he would reduce the population of Richmond by sending government departments elsewhere. Seddon concurred, as did Davis. When Bragg discussed the idea with General Gorgas, however, the chief of ordnance thought Bragg was "a *little cracked*." Diarist Robert G. H. Kean sarcastically pronounced, "The idea was worthy of the hero of Missionary Ridge!"[24]

Despite complaint, the plan went forward. Various bureaus prepared to send off the personnel who could conduct their business outside the capital. As with most of war's burdens, this one fell most heavily on women. The Treasury Department had employed many females, and now their chief, Secretary of the Treasury Christopher G. Memminger, ordered them to Columbia,

---

[23] Bragg to W. M. Gardner, September 16, 1864, Confederate Generals and Staff Officers, Compiled Service Records, National Archives and Records Administration, Washington, D.C.; *OR*, Series 4, III, 724-25.

[24] *OR*, LI (pt. 2), 852; Gorgas, *Diary*, p. 95; Kean, *Inside*, p. 145.

South Carolina. On April 25 Kean reported that after two long cabinet meetings, the whole plan was deferred "except in the case of the ladies who sign Memminger's notes." When the women protested, Memminger told them they must either go or resign. He knew, of course, it was impossible for them to resign, as their incomes often provided the sole means of support for themselves and their families. Sadly, "in sorrow and in tears they bade adieu to Richmond." Bragg also had the hospitals send off some of their personnel, to the disgust of one matron. "Gen. Bragg has been putting his fingers in the Hospital pies," reported Phoebe Yates Pember, who presided over the Chimborazo Hospital in Richmond, "closing them and dispersing all the corps just when the spring campaign is about to open."[25]

It is unlikely that Bragg expected to go uncensured for these measures, and he was not disappointed. "The *Examiner* cries," Chesnut wrote in her diary, "parodying the Mexican War order of General Taylor, 'A little more *brains*, Captain Bragg.'"[26]

Civilian disaffection elsewhere also became Bragg's responsibility, although what anyone expected him to do about it is unclear. Reports reached his office from all areas of the Confederacy. People in northern Mississippi had become demoralized through trading cotton with the Federals; those in southern Mississippi were in rebellion, calling themselves "Southern Yankees"; and in the state capital "the women are losing their real faith and patriotism. . . . And the men, what can they be when the women are lost to their country?" In the East, Governor Zebulon B. Vance of North Carolina reported his mountain counties "filled with tories and deserters, burning, robbing, and murdering. They have been robbed and eaten out by Longstreet's [Confederate!] command, and have lost their crops by being in the field nearly all the time trying to drive back the enemy"—whether

[25] Kean, *Inside*, p. 145; Sallie Brock Putnam, *Richmond during the War: Four Years of Personal Observation* (New York, 1867), p. 288; Phoebe Yates Pember, *A Southern Woman's Story*, ed. Bell Irvin Wiley (Covington, Ga., 1977), p. 140.
[26] Chesnut, *Civil War*, p. 596.

Longstreet's troops or the Federals, he did not say. Some of the disaffected banded together in secret societies, which Bragg ordered investigated. "The whole thing . . . is of such magnitude that I hardly know at what point to grasp it," one inspector complained, and Bragg, too, appeared stymied by the immensity of the problem.[27]

Bragg's greatest challenge was keeping soldiers in the ranks. By late 1863 disaffection prompted not only rampant desertion but threats of outright rebellion. In December 1863 a Union soldier reported refugees entering the Federal lines, many of them deserters from the Confederate army. General Dabney H. Maury reported from Mobile that regiments in General James H. Clanton's Brigade had resolved that on Christmas Day they would simply lay down their arms and go home. Manigault believed soldiers from the poorer classes were ready to accept peace on any terms, attributing this attitude to the fact that "many of them were reluctantly drawn from their homes."[28]

Here was the real nub of the problem—conscription. A Union soldier in the Chattanooga area reported that refugees flooded into the Union lines to avoid being conscripted into the Southern armies. In February 1864 Representative W. N. H. Smith requested conscription be suspended in Bertie County, North Carolina, but Bragg, drawing on his experience in the West, demurred. "I have never known any good to result from a suspension of our laws in disaffected districts," he asserted. "In East Tennessee it undoubtedly resulted in evil." The petition was denied. In April Governor Vance tried again to have conscription suspended in parts of North Carolina. Seddon could not recom-

---

[27] *OR*, XXXII (pt. 1), 346; (pt. 3), 662–63; XXXIX (pt. 2), 729; Series 4, III, 645–51, 393–94, 805–7; LIII, 324; J. B. Jones, *Rebel War Clerk's Diary*, II, 230; Henry T. Shanks, "Disloyalty to the Confederacy in Southwestern Virginia, 1861–1865," *North Carolina Historical Review*, XXI (1944), 118–35; Henry J. Leroy to Bragg, September 21, 1864, Davis Papers, Duke University Library. For a full discussion of disaffection in the mountain counties of western North Carolina, see Phillip Shaw Paludan, *Victims: A True Story of the Civil War* (Knoxville, 1981).

[28] Mosman, *Rough Side*, pp. 139–40; *OR*, XXVI (pt. 2), 548.

mend such a course, and Bragg agreed. "My experience in East Tennessee," he repeated, "satisfies me of the correctness of the . . . Secretary's view. More harm than good has resulted from relaxation." Again, the request was denied. From South Carolina General James Chesnut reported he had been compelled to send forces to aid the conscription officer in suppressing violence and punishing marauders.[29]

Conscription itself seemed to be not as repugnant to Confederates as was the unjust manner in which the bureau carried it out. Bragg devoted much time and effort to improving its operations and image, frequently sending inspectors to gather information on the workings of individual units within the bureau. In Augusta, Georgia, Inspector H. W. Walter discovered that many draftees received exemptions to which they were not entitled. At Milledgeville, he found that the department was "a farce and could be dispensed with without injury to the service." A particular evil, Walter reported, was the practice of the state governor of enlisting men into "Supporting Forces," or units that would not leave the state. He found three companies of cavalry at Macon who, after six months, remained unarmed and had done little or no service. Although he believed them worse than useless, there was one thing in their favor: unlike other such units, "being unarmed, they have not straggled over the State, and under the pretext of performing duty, plundered the citizen." Bragg forwarded this startling report to Davis, adding that reports from other states were equally unsatisfactory. He firmly believed, "Stern, rigid administration can correct the evil; nothing else will."[30]

The poor suffered most from conscription. A correspondent informed Bragg that in Mobile many men were exempted from military duty—generally those with money. "It is a notorious and dangerous fact," he wrote, "that the poor men, . . . men of no influence are never *improperly* exempted as in the case of those who

[29] Mosman, *Rough Side*, p. 140; *OR*, LI (pt. 2), 821–22; LIII, 324–25, 329, 342.
[30] H. W. Walter to Bragg, August 20, 1864, Davis Papers, Duke University Library; *OR*, Series 4, III, 624–25.

have means and influence." An old family friend believed that only martial law would solve the problem, as elected officials passed legislation that allowed their relatives and friends to avoid dangerous military service.[31]

Bragg submitted a devastating report on the Bureau of Conscription in September. Forwarding a list of officers employed at the Richmond office, Bragg noted there were several points inviting attention, a sure indication that he was out for blood. These several points reveal his vindictive nature. He took issue with allowing an able-bodied colonel to do two years of office duty while his regiment served in the field. Bragg believed the job could be performed by a disabled officer, in which event "this colonel might see a little field service yet before the war is over and learn something of the rules of discipline and respect for his superiors, of which he appears to be much in need from the inclosed copy of a letter recently addressed to this office." This letter included a long lecture that Bragg had received from the colonel in which he instructed Bragg that conscription officers only recognized inspectors authorized by the president or the secretary of war, citing the general orders setting forth this protocol. "None of its officers," this impertinent colonel went on, "should, therefore, be held liable to obey any exceptional orders from an eccentric source." Bragg also criticized an officer who "does not seem to devote much time" to his duties, and another who appeared too young for the duties assigned him. Overall, Bragg reported the whole organization appeared defective and inefficient. This caustic report prompted the supervisor, General J. S. Preston, to tender his resignation.[32]

Bragg soon had satisfaction, both personal and professional. Unable to reform the conscription department, in September he

[31] B. F. Jones to Bragg, October 10, 1864, P. W. Alexander Papers, Columbia University, New York; Samuel E. Phillips to Bragg, October 2, 1864, Bragg Papers, Western Reserve.
[32] *OR*, Series 4, III, 609–10, 568, 641; Thomas P. August to Bragg, August 2, 1864, Bragg Papers, Western Reserve.

)

persuaded Davis to dismantle it. As embodied in an act of Congress the following March, commanders of the reserves in each state took charge of conscription. All of the department's personnel fit to bear arms found themselves ordered into the ranks.[33] Bragg must have been exultant. Not only had Davis accepted his recommendations, but at the same time he had put the bumptious colonel into the field.

There was another source from which to recruit—the black people held in bondage in the South. Their presence had both caused and complicated the Confederacy's waging of war. From the start, they performed much of the army's menial labor but were never uniformed or even considered part of the army. The North, however, began using blacks as soldiers, hesitantly at first, but then with growing confidence and enthusiasm, prompting the Confederate Congress in 1863 to authorize the execution of captured black soldiers and their white officers. When Union officials protested this policy, the South found it easier not to deal with black prisoners at all, choosing instead to execute them on the spot even after they had surrendered or, should they be taken prisoner, to return them quietly to slavery. Bragg faced this problem in April when the Confederates captured a number of blacks at Plymouth, North Carolina. He asked Governor Vance to take possession of the black prisoners and, if possible, to restore them to their owners. Bragg wished, however, to avoid complications with Union authorities and instructed Vance to keep the matter out of the newspapers.[34]

Despite this hard line, some Southerners began to suspect that the Confederacy's only chance of success required using blacks as soldiers. In December 1863 General Patrick Cleburne, a former subordinate of Bragg's in the Army of Tennessee, drew up a docu-

[33] J. B. Jones, *Rebel War Clerk's Diary*, II, 189–90; *OR*, Series 4, III, 1176–77.
[34] Mary Frances Berry, *Military Necessity and Civil Rights Policy: Black Citizenship and the Constitution, 1861–1868* (Port Washington, N.Y., 1977), pp. 39, 61; James M. McPherson, *Battle Cry of Freedom: The Civil War Era* (New York, 1988), pp. 565–67, 792–96; Phillip Shaw Paludan, *"A People's Contest": the Union and Civil War, 1861–1865* (New York, 1988), pp. 213–14; *OR*, Series 2, VII, 78–79.

ment urging that slaves be enlisted, with a provision for their freedom if they remained loyal to the Confederacy. Several brigade
and regimental commanders supported Cleburne's view. "The
document," one historian understated, "startled both the high
command and Richmond." Davis ordered Johnston, commanding
the Army of Tennessee, to suppress all discussion of the proposal.
Johnston did so, but by spring 1864 he called for Negroes to fill
army positions such as cooks, pioneers, and laborers, thus freeing
an estimated 10,000 to 12,000 whites to serve in the fighting
forces. In September Lee also requested blacks to replace whites
in the same positions, believing this would give him hundreds
more in the fighting ranks.[35]

Bragg was jubilant when he saw that many of his detractors in
his old army were involved in the scheme to enlist blacks. In early
February he told General Marcus J. Wright, "A great sensation is
being produced . . . by the Emancipation project of Hardee,
Cheatham, Cleburne & Co. It will kill them," he gloated. A
month later Bragg advised letting "the abolition gentlemen
subside for the present, but they are agitators, and should be
watched." "We must mark the men," he cautioned.[36]

Nevertheless, Bragg continued to receive proposals regarding
the arming of blacks. In March another correspondent from the
Army of Tennessee informed Bragg, "The Free Negro scheme
seems to be down with chill and fever," but he went on to suggest
that "the experiment be tried on a small scale" with a mixed brigade assigned "to the originator of the 'Scheme.'" Although he may
have been remarking facetiously, others no longer believed the
idea so outlandish. One negrophobe urged Bragg to consider em-
ploying blacks as soldiers, proposing they be used "to push the
bayonet in pursuit." He did not suggest that black soldiers should
be rewarded with freedom but rather pointed out, "He is already
half a machine and strict discipline will make him a better slave

[35] Connelly, *Autumn of Glory*, pp. 318–20; Gilbert E. Govan and James W.
Livingood, *A Different Valor: The Story of General Joseph E. Johnston, C.S.A.* (New
York, 1956), p. 245; Robert F. Durden, *The Gray and the Black: The Confederate
Debate on Emancipation* (Baton Rouge, 1972), pp. 22–24.
[36] Bragg to Marcus J. Wright, February 6, March 6, 1864, Wright Papers.

after the war." Just how blacks were to be convinced they should fight for their continued enslavement did not seem to concern the writer.[37]

Besides his bureaucratic duties, Bragg also focused his energy on military crises. When Bragg became Davis's military adviser, General Jones M. Withers, who once commanded a division under Bragg, told him, "No man in the Confederacy knows the condition of the country, . . . the wants of the army, and the material of which it is composed, better than yourself."[38]

Having this knowledge, Bragg recognized the critical nature of his responsibility. Confederate territory had seriously diminished since the early days of high hopes and successes. The Federals controlled much of its industrial raw material, as well as much of its farming and animal-producing land. The number of people available for agricultural and industrial labor also diminished as the advancing Union armies freed slaves. As if this were not enough, General Ulysses S. Grant, who had forced Bragg out of Chattanooga and out of the Army of Tennessee, now commanded all of the Northern armies.

On May 5 Grant began an unrelenting advance. Battles raged to the north and east of Richmond—the Wilderness on May 5–6, Spotsylvania on May 8, North Anna on May 23–26, Cold Harbor on June 1–4—as Grant inexorably sidled the Army of the Potomac around Lee's Army of Northern Virginia. This advance eventually ended in the siege of Petersburg, south of the capital.

Other than gathering troops for Lee, however, Bragg had little to do with these events, as they took place in Lee's area of command, so Bragg focused his attention on events taking place to the south and east, and for a critical period he acted as the overall coordinator for this area.[39]

---

[37] F. G. Robertson to Bragg, March 14, 1864; H. B. Shepard to Bragg, March 4, 1864, Bragg Papers, Western Reserve.

[38] Jones M. Withers to Bragg, February 26, 1864, *ibid.*

[39] William Glenn Robertson, *Back Door to Richmond: The Bermuda Hundred Campaign, April–June 1864* (Newark, Del., 1987), p. 92; Richard J. Sommers, *Richmond Redeemed: The Siege at Petersburg* (Garden City, N.Y., 1981), p. 109; Herbert M. Schiller, *The Bermuda Hundred Campaign* (Dayton, Ohio, 1988), p. 57.

When Bragg first took up his post, General George E. Pickett commanded the Department of Southern Virginia and Northern North Carolina. Pickett, famous for his charge at Gettysburg, bombarded Bragg with information, forwarding every report of the enemy he received. Pickett no doubt felt obliged to do so, as Bragg had instructed him to report all enemy movements. However, by April 16 Bragg had had enough. "You should keep the enemy closely watched, and report his movements frequently," Bragg reprimanded Pickett, "but I must warn you of the evil resulting from exaggerated or unreliable reports. . . . The reports sent recently are so contradictory," he scolded, "as to render them all useless, if not injurious." Pickett naturally took umbrage. "The tone is as harsh as the inferences to be drawn are unmerited," he complained. "Your instructions to me were 'to keep me advised.' This I attempted to do by sending you all the telegrams and reports . . . I received. These combined with your many other sources of information," he snarled, "I supposed would enable you to form your own conclusions." In addition, Pickett presumed to give Bragg a lesson in intelligence. "The enemy occupying an extent of country such as they did," he lectured, "it was not at all surprising that the reports of scouts should be conflicting."[40]

Believing Pickett incapable of commanding the heavily threatened Richmond area, Bragg persuaded Davis to appoint Beauregard commander of the area. Although Beauregard required much prodding, he managed to check General Benjamin Butler's advance and to contain Butler's troops on Bermuda Hundred until forced to fall back to defend Petersburg in mid-June.[41]

Two vignettes afford a glimpse of Bragg's character and job demands during this busy period. In mid-May, as the Federals made a concerted effort to capture Richmond, General J. E. B. Stuart

[40] *OR*, LI (pt. 2), 861, 863–65; George E. Pickett to Bragg, May 5, 1864, Bragg Papers, Western Reserve.
[41] *OR*, LI (pt. 2), 872, 953, 928; G. T. Beauregard to Bragg, May 11, 14, 15, 1864, Bragg Papers, Western Reserve.

sent Major Henry B. McClellan to see if Bragg had the city prepared for defense. McClellan found Bragg, "a stolid man, serenely eating breakfast, and unperturbed." Bragg had put all the city forces, plus the old men, boys, clerks, and invalids into the fortifications, and had ordered up troops from Petersburg. "He has done all he can, says Bragg, but he thinks he can hold out," McClellan reported. "If there comes a disaster, he just cannot help it. That is Bragg." One wonders just how stolid, serene, and unperturbed Bragg remained when, during one critical night, a woman noted, "Congressmen besieged the war department all night—so that Gen. Bragg was called out of bed to go down to them after midnight."[42]

Bragg's efforts to defend Richmond resulted in more controversy. By late May an order Bragg had sent General W. H. C. Whiting to assist Beauregard at Drewry's Bluff became public and misconstrued. Some apparently interpreted it to mean that Petersburg had been written off by the Confederate high command. Whiting himself may have promoted this idea when he wired Beauregard, "I think the enemy intends Petersburg, and that this move will seal its fate." It appeared that Whiting also spoke his mind freely to subordinates in Petersburg. General Henry A. Wise reported that Whiting stated that Bragg had said in his order, "The defense of that city [Petersburg] was not as vital as that of the metropolis [Richmond]." Wise went on to say that Whiting had freely and openly criticized the order in the presence of several people.[43] As no one else ever claimed to have seen this order, the entire responsibility for the rumor appears to rest with Whiting. For his own reasons, perhaps reluctance to leave the comparative safety of Petersburg, Whiting loosely interpreted Bragg's language and then complained equally loosely and irresponsibly.

[42] John W. Thomason, Jr., *Jeb Stuart* (New York, 1941), p. 496; Katherine M. Jones, *Heroines of Dixie: Winter of Desperation* (St. Simons Island, Ga., 1975), pp. 98–99.
[43] W. H. C. Whiting to Beauregard, 5:00 P.M., May 15, 1864, Bragg Papers, Western Reserve; *OR*, XXXVI (pt. 3), 859–60.

Jones reported in his diary on May 27 that two newspapers had denounced Bragg and that "the city is excited with rumors." One rumor purported that when Bragg ordered Beauregard to evacuate Petersburg, "certainly an insane measure," Beauregard wired Davis for confirmation. Davis replied that he had indeed authorized the orders sent by Bragg. However, Jones wrote, Beauregard *"disregarded* the order and fought the battle, saving Petersburg."[44]

Many people were quite willing to believe these rumors. Diarist Catherine Edmondston declared, "Beauregard interfered & said 'No! No! a thousand times No! it was suicidal to think of it, if they took it it must be through oceans of blood, he would defend it to the last at all extremities.'" She concluded with what must have been on many minds—"Just like Bragg!" A Richmond editor agreed. "The evacuation of Petersburg," he averred, "would have been exceedingly natural . . . for General Bragg, and . . . he may have suffered injustice only by anticipation."[45]

Even Beauregard's disclaimer of any knowledge of such an order failed to still the rumor. On May 27 Gorgas wrote, "Bragg is bitterly assaulted in two journals this morning, without much harm done." Despite Gorgas's impression of little harm done, the next day Jones reported, "It is thought, to-day, that Bragg will resign. . . . But I doubt the story; I don't think the President will permit Bragg to retire before his enemies, unless," he accurately predicted, "affairs become desperate by the defeat of our army in this vicinity."[46]

The rumor caused enough harm for Bragg to feel obligated to explain himself in a postwar defense. In attempting to save both Richmond and Petersburg, he wrote, he had ordered all the troops from both Richmond and Petersburg to join Beauregard. To illustrate the good sense of this decision, he pointed out that at

[44] J. B. Jones, *Rebel War Clerk's Diary*, II, 220.

[45] Edmondston, *Secesh Lady*, p. 564; F. S. Daniel, *Richmond Examiner*, pp. 201–2.

[46] *OR*, LI (pt. 2), 967; Gorgas, *Diary*, p. 110; J. B. Jones, *Rebel War Clerk's Diary*, II, 221.

about the same time Beauregard had also given Whiting the same orders, "it being evident if Butler was discomfited Petersburg was saved, but if he was not Whiting and his garrison . . . would only be sacrificed. The result," Bragg boasted, "proved what common sense dictated. Yet some persons," he complained, "under the excitement of the times, ignorant, probably, of the facts and their bearings, have denounced Gen'l Bragg as guilty of a heinous offence towards the people of Petersburg in advising the evacuation of that city, when, indeed, the movement, which was simultaneously directed by Beauregard, and had been previously ordered by the Sec of War, was all that could have saved them."[47] Bragg thus pointed out not only that he had used common sense in the emergency but that his decision had been supported by others more popular than himself. The bad feeling that this controversy generated between Bragg and Whiting boded ill for their future relations.

Bragg took the blame for other things he had no hand in. In late June and early July General Jubal Early forayed north, pushing into the outskirts of Washington, D.C. One of his own countrypeople accurately described Early's chances of success. "Early is careening around Washington and Baltimore and frightening the eternal Yankee nation into fits," he wrote, "but I fear will not be able to capture the former." Nor was he able to capture the latter, or accomplish anything else of lasting importance. Although Early's careening had been ordered by Lee, it, too, became Bragg's fault. "It looks very much like the style of military blundering usual with Bragg," another Confederate complained.[48]

In addition to coordinating military activity around Richmond, Bragg also spent time on Western military matters, receiving reports from various commanders, ordering troop transfers, and suggesting responses to enemy activities. In the West he also had

---

[47] Bragg, "Notes," Bragg Papers, Western Reserve.
[48] Edgeworth Bird and Sallie Bird, *The Granite Farm Letters: The Civil War Correspondence of Edgeworth and Sallie Bird*, ed. John Rozier (Athens, Ga., 1988), p. 176; *OR*, XLI (pt. 2), 1012.

to mediate among the commanders. Generals E. Kirby Smith, Richard Taylor, and Stephen D. Lee proved incapable of co-operating with one another, each running to Bragg with tales about the others' dilatory, or nonexistent, execution of orders. After several months of attempting to move some of Smith's troops across the Mississippi to Taylor's aid, Taylor reported to Bragg that Smith had pardoned those who deserted from the army when ordered to Taylor. "This," he wailed, "after I had captured most of the deserters. Under these circumstances," he concluded, "it seems to me to be useless to send further orders to cross the troops." It is no wonder Taylor wrote Bragg in July, "I will not entirely forego the hope that the Trans. Miss. Dept. may get placed under your control [as field commander]," and a few months later he informed Bragg, "In my judgement [*sic*], it is a great misfortune you were not sent there [Trans-Mississippi] when you left the Army of Tenn. You would have been welcomed by the army and the great body of the people."[49]

Fortunately for the Confederacy, Bragg did not go to the Trans-Mississippi; he remained in Richmond eight months, accomplishing much under difficult circumstances. The management of the various military institutions had improved, either through the removal of incompetent department heads or by the dismantling of entire corrupt bureaus. Army supply had improved, but not to the extent it might have if Davis had heeded Bragg's advice on military supervision of the railroads. Davis relied heavily upon Bragg's understanding of military affairs and institutions. Although he did not always agree with Bragg, Davis consistently sought his expertise and opinion on a variety of matters. By un-

[49] *OR*, XXXII (pt. 3), 812; XXXVIII (pt. 4), 668; (pt. 5), 876, 887, 894, 897, 898, 902, 904, 905, 907, 926, 930, 939, 944, 948, 952, 954, 959–60, 972, 979, 986, 1000, 1006; XXXIX (pt. 2), 647, 687, 688–89, 700, 710, 714, 719–20, 721, 733, 746, 751, 777, 784, 798, 826, 829, 831, 860, 862, 865, 866, 867; (pt. 3), 782; XLI (pt. 1), 103, 108, 118; LII (pt. 2), 752. See also *OR*, XXXIV (pt. 4), 697; XXXVI (pt. 3), 894–95; XXXIX (pt. 2), 657–58, 668, 690, 694, 696, 727; XLI (pt. 1), 89–91, 111–12, 117, 119–22; (pt. 2), 990–93, 1029–31, 1037; LII (pt. 2), 731–32; Richard Taylor to Bragg, July 22, September 25, 1864, Bragg Papers, Western Reserve.

tiringly assuming many of the duties and much of the criticism that had burdened and perplexed Davis, Bragg eased some of the president's vexations. In the process he maintained old enmities and created many new ones.

CHAPTER X

This shows very badly for Bragg

July, 1864

EVEN AFTER BRAGG LEFT the Army of Tennessee, he remained a determinative influence in its affairs, and he ultimately aided in its destruction through the removal of General J. E. Johnston as its commander. Many people believed that Bragg's experience as that army's commander and his knowledge of conditions in the Western theater made his appointment as Davis's military adviser particularly important to that area. General Alexander P. Stewart informed Bragg that his friends in the Army of Tennessee believed that his position in Richmond would enable him to see that the Western army was "more fully appreciated at the seat of government than perhaps they have been heretofore." Cavalry commander General Joseph Wheeler concurred. "This army is much pleased," he avowed. "The entire Southwest has felt that its military geography and military resources have not been fully comprehended in Richmond and they have long felt the want of having a directing hand which understood this country."[1]

Bragg did keep his eye on his old army, and he continued to influence its administration. His position sometimes afforded Bragg opportunities to strike at his enemies in that organization: "His actions," a historian contended, "would be colored by his firm belief that the mistakes of the army were those of his subordinates and not his own." On other occasions he saw to promotions and transfers of his supporters and friends in the army. In March Major Felix G. Robertson complained to Bragg of juniors from the East being promoted over his head, expressing the hope that

[1] Alexander P. Stewart to Bragg, March 19, 1864; Joseph Wheeler to Bragg, March 3, 1864, Bragg Papers, Western Reserve.

Bragg would do justice for him. Bragg did indeed try to see justice done his old friend. "Recently some complaints, I learn privately," Bragg informed Johnston, "have been heard from your Artillery officers, that they were being oversloughed by their juniors from the Army of Northern Virginia. . . . I should very much fear the effect of such transfers, unless there was some transcendant or overshadowing ability or achievement to silence all complaints." Johnston explained that his reason for overlooking the artillery officers already with the Army of Tennessee was in part their "childish eagerness to discharge their pieces,"[2] a charge Bragg does not seem to have disputed. Robertson, however, did receive a promotion to lieutenant colonel.

Bragg and Johnston soon began working at cross purposes. While Johnston repeatedly called for more of everything, from troops to equipment to horses to wagons, Bragg insisted that Johnston must strike the enemy at once. This became a constant theme in their correspondence. Bragg pressured Johnston to do things that Bragg had found impossible to do when he commanded the army, and Johnston in turn asserted that it was still impossible to accomplish what Bragg asked.[3] Bragg seemed to have forgotten the problems facing field commanders. How he expected Johnston to achieve what he himself never attempted is beyond comprehension.

By April both generals felt the pressure. On the thirteenth Colonel Benjamin S. Ewell arrived in Richmond to explain Johnston's views on the approaching campaign to Davis and Bragg. Ewell contacted Bragg first in the belief that Bragg might be able to "pour oil on the troubled waters," a reference to Davis's

[2] Connelly, *Autumn of Glory*, p. 278; *OR*, XXXV (pt. 2), 488; XXXVIII (pt. 4), 733, 788; (pt. 5), 882; LI (pt. 2), 658–59; Bragg to Joseph E. Johnston, March 7, April 4, 16, July 6, 1864, Joseph E. Johnston Papers; Felix G. Robertson to Bragg, March 14, 1864, Bragg Papers, Western Reserve; Bragg to Joseph E. Johnston, March 24, 1864; Joseph E. Johnston to Bragg, March 30, 1864, Joseph E. Johnston Papers; L. J. Daniel, *Cannoneers*, p. 138.

[3] *OR*, XXXII (pt. 3), 592, 613–15, 636–37, 666; Bragg to Joseph E. Johnston, March 4, 12, 1864; Johnston to Bragg, March 16, 20, 1864, Joseph E. Johnston Papers.

dislike of Johnston since early in the war. Bragg received Ewell cordially, and although he agreed that Johnston needed reinforcing, he doubted it could be done, given the situation in the East. As it turned out, this rationale became the administration's final response to Johnston's request. In addition, Davis and Bragg blamed Johnston for Grant's ability to mass as many troops in the eastern theater as he did, mistakenly believing that a good number of those soldiers came from the West. Had Johnston attacked when Richmond told him to, they believed, Virginia would not now be facing a crisis.[4]

Bragg, meanwhile, sent two inspectors to the Army of Tennessee, who sent back conflicting reports. Colonel Brent reported he could discover no evidence that Johnston planned to advance. "I came to the conclusion from all I could observe," he wrote, "that he was opposed to taking the offensive." Another inspector, W. N. Pendleton, reached a different conclusion—he believed Johnston would move soon.[5]

Pendleton was right about Johnston moving, but wrong concerning the direction the move would take. As Federal general William T. Sherman, with nearly 100,000 soldiers, pushed against Johnston's 65,000, the Army of Tennessee evacuated Dalton, Georgia, on May 12. Over the next three months Johnston continued retreating while maintaining the army's morale and keeping in constant contact with the enemy, until he reached the outskirts of Atlanta. "Of course," William Mackall (now Johnston's chief of staff) informed his wife, "the friends of the Prest. will now try to show that Johnston has done exactly like Bragg—but the army sees that it is not so. We came back step by

[4] Benjamin Stoddard Ewell to Bragg, April 13, 20, 1864, Bragg Papers, Western Reserve. For discussion of Davis's dislike of Johnston, see Connelly, *Autumn of Glory*, pp. 34–36; and Richard M. McMurry, "'The *Enemy* at Richmond': Joseph E. Johnston and the Confederate Government," *Civil War History*, XXVII (1981), 5–31; Benjamin Stoddard Ewell to Joseph E. Johnston, April 29, 1864, Joseph E. Johnston Papers.
[5] George Brent to Bragg, April 16, 1864, Bragg Papers, Western Reserve; Susan P. Lee, *Memoirs of William Nelson Pendleton, D.D.* (Philadelphia, 1893), p. 320.

step—never out of the sound of the enemy's guns and have hit them many hard blows." A soldier agreed. "The morale of the army was never better than it is now and the men are sanguine of success and their confidence in Johnston is undiminished." He, too, could not resist a comparison with his former commander. "I will venture to say that if Bragg conducted this order, that he would now have had a discontented and demoralized army. It has been remarked by everybody that there is less straggling than ever was known before, and every man is at the post assigned him."[6]

Davis was less generous. "I cannot judge of the circumstances which caused General Johnston to [retreat]," he reported to Lee in May. "I hope the future will prove the wisdom of his course, and that we shall hereafter reap advantages that will compensate for the present disappointment." But in July Davis informed Johnston that his movement "renders me more apprehensive for the future."[7]

Constant carping from Richmond did not make Johnston's job easier. "Johnston has much to contend with," Mackall complained. "It is unjust to the country to put a man at the head of an army and then try to destroy his capacity for usefulness by expressing fears and distrust." He did have some hope for the situation, however, for "the Lord will work his own way in spite of either Presidents or people."[8]

The Richmond administration, however, had other plans for Johnston. As the Eastern armies settled into comparative quiet in their Petersburg trenches, Bragg and Davis turned fuller attention to the West.

On July 9 Davis ordered Bragg to Georgia to confer with Johnston on the military affairs there, "with a view to such dispositions and preparations as may best promote the ends and objects which have been discussed between us."[9] A careful scrutiny

6 William W. Mackall to Mrs. Mackall, June 3, 1864, Mackall Papers; R. D. Patrick, *Reluctant Rebel*, p. 182.
7 *OR*, LI (pt. 2), 952; XXXVIII (pt. 5), 867.
8 Mackall to Mrs. Mackall, June 3, 1864, Mackall Papers.
9 *OR*, XXXIX (pt. 2), 695–96.

of the extant correspondence passing between Davis and Bragg over the next several days clearly indicates that the ends and objects under discussion concerned the removal of Johnston from command of the Army of Tennessee.

Before Bragg even arrived in Atlanta, Davis wired Lee that it appeared Johnston planned to abandon the city and should be relieved at once. The following day Davis informed Lee that Bragg had reached Atlanta but had not yet filed a report. Still, he pressed the issue of Johnston's relief from command, stating, "The case seems hopeless in present hands." The fault, Davis maintained, was entirely Johnston's, since "the measures are surely adequate if properly employed."[10] Clearly, Davis had already made up his mind. Bragg's primary mission appears to have been that of public relations—to give the semblance of having carefully weighed the evidence on the spot before axing Johnston.

Mackall understood what was going on, although he did not guess the end result. On July 12 he told his wife, "Mr. Davis sent Johnston a very sneering telegram yesterday. . . . I hailed it as a sign that he thought things were safe in Virginia and that he could afford to be impudent." The next day Mackall reported that Bragg would visit the army. "I fancy," he wrote, "it is the design of Mr. D. to take advantage of the discontent he has received in Richmond and the temporary excitement in Ga. produced by our near approach to Atlanta to make a display of his distrust of Johnston & if he finds he can infuse it into the army, to relieve him." Johnston, too, may have suspected something; "Joe looks uneasy this morning," Mackall reported.[11]

Bragg's arrival in Atlanta early on July 13 did not go unnoticed. "That bird of evil omen, Gen. Bragg, has arrived," Robert D. Patrick reported. "I think we will be defeated if he has anything to do with it. . . . I presume his first act will be to have someone court martialed and the next will be to have him shot." Even the Federals knew Bragg was abroad. A report reached Sherman that

[10] *Ibid.*, LII (pt. 2), 692.
[11] William W. Mackall to Wife, July 12, 13, 1864, Mackall Papers.

Bragg was in Atlanta. "All bosh of course," was Sherman's first reaction, yet later that day he informed General John B. McPherson that "Bragg's arrival from Richmond must be to consult."[12]

Mackall believed Bragg had no particular mission but rather had come to sooth Davis's general uneasiness about affairs in the West. Bragg immediately proved Mackall wrong. On his arrival, before he even saw Johnston, Bragg wired Davis, "Indications seem to favor an entire evacuation of this place." Thus began the creation of evidence justifying the removal of Johnston. Later that day Bragg added to the file, reporting, "Our army is sadly depleted. . . . I find but little encouraging."[13]

By July 15 Bragg had visited Johnston, and his facade of evidence against the general grew. "Nearly all available stores and machinery are removed," he reported to Davis, "and the people have mostly evacuated the town." His next dispatch informed Davis, "I have made General Johnston two visits, and been received courteously and kindly. He has not sought my advice, and it was not volunteered." Bragg's actions reveal his duplicity. After admitting he had not discussed or questioned Johnston's plans, he continued, "I cannot learn that he has any more plan for the future than he has had in the past."[14]

Having established one layer of spurious evidence against Johnston, Bragg now got down to the real business of his mission. Davis had cryptically prompted him the previous day, apparently in reference to the possibility of replacing Johnston with his second in command, General William Hardee, "If C. [probably a code for change of commanders] is thus indicated adopt advice and execute as proposed." Bragg, however, proved reluctant to turn the command over to an old enemy. "I am decidedly opposed," he replied to Davis, "as it would perpetuate the past and present policy which he [Johnston] has advised and now sustains.

---

12 R. D. Patrick, *Reluctant Rebel*, 194–95; *OR*, XXXVIII (pt. 5), 144, 147.
13 William W. Mackall, *A Son's Recollections of His Father* (New York, 1930), p. 217; *OR*, XXXVIII (pt. 5), 878.
14 *OR*, XXXVIII (pt. 5), 881.

Any change will be attended with some objections. This one could produce no good."[15]

Bragg followed this short message with a longer dispatch. After stating that Generals John B. Hood and Joseph Wheeler believed it imperative to mount an offensive, Bragg pointed out, "On the contrary, General Hardee generally favored the retiring policy."[16]

The next sentence in this document has misled some people as to Bragg's intentions: "You will see at once that the removal of the commander, should such a measure be considered, would produce no change of policy, and it would be attended with some serious evils."[17] This comment has been interpreted to mean that Bragg did not favor the removal of Johnston. However, he merely pointed out that simple removal of the commander was not enough. The removal, in Bragg's opinion, had to be followed by the promotion of a junior officer over Hardee. This interpretation is borne out by the next paragraph of the dispatch, a paragraph excised from the document in the published *Official Records*.[18] Bragg wrote that he enclosed a copy of Governor Joseph Brown's proclamation, which stated Brown's objections to the strategic schemes cooked up in Richmond, particularly blaming Davis for the situation in which Georgia found itself. Bragg pointed out that many of Davis's enemies "compose the Cabal," and he included a note that Johnston had appended to the governor's proclamation. "It has been most unfortunate for Genl. Johnston that his name has been associated with this weak but treasonable document," Bragg equivocated. "His influence in the Army is injured by it," a statement for which he had no proof, or at least offered none.[19]

Bragg had played his assigned role well. "I am directed by the

[15] *Ibid.*, LII (pt. 2), 704, 707.

[16] *Ibid.*, XXXIX (pt. 2), 712–14.

[17] For examples of misinterpretation, see Don C. Seitz, *Braxton Bragg, General of the Confederacy* (Columbia, S.C., 1924), pp. 450–51; and Dowdy, *Lee's Last Campaign*, pp. 47, 332.

[18] *OR*, XXXIX (pt. 2), 712–14; Bragg to Jefferson Davis, July 15, 1864, Civil War Collection, Huntington Library.

[19] Govan and Livingood, *Different Valor*, pp. 304–5; Bragg to Davis, July 15, 1864, Civil War Collection.

Secretary of War," Cooper wired Johnston on July 17, "to inform
you that as you have failed to arrest the advance of the enemy to
the vicinity of Atlanta . . . and express no confidence that you can
defeat or repel him, you are hereby relieved from the command of
the Army and Department of Tennessee."[20]

Johnston's removal shocked the army and the country. "Quite
an unexpected and startling announcement this morning," reported Patrick. "I have no doubt old Bragg has had something to
do with this." "True, that bird of ill omen, Braxton Bragg, had
been seen ventilating his . . . countenance around our lines for a
day or two past," wrote Adolphe Chalaron, "and many presaged
no good from his presence, yet I venture to say that it never entered the mind of a single man in this army that the victim of the
machinations at Richmond was to be our noble, our beloved
leader, Joseph E. Johnston." Another soldier reported, "When the
news reached the troops that Johnston had been relieved the administration received its quota of abuses, and Bragg was immediately implicated." A Maryland journalist commented upon the
sorriest aspect of the affair. "The worst feature about the whole
business was the sending out Bragg as a spy to report on affairs at
Atlanta. Bragg was the man who had been displaced to make
room for Johnston. The wound to his personal vanity made it
impossible for him to do justice to the handsome manner in which
Johnston had treated him on that occasion."[21]

Johnston, however, no longer treated Bragg handsomely. In
early September he explained that Bragg, during his sojourn,
"gave me the impression that his visit to the army was casual, he
being on his way farther west. . . . I thought him satisfied with
the state of things. . . . He said nothing of the intention to relieve," but he had, Johnston discovered, discussed it with at least

[20] OR, XXXVIII (pt. 5), 885.
[21] R. D. Patrick, Reluctant Rebel, 197; Adolphe Chalaron to Sister, July 18, 1864,
Chalaron Papers, Louisiana Historical Association Collection; Charles Galliveiz
[?] to My dear Willie, July 24, 1864, Polk Papers, University of the South; William
Wilkins Glenn, Between North and South: A Maryland Journalist Views the Civil War:
The Narrative of William Wilkins Glenn, 1861–1869, ed. Bayly Ellen Marks and Mark
Norton Schatz (Teaneck, N.J., 1976), p. 177.

one of his subordinates. "It is clear," Johnston declared, "that his expedition had no other object than my removal *and the giving proper direction to public opinion upon the subject.*" He concluded with a devastating assessment. "A man of honor in his place would have communicated with me . . . upon the subject."[22]

As he traveled further south and west, Bragg continued the public relations campaign he and Davis had devised to solicit support for Johnston's removal. Johnston stated that he received "concurring reports from all the towns at which Genl. Bragg stopped . . . that he exerted himself either falsely or unfairly, to disparage me . . . saying that I had disregarded the wishes & instructions of the administration, that he had implored me to change my course. He did nothing of the sort. . . . He seems to have been disseminating his slanders by staff officers stationed on the rail roads for the purpose." Johnston reported that Bragg, adding insult to injury, "compared my loss with his at Chickamauga," Bragg's one decisive victory. "He ought," Johnston fumed, "to have included his retreat from Duck River, & that from Missionary Ridge to Dalton. The latter, however, was no retreat. Those operations of his," Johnston marveled, "seem to have gained him the highest position in the confederate armies. I should have nothing to fear from a comparison of them with those for which I have been put aside."[23]

Johnston saved his most pointed barb at Bragg for a congressional committee. "I know Mr. Davis thinks that he can do a great many things that other men would hesitate to attempt," the general told the representatives. "For instance, he tried to do what God had failed to do. He tried to make a soldier of Braxton Bragg and you know the result. It couldn't be done."[24]

And so Bragg created one more enemy. A man who had defended and supported Bragg in his hours of need now distrusted and despised him. "When we take into consideration Johnston's

[22] *Confederate Veteran*, XXVI (1918), 395, author's emphasis.
[23] Joseph E. Johnston to Louis T. Wigfall, August 27, 1864, Wigfall Family Papers, University of Texas.
[24] Seitz, *Bragg*, p. 445.

behavior towards Bragg when he was sent into Kentucky on a similar mission," a journalist remarked, "this certainly shows very badly for Bragg."[25]

Bragg's involvement in Johnston's removal is clear. "It is evident from [Johnston's] report that Bragg was with him under false colors," contended a contemporary, "that he asked no questions & demanded no explanations, although he had been sent there by Davis to report." Kean stated in July that "Bragg went out some days ago to consult with Johnston, and telegraphed to the President advising his removal." Despite this entry, in November Kean claimed that he had earlier thought Bragg "wholly innocent" in the removal, "but I now hear from Judge [John A.] Campbell [assistant secretary of war] that Bragg had telegraphed from Atlanta to the President that Johnston ought to be removed."[26]

Major A. D. Banks wrote Johnston from Montgomery in late August that Bragg had been boasting of his role in the removal. Banks reported that the day after Johnston's removal was announced, Bragg arrived in Montgomery. He had wired ahead to two of Banks's acquaintances for a meeting. Before meeting with Bragg, both men unhesitatingly declared that the removal "was done against the views and wishes of General Bragg." However, after the meeting one of the men told Baker that Bragg had explained Davis's alarm at Johnston's campaign and that the president suggested Hardee as the successor to the command. Bragg stated he had told Davis that replacing Johnston would not alter the policy of retreat, as Hardee agreed with Johnston's views. Bragg then asserted, "It was important the change should be sustained by the press and public opinion set right on the causes of the change." These comments so far tally perfectly with the dispatches Bragg had sent to Davis. However, Bragg now prevaricated again, saying that he had implored Johnston to change his policy but to no avail. This claim is in direct contradiction to both Bragg's and Johnston's statements that they did not, in fact, dis-

[25] Glenn, *Between North and South*, p. 158.
[26] *Ibid.*; Kean, *Inside*, p. 166; Connelly, *Autumn of Glory*, pp. 410–21.

cuss Johnston's plans at all. Banks concluded, "Abundant material
. . . can be gotten to implicate General Bragg as the chief operator
in the transaction."[27]

Banks was incorrect in pointing to Bragg as the *chief* instigator,
although he undoubtedly served as one of many. Former secretary
of war George W. Randolph reported that Davis's cabinet generally supported Johnston's removal. A historian of the Confederate cabinet agreed, maintaining that Bragg "undoubtedly . . .
strongly favored it, but the entire Cabinet held a similar opinion."
It is possible that Elise also had a hand in all of this. "Rumour
whispers that Mrs Davis has much to do with it," a Southern
woman wrote. "Mrs Johnston and herself do not visit[,] whilst
Mrs Bragg is her warm personal friend." Perhaps unrealistically,
she admitted, "I must believe, however, that Mr Davis is superior
to such influences."[28]

At first Bragg appeared pleased with his role in the affair, boasting about it everywhere, but within months his circumstances
changed, and so did his story. Not only had Johnston's successor
destroyed the army that Bragg had recommended him to command; Bragg also found himself in a position subordinate to
Johnston. Now Bragg attempted to extricate himself from the
whole business. In February 1865, while Bragg commanded at
Wilmington, his military secretary, John B. Sale, warned that
Davis "wants your books and papers left with him, although Lee
took *his* away. Generally this would be right:—but your correspondence about Johnston and the appointment of Hood, is there
recorded, and make it look as if you originated that programme.
This might become unsafe."[29] As Davis would later try to justify

[27] A. D. Banks to Joseph E. Johnston, August 21, 1864, Montgomery, Alabama, Joseph E. Johnston Papers; Joseph E. Johnston, *Narrative of Military Operations Directed, during the late War between the States* (Bloomington, Ind., 1959),
pp. 363–64.
[28] Glenn, *Between North and South*, p. 177; Rembert W. Patrick, *Jefferson Davis
and His Cabinet* (Baton Rouge, 1944), p. 139; Connelly, *Autumn of Glory*, pp. 406–7;
Edmondston, *Secesh Lady*, p. 617.
[29] Seitz, *Bragg*, p. 505.

his removal of Johnston, perhaps he already had in mind making Bragg the scapegoat.

Bragg's deviousness blossomed as he wrote a third-person disclaimer after the war. Explaining that Davis was bent on dismissing Johnston, Bragg declared that he "asked for and obtained the order to visit Atlanta and see Gen'l Johnston, to whom he had ever been most friendly, with a view, if possible of obviating his removal. Upon arriving at Atlanta," Bragg insisted, "he telegraphed the President the exact situation of the two armies, without comment, and advised a suspension of all action till his written report could be received. Without waiting, however, the President promptly ordered the removal, and said to the Sec'y who handed him the dispatch, 'I regret now that Gen'l Bragg was permitted to go to Atlanta, as he will no doubt be charged with complicity in this act when it is whol[l]y my own.'" Bragg claimed that several days later, when he was in Montgomery, "he heard with some surprise of the President's action in removing Gen'l Johnston."[30] The official correspondence between Bragg and Davis at the time of the removal, however, demonstrates that this account is pure fabrication.

By the time he wrote this disclaimer, Bragg believed Davis had slighted him in several instances, perhaps the first affront having been Davis's failure to appoint Bragg as Johnston's replacement. Enough people had assured Bragg that they believed he should again command the Army of Tennessee for Bragg to have expected the appointment. "Your numerous friends here speak of you often," wrote General Edward C. Walthall from the western army, "and would be glad to see you soon again among us." In April, during an inspection tour of the army, Brent assured Bragg "that you possess the confidence & affection of the Army of Tennessee." A civilian wrote, "I do Say, & thousands say the same, I wish Genl. Bragg commanded the Tenn Army." General Robert C. Tyler informed Bragg, "Amidst all the excitement, di-

---

[30] Bragg, "Notes," Bragg Papers, Western Reserve.

saster and disappointment of the past few weeks I have anxiously been looking for something that would justify a hope and belief that you would once more be placed in command of the grand old Army of Tenn." [31]

But Bragg did not receive the appointment. In his recommendations to Davis, Bragg halfheartedly suggested General John Bell Hood for the position. After presenting Hood's name, which had certainly been discussed before Bragg even left for Atlanta, Bragg hedged. "Do not understand me as proposing him as a man of genius, or a great general, but as far better in the present emergency than any one we have available"—anyone, that is, except himself. [32]

Nevertheless, on July 17 Seddon assigned Hood to command the Army of Tennessee. "You are charged with a great trust," he wrote, and counseled, "Be wary no less than bold." [33] This advice went unheeded.

Hood had been campaigning for Johnston's position for months and may have aided in Bragg's spawning of evidence against Johnston. Since March he had been writing directly to Bragg, Davis, and Seddon on the affairs of the Army of Tennessee, without Johnston's knowledge: "I am eager to take the initiative"; "How unfortunate . . . it is for the Generals in the field to fail to cooperate thoroughly with the authorities of the Government"; "You know how anxious I have been to advance"; "You know I am fond of large engagements and hope you will not forget me." And finally Hood wrote: "I . . . am sorry to inform you, that I have done all in my power to induce Genl Johnston to accept the proposition you made to move forward. He will not consent. . . . I regret this exceedingly as my heart was fixed upon our going to

[31] Edward C. Walthall to Bragg, March 11, September 8, 1864; George W. Brent to Bragg, April 16, 1864, Bragg Papers, Western Reserve; George D. Phillips to Bragg, June 22, 1864, Davis Papers, Duke University Library; Robert C. Tyler to Bragg, January 22, 1865, Bragg Papers, Western Reserve; Connelly, *Autumn of Glory*, pp. 410–13.

[32] *OR*, XXXIX (pt. 2), 714; LII (pt. 2), 692.

[33] *Ibid.*, XXXVIII (pt. 5), 885.

the front." Hood thus spoke of the man who trusted him as a confidant. When Bragg arrived in Atlanta, Hood submitted one further report. "I have, general, so often urged that we should force the enemy to give us battle as to almost be regarded reckless by the officers high in rank in this army, since their views have been so directly opposite. I regard it as a great misfortune to our country that we failed to give battle to the enemy many miles north of our present position." Hood's proclamations of his own aggressive instincts are not borne out by the records. At least twice during the retreat toward Atlanta, Hood had failed to execute attacks ordered by Johnston, and he consistently advised further withdrawals.[34]

Hood's appointment failed to cause elation among Confederates, and rightly so. A soldier predicted, when Bragg visited Atlanta, "We may expect to hear of something going wrong in a few days." He was right. Within six weeks Hood had to explain why he had evacuated Atlanta on September 1, blaming everyone except himself. A Virginian sympathized with the Army of Tennessee. "Our army in North Georgia seems unfortunate," he understated. "It is composed of splendid material, and was effective in the hands of a master mind like Johnston. Hood is a nice fellow, but isn't owner of sufficient mental calibre for the crisis." In early September he lamented, "Atlanta has fallen. What a triumph for Johnston at the expense of our cause. Hood was outgeneraled. He is not able to cope with Sherman."[35]

In mid-October, Hood turned his back on his opponent and marched the bulk of the Army of Tennessee to destruction at Franklin and Nashville, Tennessee, while Sherman, virtually unopposed, cut a swath of destruction through Georgia. In November,

[34] Connelly, *Autumn of Glory*, pp. 416–18, 406–7; McMurry, *Hood*, pp. 117–19; John Bell Hood to Bragg, March 10, April 3, 13, 1864, Bragg Papers, Western Reserve; *OR*, XXXII (pt. 3), 606–8; XXXVIII (pt. 3), 978–91; (pt. 5), 879–80; McMurry, *Hood*, pp. 103, 106, 108–14, 118; Govan and Livingood, *Different Valor*, pp. 311–12.
[35] R. D. Patrick, *Reluctant Rebel*, 195; John Bell Hood to Bragg, September 4, 1864, Bragg Papers, Duke University Library; McMurry, *Hood*, p. 152; Bird and Bird, *Letters*, pp. 185, 202.

as things in Georgia went from bad to worse, a native of the state wrote, "I think there has been a great mismanagement about our Georgia affairs, and, when Johnston's great intellect was taken from us, their solution became much more difficult. Our subsequent misfortunes have all proven his long sighted sagacity."[36]

Bragg's role in Johnston's removal remains the most ignoble incident of his career. Davis has been censured for sending Bragg in the first place. At the time, though, Davis strongly believed that something had to be done and that public opinion had to support the move. He may have thought Bragg his only choice in these circumstances. As one contemporary acknowledged, "Bragg was the only man of any mark in the army who supported the President."[37] Bragg, despite his possible motive of hoping to secure the command of the Army of Tennessee himself, was torn between loyalty to Davis, his commander in chief, and to Johnston, an old friend. In the end, his determined devotion to the Confederate nation led him to choose duty over friendship.

[36] McMurry, *Hood*, pp. 161–83; Bird and Bird, *Letters*, p. 211.
[37] Glenn, *Between North and South*, p. 177.

CHAPTER XI

All personal questions should be adjourned

February 24–October 14, 1864

BRAGG'S EIGHT MONTHS as military adviser made him a highly public figure, thus providing a glimpse at how his contemporaries viewed him. Few people were neutral—they either admired or despised him. Continually involved in controversy, Bragg delighted in striking at those he disliked. Although he had friends in Richmond, there are few references to his social life. Gorgas mentioned that a talkative Bragg played a game of whist at his home in late February, and in mid-March several observers spotted him attending church with a number of high-ranking Confederate officers. Bragg's apparent lack of socializing prompted one investigator to contend that "his social enjoyment was confined to his own company."[1] As Elise had accompanied him to Richmond, they may have chosen to spend what free time he had with one another.

Bragg approached his duties in Richmond with such vigor and determination that it is not surprising he surrounded himself with controversy. Much of it, as usual, he brought upon himself, as comments by contemporaries and historians illustrate. "Gen. Bragg is now in hot water with the Quartermaster-General," reported War Department clerk John B. Jones, and as to his troubles with one of the war bureaus, "Bragg may aim another bomb at the refractory concern." When Bragg had been absent from Richmond for nearly a month, Robert Kean stated, "hence no further trouble with him." A historian contended, "He was bit-

---

[1] Gorgas, *Diary*, p. 84; John R. Thompson, "Diary," *Confederate Veteran*, XXXVII (1929), 98; Chesnut, *Civil War*, p. 585; Barrie Almond to author, June 6, 1987.

terly and constantly criticised by the anti-administration politicians and busy getting out of one disagreement only to get into
another."[2]

Bragg gave as good as he got. His attitude, revealed in a letter to
General Alpheus Baker, suggested little sympathy with some of
his compatriots. Baker professed himself very gratified by Bragg's
"most valuable and remarkable letter in which [with] rabid but
most discriminating pencil you drew some striking portraits." He
would like to have kept the letter "as an intellectual work of art if
nothing else" but feared that if it fell into enemy hands it would
be published by Northern newspapers, creating "a flutter in the
Pigeon roost." Therefore, Baker explained, "I deemed it wiser
after reading it again and again to commit it to the flames."[3]

Despite Bragg's penchant for creating turmoil, he and Davis,
another difficult personality, remained loyal to one another. Prior
to Bragg's assignment in Richmond, Davis had repeatedly supported Bragg against discontented subordinates. One historian
believes that Davis's support grew out of his respect for Bragg's
seeming qualifications for high command early in the war and that
Davis continued to support him because there was no one of equal
or greater competence with whom to replace him. Too, Bragg's
loyalty to Davis may have been the basis for his continued support
by the president.[4] During his stint in Richmond, the mutual admiration between Bragg and Davis remained firm.

Bragg's relations with Seddon, however, became strained. Born
in 1815, Seddon was a proud Virginia aristocrat. After graduating
from the University of Virginia Law School, he served in the
U.S. Congress until 1851, when ill health forced him to retire. In
November 1862, having already run through four War Depart-
ment secretaries, Davis called on Seddon to accept the position.
Although he looked like he had been "in his grave a full month,"
Seddon agreed, holding the post longer than any other person

---

[2] J. B. Jones, *Rebel War Clerk's Diary*, II, 301; Kean, *Inside*, p. 168; Hay, "Bragg,"
p. 307.
[3] Alpheus Baker to Bragg, April 18, 1864, Bragg Papers, Western Reserve.
[4] McWhiney, *Bragg*, pp. 326–28.

because in most instances he acquiesced to Davis. Seddon retained his post until a congressional censure in early 1865 injured his pride and he resigned, citing poor health as the reason. Ailing since at least 1851, Seddon lived until 1880.[5]

Perhaps their mutual poor health exacerbated problems between Bragg and Seddon. Seddon, however, held a dim view of Bragg's military abilities. It was he who had prodded so persistently for Johnston to take over Bragg's command after Murfreesboro, and one student of the war contends Seddon resented Bragg's appointment; although he remained influential, his authority in military councils declined after Bragg's arrival.[6]

It appears that Seddon tried to make the best of the situation. He and Bragg frequently concurred in the opinions expressed to Davis, particularly early in their relationship. However, Bragg soon invaded Seddon's domain to such an extent that "nothing but a sense of duty can make a high spirited man like . . . [Seddon] put up with it," according to Kean. "The effect of the *manner* in which these things are done is to prejudice the position of the Head of the Department in the eyes of his subordinates, and this effect has as a matter of fact been produced." Jones remarked in mid-April that in Davis's view, Bragg seemed to outrank the secretary of war, and within a month Bragg penned a "pretty tart letter" to Seddon. In June Kean reported that "this dealing with Mr. Seddon looks like a want of sincerity. . . . With this feeling on the President's part, . . . added to the endless meddling of Bragg, I do not think a man of spirit, as I take Mr. Seddon to be, can stand it long." Later, an incident occurred that raised Jones's hopes that Seddon would "*flare up*, and charge Gen. B. with interference, etc.—but no," he lamented, "he must see that Gen. B. is acting with the concurrence of the President."[7]

---

[5] Boatner, *Dictionary*, p. 730; Patricia L. Faust, ed., *Historical Times Illustrated Encyclopedia of the Civil War* (New York, 1986), pp. 664–65.

[6] Bragg to James H. Hammond, October 18, 1864, James J. Hammond Papers, Library of Congress; R. W. Patrick, *Davis*, pp. 136, 139–40; McWhiney, *Bragg*, pp. 338, 384–85.

[7] Kean, *Inside*, pp. 144, 161, 194; J. B. Jones, *Rebel War Clerk's Diary*, II, 190, 215, 278.

In August the relationship became even more heated. Bragg complained to Seddon that he no longer received copies of orders and instructions issued from the adjutant general's office. "I have called attention to this matter verbally . . . in your own office," he charged, "but being still without the needful files, I presume to remind you again in this form, lest perchance it might escape your memory." In recording this incident, Jones commented, "They are all inimical to Bragg—all but the President, who is bound in honor to sustain him." At some point Seddon offered his resignation in favor of Bragg, whereupon "Davis had assured him that there was *no one he preferred to him* in the War Office; that General Bragg had not the qualifications at all for that position."[8] This response apparently satisfied Seddon, as he continued in that office for several months after Bragg left Richmond.

Bragg's relations with Northrop proved even more acerbic. They had already bickered during Bragg's command in the West. Severely criticized throughout his tenure, Northrop was one of Davis's most unpopular appointees. Mary Chesnut called him "the most cussed and vilified man in the Confederacy," whose appointment many attributed to his having been Davis's classmate and crony at West Point, a fact which, Chesnut declared, "I hear . . . alluded to oftenest of his many crimes."[9]

It did not take long for Bragg and Northrop to tangle again. In a report to Seddon, Bragg deemed that Northrop's language to a field general was "unfortunate; can do no good, and may do harm." At about the same time Bragg reported to Davis that in another dispute, both Beauregard and Northrop had gone out of their way to bring into a discussion "much extraneous matter better omitted, and only calculated to complicate and embarrass." Northrop quickly responded, "General Bragg's criticism about the Commissary-General is illogical."[10]

[8] Bragg to James A. Seddon, August 20, 1864, Pritchard Von David Papers, University of Texas; J. B. Jones, *Rebel War Clerk's Diary*, II, 267–68; Kean, *Inside*, p. 171.
[9] Boatner, *Dictionary*, p. 601; Charles L. Dufour, *Nine Men in Gray* (Garden City, N.Y., 1963); Chesnut, *Civil War*, p. 124.
[10] *OR*, XXXII (pt. 3), 715; LIII, 321–22.

These were just the opening shots. In April Bragg had his secretary direct Northrop to send commissary stores to Longstreet.
Northrop returned the paper, "calling the attention of Gen. B's
secretary to the Rules and Regulations, involving a matter of red
tape etiquette," that he "can only be *ordered* or *directed* by the Secretary of War." Bragg took this up with Seddon, remarking that
"if he [Bragg] is to be restricted, etc., his usefulness must be nec-
essarily diminished." Seddon apparently managed to smooth
things over. However, as Northrop boasted a couple of days later
that "he had carried his point, in causing Gen. Bragg to address
him according to military etiquette," Seddon must have called
upon all of his powers of diplomacy. Davis, too, was forced to
referee. "The President says that Gen. B. certainly has the right
to give orders," reported Jones, "but that any one of his staff . . .
ought to give commands 'by order' of Gen. Bragg." Northrop's
response was predictable: "Col. N. says that don't satisfy him;
and that no general has a right to issue orders to him!" In June
Bragg noted on an explanation from Northrop regarding subsistence, it "does not meet the complaint." Northrop, in turn, replied, "It being presumed that the Secretary of War does not
concur in the comments of General Bragg, no remark upon the
inaccuracy is deemed necessary."[11]

Much to Bragg's delight, no doubt, in early 1865 a congressional committee discovered Northrop's office to be in extremely poor condition. The committee believed that under the
supervision of Northrop, "celebrated as much for his want of
judgment as for his contempt of advice, there seemed little prospect for its improvement."[12] This report forced Davis to remove
Northrop from office on February 15, 1865.

Bragg had supporters in the Confederate Congress, but his de-
tractors seem to have been more vocal than his friends. Senator
James L. Orr remarked that "the President's attattchment [*sic*] for
Genl. Bragg could be likened to nothing else than the blind &

[11] J. B. Jones, *Rebel War Clerk's Diary*, II, 186–88; *OR*, XXXVI (pt. 3), 898–99.
[12] Putnam, *Richmond*, p. 352.

gloating love of a mother for a deformed & misshapen offspring."
Part of Bragg's problem arose from his penchant for blaming his
military defeats on subordinates, many of whom had their spon-
sors in Congress. Viewing Bragg's appointment to military adviser as a reward, several members watched his activities closely
and even tried to reduce his pay. Bragg did not believe in giving
quarter, especially to nonmilitary elected officials. "It is plain to
me that there is to be a row between Bragg and Congress," reported Kean. "General Bragg has already made two or three slaps
at Congress over interfering into military matters. If he brings his
former bitterness to wound what he calls 'politicians' here as he
has done, he will be in no end of trouble." Kean was right. "From
yesterdays proceedings of Congress," Bragg complained to Davis
in early April, "I find myself again assailed and falsely maligned
in the Confederate State Senate." As Congress prepared to reas-
semble at the end of the month, Kean wrote, "It will be amusing
to watch the relations between them and Bragg. A row is nearly
certain."[13]

Bragg's relationship with Robert E. Lee appears to have been
satisfactory, probably due to Lee's ability to dissemble. Lee continued his usual mode of communication with the government,
and Bragg had the good sense not to interfere; given Davis's strong
attachment to Lee, Bragg wisely chose the expedient course. For
his part, Lee punctiliously observed polite form; Lee "addresses
Gen. Bragg as 'commanding armies C.S.,'" reported Jones. "This
ought to be an example for others to follow." Bragg, however, was
not above misleading Lee, as indicated by a cryptic warning to a
correspondent. "It was necessary to use some little circumspec-
tion to keep Genl Lee from knowing the object, or he never would
have yielded his assent."[14]

[13] J. H. Claiborne to Dear Wife, March 29, 1864, J. H. Claiborne Papers, University of Virginia, Charlottesville; Wilfred Buck Yearns, *The Confederate Congress*
(Athens, Ga., 1960), p. 148; Kean, *Inside*, pp. 142–43, 146; Bragg to Jefferson
Davis, April 4, 1864, Bragg Papers, Western Reserve.
[14] Robert E. Lee, *Lee's Dispatches: Unpublished Letters of General Robert E. Lee,
C.S.A., to Jefferson Davis and the War Department of the Confederate States of America,
1862–65*, ed. Douglas Southall Freeman (New York, 1915), p. 139; J. B. Jones,

But Bragg found his authority infringed when he dealt with Lee. Davis relied heavily upon Lee's judgment. After reporting to Lee on conditions elsewhere in the Confederacy, Davis assured him, "I am willing, as heretofore, to leave the matter to your decision." Further indicating to Lee that, despite Bragg's position as military adviser, Lee's opinions carried more weight with the president, Davis continued, "You are better informed than any other can be of the necessities of your position . . . and I cannot do better than to leave your judgment to reach its own conclusions."[15]

In some instances Bragg received blame for Lee's doings. Lee maintained jurisdiction over military affairs in the Shenandoah Valley. Although Bragg received communications from commanders there, he could not interfere with Lee's plans. On June 5 the Confederates suffered a portentous defeat at Piedmont, opening the entire valley to Federal depredations. When Bragg pointed out that since the valley was in Lee's command, "all was left to his better judgment, especially as he has directed all the movements . . . [there] down to this time," two war department diarists expressed resentment at this cavalier dismissal of Lee. "General Bragg coolly in a note to the Secretary of War shuffles off on General Lee in a single instance the responsibility and the work of repairing this disaster," complained Kean. John B. Jones produced a more accurate record in his account. Bragg "says Gen. R. E. Lee has command there as well as here, and was never interfered with." And that was the truth of the matter. "Gen. B.," Jones continued, "says he had tendered Gen. Lee his services, but they had not been accepted." Indeed, Lee seldom informed Bragg of his movements or intentions, and Bragg often had to plead with Lee to maintain contact with him.[16]

Although Lee clearly held responsibility for the valley, Bragg

Rebel War Clerk's Diary, II, 277; Bragg to unknown, April 15, 1864, Howard F. Jones Papers, North Carolina Department of Archives and History.

[15] *OR*, LI (pt. 2), 952.

[16] *Ibid.*, XXXVII (pt. 1), 732–33, 150–51; Kean, *Inside*, p. 154; J. B. Jones, *Rebel War Clerk's Diary*, II, 227; Bragg to R. E. Lee, June 9, 15, 1864, Charles Scott Venable Papers, Southern Historical Collection.

received the blame for its loss. Hearing that Bragg was being censured for the loss of Staunton, Edmondston remarked, "Justly I dare say, he has lost us so much elsewhere that it would not be 'Bragg, the Unlucky' were he now to fail. Let us hope," she declared, "his evil genius may exhaust itself in that last 'coup' & that he may have no heavier misfortune in store for us."[17]

Bragg was not the only one to deflect blame from Lee. After failing to destroy Lee's army at Cold Harbor on June 1–4, Grant began another sidle to his left, intending to cross the James and approach Richmond from the south. By June 7 Beauregard sent the first of many warnings about Grant's intentions, which were obvious to him.[18] Lee, however, could not be convinced and refused to begin a corresponding move. Even after a June 9 attack on Petersburg, Lee remained steadfast in his belief that Grant could not have crossed his army over the James.

Largely because of Davis's trust in Lee and his distrust of Beauregard, Beauregard's pleas for help during the attack met with a nonchalant reaction from Richmond. Seddon and Bragg had concluded that there were no reinforcements to be sent. "As commandant of the department he must decide on the proper employment of his forces under the emergency. This," Seddon asserted, "will place the responsibility where it properly belongs"[19]—right on Beauregard's shoulders.

In the circumstances, Beauregard performed a miracle. On June 14 he reported to Bragg that Grant had indeed crossed the James and that his own position was critical. He warned that he could not reinforce Petersburg without abandoning the Bermuda Hundred line, thus allowing Butler's troops to join Grant's. In an effort to determine the feeling in Richmond, Beauregard wired Bragg at 1:45 P.M. on June 15 that, as he could not hold both, he wished to know which the War Department wanted defended, Petersburg or the lines across Bermuda Hundred Neck. Nearly

---

[17] Edmondston, *Secesh Lady*, p. 577.
[18] *OR*, XXXVI (pt. 3), 878–79, 889; XL (pt. 2), 647, 648; LI (pt. 2), 996, 998.
[19] *Ibid.*, LI (pt. 2), 999–1000.

ten hours later Richmond had not responded, so he took matters into his own hands. At 11:15 P.M. he wired Lee that he had abandoned the lines on Bermuda Hundred and concentrated at Petersburg. He asked Lee to send some of his own troops to Bermuda Hundred.[20]

Lee finally and belatedly saw the light and began his own movement to defend the southern approaches to Richmond. "I heard today of Bragg's having blamed Lee for the enemy's getting into the outer line between here and Petersburg," reported Kean on June 17. If Bragg did so, he had good reason. By the time Lee arrived at Petersburg on June 18, Beauregard's efforts had staved off numerous Union assaults. Both sides now settled into a siege that would last nearly ten months, ending only just before the fall of the Confederacy.[21]

No matter what he did, however, Beauregard received no credit or praise from his superiors. Davis had never liked Beauregard, and Bragg seems to have shared this feeling. Although Bragg had appeared friendly, as early as 1862 he reportedly disparaged Beauregard in his Shiloh report in order to please Davis. Bragg now maliciously questioned Beauregard on his abandonment of the Bermuda Hundred lines. This showed poor judgment on Bragg's part, as Beauregard had warned Bragg that he could hold either the lines on the neck or the lines around Petersburg and had asked Bragg which should be defended. Not receiving a reply, he had acted on his own, thus allowing the Confederacy to hold Petersburg and Richmond for another year.[22]

Beauregard submitted an eight-page defense of his decision. Davis's comments on the document reveal his attitude toward Beauregard. He first castigated the general for evacuating the Bermuda Hundred lines without notice. A perusal of the telegrams included in the document would have shown that Beauregard had indeed given several warnings. Then, after having agreed with

[20] *Ibid.*, XL (pt. 2), 652, 653, 656–57.
[21] Kean, *Inside*, p. 157; *OR*, XL (pt. 2), 658, 659, 660, 666, 667, 668.
[22] Kean, *Inside*, p. 157.

Seddon and Bragg on June 9 that the whole responsibility for Petersburg was Beauregard's, Davis had the temerity to now assert that "Genl. Lee was in command and it was for him to decide whether further reinforcements would . . . be immediately required at Petersburg." Lee, of course, had no idea of what was going on at this point, largely because he had ignored Beauregard's reports of Grant's movement across the James. "That greater injury did not result from the abandonment of the line of Bermuda Hundred . . . is due to the prompt and decided action of Genl. Lee," Davis lied. Then, apparently in an effort to damage further relations between Beauregard and Bragg, Davis called Bragg's attention to a remark Beauregard had made about Bragg's lack of response to a telegram. Bragg, of course, insisted "Genl. Beauregard is mistaken in saying no reply was made to his dispatch."[23]

In addition to bickering about Beauregard's decision to save Petersburg, Bragg kept up a running controversy with Beauregard in reference to a North Carolina cavalry unit which Bragg contended Beauregard had detained without authority. Beauregard replied that he did indeed have permission from Bragg to retain the troops, and he did so as long as it was necessary. Beauregard became so incensed over this matter that he demanded a court of inquiry. Not unexpectedly, when faced with facts, Bragg backed down. "I was pleased to see a few days ago that Beauregard had made Bragg eat dirt," reported Kean. "Beauregard exploded Bragg [sic] statements, and then closed by demanding a court of inquiry. . . . Bragg wrote asking to withdraw his letter."[24]

Much of Bragg's anger toward Beauregard may have stemmed from a March incident. Leading citizens of Charleston, then in Beauregard's department, had protested the removal of several companies of cavalry from their area, and their petition to Congress had been approved by Beauregard's chief of staff. Jones re-

---

[23] G. T. Beauregard to Bragg, June 21, 1864 (with endorsements by Bragg and Davis), Pierre Gustave Toutant Beauregard Papers, Duke University Library.
[24] *OR*, XL (pt. 3), 801–5; Kean, *Inside*, p. 172.

ported that Bragg sent it back with an indignant note which
revealed that Bragg was primarily concerned with his own image.
He informed Beauregard that "the offense of having the military
orders of the commander-in-chief . . . exposed to civilians, to be
criticized and protested against . . . ought not to . . . pass without
a merited rebuke. And I am sure," Jones sighed, "poor Beauregard will get the rebuke."[25]

Despite his constant carping at Beauregard, Bragg professed to
admire the general "as a man and soldier." A mutual acquaintance
told Beauregard that Bragg "regretted that any misunderstanding
had ever existed between the Administration and yourself, and
that he hoped, that in his present position, he would be able to
prevent the occurrence of any further trouble." Nevertheless,
Beauregard never forgave Bragg. In late August he told Representative William Porcher Miles that "he had always considered
Bragg his friend, but he knew now that he was an enemy." "I have
nothing to ask of him or his 'Master [Davis],'" Beauregard ex-
postulated. "I defy them both."[26]

Bragg's relations with former subordinates in the Army of Tennessee remained even less cordial. In May Buckner complained of
Bragg's issuing an impossible order to one of his subordinates.
Bragg replied that Buckner had already been relieved of his command before the order was given. Buckner's removal may have
been due in part to a report Bragg received that a particularly
virulent anti-Bragg article appearing in the *Richmond Enquirer* had
been written, or at least revised, by Buckner.[27]

Bragg also continued to skirmish with Polk. In March Bragg
still dwelt on Polk's intransigence while under Bragg's command,
writing his friend Wright that a Polk supporter had been proven
guilty of drunkenness, profanity, and wasting his wife's patri-

[25] J. B. Jones, *Rebel War Clerk's Diary*, II, 176.
[26] S. Chaffin to G. T. Beauregard, August 26, 1864, Beauregard Papers;
T. Harry Williams, *P. G. T. Beauregard: Napoleon in Gray* (Baton Rouge, 1955),
p. 238.
[27] *OR*, XXXII (pt. 3), 854; Lafayette McLaws to Bragg, April 24, 1864, Bragg
Papers, Western Reserve.

mony. "Here you have a fair illustration of the means and men employed to assail a commander," Bragg fumed. On April 18 Polk presented Bragg with a splendid opportunity for reprisal when he requested that General Cheatham (also an enemy of Bragg's) and his division be transferred to Polk's command. This request enabled Bragg to strike at two hated foes with one vengeful blow. "The transfer of the division to that locality," he gleefully wrote in denying the request, "would soon see another large portion of them on stolen horses marauding over the country."[28]

Longstreet, too, failed to escape unscathed. On a report from the general regarding the enemy's return, Bragg remarked, "These dispatches, with their antecedents, evince a want of information & unsteadiness of purpose not calculated to inspire confidence." This comment was totally gratuitous, serving no purpose beyond amusing Bragg.[29]

Forrest also felt Bragg's continued animosity. Finding nothing else to complain about on a report from the cavalry leader, Bragg found fault with the messenger. "If Mr. William McGee . . . belongs to a Louisiana battery [as Forrest had stated], he is employed by the general without authority, and is one of the cases of men enticed from their commands and employed in violation of orders. He should be arrested and sent to his proper command, and General Forrest made accountable for his unauthorized absence." Davis, perhaps flummoxed, passed this along for Cooper's attention.[30]

The newspapers continued their extensive coverage and comment on Bragg. Many remained anti-Bragg. In early June the *Richmond Examiner* editorialized, "If the Southern community realized the fact that Bragg had his hand on the reins, a loud and stern protest would rise from every quarter of the land." The *Richmond Enquirer* appeared schizophrenic on Bragg. Prior to his appointment, the paper published a long editorial, "denouncing in

[28] Bragg to Wright, March 6, 1864, Bragg Papers, Western Reserve; *OR*, XXXII (pt. 3), 791.
[29] *OR*, LII (pt. 2), 633.
[30] *Ibid.*, XXXII (pt. 1), 613.

advance his assignment to any prominent position, and severely criticized his conduct in the West. To-day *it hails his appointment as Commander-in-Chief with joy and enthusiasm!*" However, in early April the *Enquirer* once again saw fit to be "terribly severe on Bragg."[31]

Bragg may have brought the journalists' wrath upon himself. In August Jones reported, "It is said Gen. Bragg prevents news, good or bad, from expanding—believing that any intelligence whatever in the newspapers affords information to the enemy." Jones approved of Bragg's actions, commenting, "He is right."[32]

Despite his censorship, some papers remained supportive of Bragg. In June, about the time the *Examiner* reviled him, he received a gift of spurs from the editors of the *Atlanta Register.* Just after Bragg's appointment in Richmond, editor L. J. Dupree claimed that he had changed his mind about Bragg. "I was misled as to your social characteristics," he admitted. "I have learned in reference to your personal peculiarities, that I did you injustice," and he promised, "I shall find an occasion to make amends worth more than this tendered apology." And he did; a few months later Dupree decided to write a laudatory history of Bragg's exploits in the West.[33]

Among others, however, discontent with Bragg as military adviser continued. Senator Louis T. Wigfall reported to Polk in April that Lee's army was very dissatisfied with Bragg's appointment. "His counsels it is feared will not be wise & it is apprehended that promotions will be regulated in accordance with his prejudices; not according to the merits of the officers." Given Bragg's nature, this was a valid concern, although as it turned out, Bragg had little to do with Lee's army. In June Jones wrote, "There is discontent . . . in the East with Bragg," while Kean reported "the deepest uneasiness pervades the army, officers and

[31] F. S. Daniel, *Richmond Examiner*, p. 200; J. B. Jones, *Rebel War Clerk's Diary*, II, 159; Kean, *Inside*, p. 142.
[32] J. B. Jones, *Rebel War Clerk's Diary*, II, 268.
[33] William G. Swan to Bragg, June 8, 1864; L. J. Dupree to Bragg, February 25, May 16, 1864, Bragg Papers, Western Reserve.

rank and file, at Bragg's being in Richmond." It appeared they feared that if something should happen to Lee, Bragg would be assigned to his command, "which they regard with universal consent as the ruin of the army and the cause." In late July Jones once again announced dissatisfaction with Bragg. "There is a revival of murmurs against the President. He will *persist* in keeping Bragg in command."[34]

Yet Bragg received many messages of praise and support. A woman from Alabama sent him "a small box of edibles," while John Forsyth assured Bragg that his pursuit by Confederate enemies "only tends to strengthen the ties of your friends." In June a party of refugees sent $1,000 in Bragg's name to an organization for the relief of maimed soldiers. Joseph Jones, from Bragg's native Warren County, North Carolina, thanked Bragg for the great service he had rendered the South. Jones also offered a place in his home for Elise, declaring, "I know of no family who would be more pleased to take care of Mrs. Braxton Bragg than my own."[35]

During his travels through the Southwest in the summer of 1864, Bragg met an appreciative civilian. As his train chugged along between Columbus and Montgomery, "An old farmer in the car became intensely excited when he heard what an illustrious passenger he was travelling with," reported an eyewitness, "and rushed up saying, 'Are you Mr Bragg? are you General Bragg? Give us your paw!' and the General very good-naturedly [one of his few reported good-natured acts] shook hands with him. Then he sat down and stared in mute admiration." Even after Bragg left the train, the farmer continued to revel in his meeting with the general.[36]

Despite the controversy he generated, these letters and anec-

[34] Louis T. Wigfall to Leonidas Polk, April 12, 1864, Leonidas Polk Papers, Library of Congress; J. B. Jones, *Rebel War Clerk's Diary*, II, 229, 257; Kean, *Inside*, p. 155.
[35] C. J. Pope to Bragg, March 30, 1864; John Forsyth to Bragg, June 2, 1864; Phil P. Neely to Bragg, June 21, 1864; Joseph S. Jones to Bragg, March 18, July 15, 1864, Bragg Papers, Western Reserve.
[36] Ross, *Cities and Camps*, pp. 191–92.

dote illustrate that Bragg's contemporaries recognized his importance and influence while serving as Davis's military adviser.
Johnston admitted, when Lee became military adviser again in
1865, "Genl. Lee will probably have less influence than his predecessor, Gen'l. Bragg." One Southerner complained that Bragg
"is placed in an office where every petition for promotion must
pass through his censorship," while another contended, "There is
no denying the privileges and power he has at Richmond in the
position he occupies." Representative Thomas J. Foster assured
Bragg, "It is clearly manifest . . . that the splendid conceptions—
combinations—and preparations that have produced those glorious results must have had their origin elsewhere than with our
generals in the field . . . and when . . . malice and prejudice
[have] yielded to calm and dispassionate reason, the impartial historian will accord to General Bragg that skill and ability as a
leader and devotion as a patriot which dishonest and time serving
politicians, and misguided (if not unfaithful) officers have vainly
attempted to deprive him of."[37]

Some historians, however, have not been impartial to Bragg.
An early biographer described Bragg's duties as "being confined
to echoing the conclusions of the civil powers above him," without acknowledging that in the Confederacy, as in the United
States, civil authority always determines military policy. Another
historian contended that in Richmond Bragg "sank to pettiness
and quarreling" instead of rising to the challenge of creating a
general staff to coordinate operations. This writer seems not to
have recognized the situation into which Bragg stepped in early
1864. The Confederacy faced crises of enormous proportion. In
those circumstances it is unrealistic to believe that Bragg could
have devoted the time it would have taken to develop and establish
an institution which, at the time of the Civil War, was in the very
earliest stages of evolution throughout Western military organiza-

[37] Govan and Livingood, *Different Valor*, p. 343; R. D. Patrick, *Reluctant Rebel*,
p. 194; Charles Galliviez [?] to My dear Willie, July 24, 1864, Polk Papers, University of the South; Thomas J. Foster to Bragg, August 30, 1864, Bragg Papers,
Western Reserve.

tions. Clifford Dowdey declared, "The neurotic Bragg was efficient and his services . . . might have been useful had he not given
Davis sycophantic support in his most irrational orders."[38]

Such conclusions indicate a failure to examine the evidence. A
careful study of Bragg's activities reveals that he approached his
job with characteristic intensity and purpose. His efforts to
streamline the various departments, notably the prison system
and the conscription bureau, met with resistance, which did not
prevent him from accomplishing some of his goals. In field affairs
Bragg helped prolong the life of the Confederacy, particularly
during the Bermuda Hundred campaign. Far from being a syco-
phant, the records show that Bragg often disagreed with Davis.
One Confederate remarked that Bragg "is virtually commander in
chief."[39] But he was not commander in chief; that was Davis's
responsibility. Bragg's duty was to carry out the directives of his
commander, a task he took seriously and executed competently.

There is no doubt that Bragg made an impact during his tenure
in Richmond. "Bragg's quick decided spirit is, I believe, felt
here," wrote Josiah Gorgas. "His presence I have no doubt does
good. Every one feels that he will *assist* the President in the conduct of military matters." Another Confederate contended that
Bragg received the appointment too late. Had he been in office
earlier, this writer believed, "judging from the benefits received
by the Federal armies from General [Henry Wager] Halleck's administration, General Bragg's great abilities in the same direction
would have accomplished quite as much for the Confederate armies." He might also have added that in addition to Halleck's
duties, Bragg also carried some of Grant's responsibilities. Lincoln, however, accorded Grant more authority than Davis ever
allowed Bragg. And Grant did not have the counterpart of the
uncommunicative Robert E. Lee. Thomas Connelly, historian of

[38] Seitz, *Bragg*, p. 410; Frank E. Vandiver, "Jefferson Davis and Unified Army
Command," *Louisiana Historical Quarterly*, XXXVIII (1955), 34; Hagerman, *Origins*, pp. xvi, 22–23, 25–27, 33–35; Dowdey, *Lee's Last Campaign*, p. 47.
[39] Galliveiz [?] to My dear Willie, July 24, 1864, Polk Papers, University of the
South.

the Army of Tennessee, argued that "Bragg in 1864 was not the stooge as general in chief which some considered him." With Davis's heavy reliance upon him, Bragg "remained far more powerful among army people than historians have given him credit for being."[40]

Historian E. B. (Pete) Long recognized Bragg's importance to the Confederacy. After perusing the materials relating to Bragg's tenure in Richmond gathered by Bragg biographer Grady McWhiney, Long stated in a note of appreciation, "It is quite clear from these letters that Bragg played a much more active role than he is given credit for. . . . I feel [Clifford] Dowdey is quite wrong in condemning Bragg as harshly as he does."[41]

Bragg explained what he believed constituted his role as military adviser to the President. "He never hesitated as to his duty in supporting the government," Bragg wrote in third person. "He ever felt and said that he could do the cause no good and might seriously injure it by opposition to government measures, even though he might not approve their policy. He . . . thought all personal questions should be adjourned."[42]

[40] Gorgas, *Diary*, p. 89; William M. Polk, *Leonidas Polk, Bishop and General* (2 vols., New York, 1915), II, 316; Connelly, *Autumn of Glory*, p. 411.
[41] E. B. (Pete) Long to Grady McWhiney, August 3, 1963, in author's possession. See also Connelly, *Autumn of Glory*, pp. 410–21.
[42] Bragg, "Notes," Bragg Papers, Western Reserve.

CHAPTER XII

If the commanding general had done his duty

October 15, 1864–January 20, 1865

AFTER EIGHT MONTHS as Davis's military adviser, Bragg received orders to resolve the crisis building in Wilmington, North Carolina. On October 15, 1864, Davis explained that the situation demanded Bragg's personal direction. Davis intended this assignment to be temporary and instructed Bragg to leave his Richmond office in his staff's charge.[1] This assignment provided Bragg another opportunity to prove himself a poor field commander, and once again he blamed others for his failure.

Wilmington provided essential services to the Confederacy. Located twenty-eight miles from the mouth of the Cape Fear River, it had railroad connections running as far north as Virginia. Two widely separated inlets from the Atlantic made it excellent for blockade-runners, and it quickly became the Confederacy's most important port. By the time Bragg appeared on the scene, Mobile Bay had been lost, leaving Wilmington the only significant port open to Confederate blockade-runners.[2]

Davis had lost confidence in the commander at Wilmington, General William Henry Chase Whiting, the man most probably responsible for the May rumor that Bragg had ordered Petersburg left to its own devises. At that time, many believed Whiting had overindulged in either liquor or narcotics, but a historian attributes his erratic behavior to physical and mental exhaustion. Whiting, a native of Mississippi, had graduated from West Point

---

[1] Jefferson Davis to Bragg, October 15, 1864, Bragg Papers, Western Reserve.
[2] Stephen R. Wise, *Lifeline of the Confederacy: Blockade Running during the Civil War* (Columbia, S.C., 1988), pp. 16, 124; Long and Long, *Civil War*, p. 559.

in 1845 and served for the next fifteen years in the Corps of Engineers, working on coastal fortifications. Resigning from the U.S. Army in February 1861, he served briefly in Virginia before his assignment to Wilmington in November 1862. During the next two years he constructed formidable fortifications on the ocean inlets that kept the Union blockaders at bay and provided covering fire for the blockade-runners. Whiting's chief problem seemed to be his inability to get along with other people. He treated the townspeople and the blockade-runners heavy-handedly and criticized fellow services.[3]

Davis expected Bragg to promote harmony and to organize an effective defense of this crucial port. These were curious assignments for the man who had a knack for creating controversy and who had lost a nearly impregnable position atop Missionary Ridge. His departure from the capital city was in no sense a demotion, as he continued to function as military adviser in addition to his new responsibilities, but there are indications that in removing him from Richmond, Davis had given in to Bragg's enemies. War clerk diarist and gossip John B. Jones explained that Bragg was being sent away because "the combination against him was too strong." Davis, finding himself relying upon General Robert E. Lee for advice and information, verified Jones's comment in a conversation with General Josiah Gorgas. "Since Bragg has gone I can get very little information of things about Richmond," he complained. "I am almost deprived of [his] assistance . . . by the prejudices existing against [him]."[4]

As usual, views on Bragg's new appointment were mixed. Diarist Catherine Ann Devereux Edmondston noted, "Bragg, I am sorry to say, has been sent [to Wilmington]—a bad augury for us! Murad the Unlucky's fate will follow him." General James Longstreet maintained that a newspaper announced, "We understand

[3] Faust, *Encyclopedia*, p. 822; W. G. Robertson, *Back Door*, p. 253; Boatner, *Dictionary*, p. 916; S. R. Wise, *Lifeline*, p. 130; *OR*, XLII (pt. 3), 1147–48.
[4] *OR*, XLII (pt. 3), 1148; Bragg to James H. Hammond, October 18, 1864, Hammond Papers, vol. 31 (1864–1875); J. B. Jones, *Rebel War Clerk's Diary*, II, 310; Gorgas, *Diary*, p. 158.

that Gen. Bragg is ordered to Wilmington! Good-bye Wilmington!" War Department clerk Robert G. H. Kean, an indefatigable gossip, best illustrated and mixed feelings when he wrote, "Everybody fears that Wilmington will 'go up' with 'Josiah' there, but is notwithstanding delighted that this element of discord, acrimony, and confusion is withdrawn from here."[5]

Bragg quickly familiarized himself with his new command. Within three days he had inspected the defensive works protecting the harbor and reported favorably on their strength and condition. He believed that any naval attack could be beaten off, but the defenses against a land attack were so limited and scattered that they could provide only a nominal resistance.[6]

In response to Davis's fears regarding Whiting's mental and physical state, Bragg devoted at least half of one report to Whiting's condition. Bragg stated that Whiting seemed worried and discontent, but he did not appear to be indulging himself in alcohol. Bragg had deemed it "prudent to so shape my order assuming command as to wound him as little as possible," leaving Whiting to exercise all of his former administrative duties, although Bragg assured Davis that he himself had assumed entire control of the situation. Bragg believed he and Whiting could work together harmoniously.[7] And so it appeared until the fall of Fort Fisher unleashed Whiting's ferocious animosity.

Bragg's new duties also brought him into close contact with thirty-four-year-old Governor Zebulon Vance, whose popularity with the people of North Carolina remained high because of his

[5] Edmonston, *Secesh Lady*, p. 627. Edmondston's "Murad" probably refers to Joachim Murat (1771–1815), brother-in-law and cavalry commander of Napoleon. Murat accompanied Napoleon on his disastrous Russian campaign in 1812, deserted him when he was defeated at Leipzig in 1813, and tried to win Italy for him when he escaped Elba in 1815. After Waterloo, Murat attempted to recover his own kingdom of Naples, at which time he was captured and executed. See also James Longstreet to E. P. Alexander, August 26, 1902, E. P. Alexander Papers; Longstreet, *From Manassas*, p. 582; Kean, *Inside*, p. 177. An example of Longstreet's unreliability in reporting is his claiming in his letter to Alexander that Bragg was not sent to Wilmington until after the December 1864 attack on Wilmington, when, in fact, Bragg had been there since October.

[6] *OR*, XLII (pt. 3), 1171–72.

[7] *Ibid.*, 1160, 1171.

efforts to ease their war burdens. Having served in the army earlier in the war, Vance understood military matters, and for the most part the relations between Bragg and Vance appeared cordial, although inevitably points of contention did arise.[8]

The resolution of the first point of contention took place without Bragg's overt interference. On October 25 Vance requested that General D. H. Hill be assigned to command the eastern portion of North Carolina. When Davis asked Lee's advice, however, Lee recommended that since Bragg commanded at Wilmington, he had better command the whole district, citing a want of harmony between the two generals, a reference to Bragg's relieving Hill of command after Chickamauga. Cooper concurred, and that settled the matter.[9]

Another point of contention, however, could have resulted in more serious repercussions, as it directly affected and impugned some of Vance's constituents. In his first report to Richmond from Wilmington, Bragg maintained that 200–300 able-bodied conscripts had been detailed by the state to make salt at the shore, work that could be done by Negroes, thus freeing the conscripts for field duty. A more important issue, though, was the contention that the salt workers were reportedly disloyal and were suspected of having contact with the enemy. On November 15 Bragg took the matter in hand, notifying Vance that he had ordered the removal of the salt workers. "This is altogether different treatment from what I expected," Vance protested, "and I inform you candidly I shall resist by every means in my power."[10]

Despite their dispute over the salt workers, the general and the governor agreed that Wilmington had too few troops for its defense. Shortly after Bragg arrived, Davis, Lee, Seddon, and Cooper agreed that Bragg and General Hardee, commanding at Charleston, South Carolina, should mutually support each other in case of an attack at either place. Hardee, who had undermined

---

[8] Wilfred Buck Yearns, ed., *The Confederate Governors* (Athens, Ga., 1985), pp. 149, 158, 160–61.
[9] *OR*, XLII (pt. 3), 1163–64.
[10] *Ibid.*, 1171, 1214; LI (pt. 2), 1052.

Bragg in the past, replied that he would cooperate but warned that owing to the smallness of his force and the many points to be defended, not much should be expected. In mid-November Vance wrote Davis requesting veteran troops from Lee's army to serve as a trained nucleus for the inexperienced troops in North Carolina, deeming it injudicious to leave the defense of Wilmington entirely to untried militia. When Lee received this communication through Seddon, who had stated his reluctance to send off any troops, Lee predictably responded, "I will send any troops to Wilmington the Secretary may direct." He went on to explain why he needed to keep every last man he had, contending that the North Carolina state troops could defend the port if properly organized and instructed. Needless to say, Lee did not reinforce the troops at Wilmington until dire emergency forced Davis to order him to do so. Elise, who had remained in Virginia, may have echoed her husband's sentiments regarding Lee's lack of cooperation. Lee, she informed Braxton, had told her that "if the Georgians are true to themselves Sherman cant escape." She wondered "why, if militia can accomplish so much does *he* not send some veteran troops to annihilate Sherman & let militia hide behind the walls here!"[11]

After Bragg arrived in Wilmington, Richmond decided to enlarge the area of his command. In advising against Hill's appointment, Lee had recommended that as long as Bragg was in Wilmington, he should command that whole district. Seddon agreed, and on November 10 Davis accepted the recommendation. The order from the adjutant general's office delineated Bragg's department as constituting the state of North Carolina east of the Blue Ridge Mountains, but at the same time, this area continued to remain under the overall direction of Lee.[12]

This additional assignment caused some confusion as to Bragg's official status. War clerk Jones believed Bragg's military-adviser position had been abolished, and Bragg, too, seemed unsure of his

---

[11] *Ibid.*, XLII (pt. 3), 1177, 1181, 1183, 1214–15; LI (pt. 2), 1048; Elise to Bragg, December 3, 1864, Bragg Papers, Western Reserve.
[12] *OR*, XLII (pt. 3), 1163, 1207, 1209.

authority. On November 17 he informed John B. Sale, his secretary in charge of the Richmond office, that several departments needed to be inspected but asked that Sale first "ascertain my status. . . .It may be that I am relieved." Davis quickly made it clear that this was not the case. On a copy of Bragg's order, Davis wrote, "This order was not intended to remove General Bragg from his position here, but only to enlarge the territory of his temporary command. I understand it has been differently construed."[13] As far as Davis was concerned, Bragg remained military adviser.

All this time rumors circulated about Federal plans to attack Wilmington. Bragg constantly received reports from Whiting and other local commanders regarding the imminence of an assault, and he became increasingly anxious about the small number of defenders available in his department. In mid-November when he sent a memorandum to Davis regarding the overall conditions in the area, this unpreparedness was his primary concern. He found the reserves undisciplined and untrained, partly because they had no experienced officers. Bragg pleaded for a proper commander. He applied to Lee, who referred him to General Theophilus H. Holmes, who said he had no one available. "The circle is squared," Bragg complained, "but the troops still remain without a commander." Meanwhile, navy personnel created more problems than they were worth. Drunkenness, rowdyism, garroting, and robbery featured prominently among their favorite pastimes. They were so bad, Bragg charged, that if they could not be put on active duty, he would rather they be removed from Wilmington.[14]

Despite these problems and the imminence of attack, Bragg had no sooner been assigned to command the Department of North Carolina than Davis ordered him to Augusta, Georgia, to meet the more immediate threat posed by General Sherman's march to the sea. Beginning in Atlanta on November 15, Sherman's forces headed toward the Atlantic coast, expecting to arrive at Savannah

13 J. B. Jones, *Rebel War Clerk's Diary*, II, 329; *OR*, XLII (pt. 3), 1219, 1210.
14 *OR*, XLII (pt. 3). 1201–2, 1206, 1207, 1218.

in late December. As it turned out, the Union army met less resistance than had been expected and arrived at the coast two weeks earlier than its target date. The 62,000 Federals moved out of Atlanta in two wings, separated by about forty miles, feinting toward Augusta and Macon in order to keep the Confederates from learning their true destination. To oppose the Federals, the Confederacy fielded 3,000 militia and state troops, some local forces, and General Joseph Wheeler's depleted cavalry corps. The *London Times'* description of Sherman's expedition as "an unknown route against an undiscoverable enemy" proved particularly apt, although the enemy was not so much undiscoverable as nonexistent.[15]

On November 22 Bragg received orders to proceed to Augusta to organize a defense against Sherman's advance. At 9:00 P.M. he notified the elected officials of South Carolina and of Augusta that he was on his way. "Exhort your people to be confident & resolute," he implored Augusta's mayor R. H. May, while he pleaded with South Carolina's governor Millege Luke Bonham to "prevail on your men to unite in protecting a sister state. Our cause is one," he pointed out. "If Georgia is saved South Carolina cannot be lost. If Georgia be lost South Carolina cannot be saved." The next day Bragg left for Augusta, taking half of the Wilmington garrison with him. With the remaining half-garrison, Whiting assumed temporary command of the Department of North Carolina.[16]

It appears Davis originally intended that Bragg and Hardee share command of the area, but by November 27 Richmond decided Bragg should coordinate all of the operations to the coast. Bragg, of course, found himself "unable to decline a responsibility of such magnitude so unexpectedly transferred to me." He warned, however, "I must candidly express my belief that no

[15] U. S. Grant, *Personal Memoirs*, II, 359–66; Burke Davis, *Sherman's March* (New York, 1980), pp. 26–27, 24; Faust, *Encyclopedia*, pp. 474–75.

[16] *OR*, XLIV, 881; Bragg to R. H. May, November 23, 1864; Bragg to M. L. Bonham, November 23, 1864, Hammond Papers, vol. 31; *OR*, XLII (pt. 3), 1228.

practicable combinations of my available men can avert disaster."[17]

Bragg was correct. The Confederacy simply lacked the people to meet this emergency. In addition, no one knew the exact location or intent of Sherman's army on a daily basis. "If our people could have arranged to hang a mammoth bell around Sherman's neck," remarked one disgusted Confederate, "they might have divined his movements."[18]

Bragg's duties at Augusta, it turned out, consisted primarily of receiving and sending reports; as diarist Jones put it, "Bragg only played the part of chronicler of the sad events from Augusta." Instructed to defend the arsenal and ordnance production there, Bragg could hardly venture far. Some historians have criticized his apparent lack of activity during this period without specifying just what it is they believe he should have, or could have, done under the circumstances. Not until December 3, when Bragg informed Sale that the enemy forces had turned toward Savannah, did it become clear that Augusta would not be assaulted after all. Four days later Bragg notified Cooper that Beauregard, who now commanded the Military Division of the West, had passed through on his journey from Montgomery, Alabama, to Charleston and Savannah, thus relieving Bragg of responsibility for events in Georgia.[19]

Grant, meanwhile, knowing of Bragg's absence from Wilmington with half of its defenders, ordered an expedition from New Berne to cut the railroad at Weldon. In reporting this plan to a subordinate, Whiting succinctly summed up the Confederacy's dilemma as exemplified in his own department: "Between Bragg and Lee, Sherman and Grant, old North Carolina is in a pretty fix."[20]

[17] *OR*, XLIV, 891, 901.
[18] Gorgas, *Diary*, p. 152; Bird and Bird, *Letters*, pp. 219–20.
[19] J. B. Jones, *Rebel War Clerk's Diary*, II, 377; B. Davis, *Sherman's March*, pp. 51, 82, 84; *OR*, XLIV, 925, 937; Edmondston, *Secesh Lady*, p. 642.
[20] *OR*, XLII (pt. 3), 748, 1264.

Actually the entire Confederacy was in a pretty fix when Brent suggested Bragg might be able to obtain troops from the Trans-Mississippi Department. Seddon had remarked that Kirby Smith consistently failed to respond to emergencies and that no future plans should be based upon his cooperation. Colonel Brent, working in Bragg's Richmond office, suggested to Beauregard that he recommend Bragg be sent to relieve Smith. That move would allow Bragg to organize and administer the department while General Richard Taylor commanded the troops. Bragg may have known of this possibility. He notified Sale on December 13 that he would go to Charleston the next day, at Beauregard's request, to see about an assignment. There is no record of what transpired at this meeting between the two antagonistic generals, but on the fifteenth Bragg informed Sale that since his services were no longer needed where he was, he planned to return to Wilmington.[21]

Upon his return, Elise joined him. On December 15 Bragg had asked Sale to notify Elise of his return and to tell her that he wanted her to join him in Wilmington. This communication seemed to be in response to a letter written by Elise on December 3, in which she complained bitterly about her situation and about the lack of news from her husband. To convince him that she should be at his side, she reminded Braxton of the trying conditions under which she existed. Staying in Petersburg with friends who "of course . . . cannot well afford giving me the shelter of their roof in my uncertain & desolate position," she prodded her husband into concern about her location. "Bettie & I walked up into Sycamore Street a few evenings ago," she wrote, "& a shell just cleared our heads, bursting . . . a square off."[22]

Elise, no doubt, saw very little of her husband during the next weeks. As soon as Grant learned of Bragg's departure from Wilmington, he urged an immediate advance upon the port. For-

[21] *Ibid.*, XLV (pt. 2), 647, 665; XLIV, 954, 958, 963.
[22] *Ibid.*, XLIV, 958; Elise to Bragg, December 3, 1864, Bragg Papers, Western Reserve.

tunately for the Confederates, General Butler, released from his pen on Bermuda Hundred, commanded the troops assigned to this task. He devised the idea of filling a vessel with explosives, anchoring it near Fort Fisher, and leveling the fort with the blast. Even as these preparations delayed the departure of the expedition, Grant doubted the efficacy of the whole plan. Butler's troops apparently had the same notion regarding their commander. One Federal soldier opined that Butler "will command the expedition—in order to insure its failure."[23]

Butler finally got off on December 13, joining Admiral David Porter's Atlantic fleet on the eighteenth, by which time Bragg had returned to Wilmington. The Federal objective was the reduction of Fort Fisher, located on the southern tip of Federal Point (renamed Confederate Point for the duration of the war), a peninsula jutting out below Wilmington, bordered on the east by the Atlantic and on the west by the Cape Fear River. The fort, greatly improved and strengthened under Whiting's administration, had earned the sobriquet "Gibraltar of the Confederacy."[24]

Bragg reported the sighting of the fleet on December 20, and Davis immediately directed Lee to dispatch General Robert Hoke's Division to the Wilmington area. Because of delays along the railroad, the unit did not arrive until the affair was about finished, although as it turned out, their arrival proved crucial to the Federal withdrawal. Bragg, meanwhile, felt confident that he could hold the city of Wilmington but made no mention of its approaches. War clerk Jones hoped that this time Bragg would be able to do more than just "chronicle the successes of the enemy."[25]

Butler's expedition proceeded with fits and starts, owing partly to the foul weather. One disgusted participant avowed, "Probably a more mismanaged expedition never left our ports. As yet

[23] OR, XLII (pt. 1), 970–71; (pt. 3), 750, 760; XLIV, 588, 611; XLVI (pt. 1), 41; Edward King Wightman, From Antietam to Fort Fisher: The Civil War Letters of Edward King Wightman, 1862–1865, ed. Edward G. Longacre (Rutherford, N.J., 1985), p. 219.
[24] Faust, Encyclopedia, p. 100.
[25] OR, XLII (pt. 3), 1283, 1056; J. B. Jones, Rebel War Clerk's Diary, II, 360.

nothing has been accomplished beyond testing uselessly the endurance of the troops, and this long two weeks of seasickness and suffering has undoubtedly harrassed and worn them [down] more than six weeks of active campaigning could have done." The mismanagement had only begun. The powder vessel which was supposed to level Fort Fisher was set off during the night of December 23 but proved ineffectual. The next day Bragg merely reported that a Federal vessel in pursuit of a blockade-runner had grounded, been abandoned, and blown up. Whiting later told Butler the explosion had "no effect at all on the fort."[26]

For the duration of the operations, Bragg assumed immediate command of all the troops in and about Wilmington and assigned Whiting to command the defenses at and near the mouth of the river, headquartering at Fort Fisher. Hoke, when he arrived, would command the troops on the sound and at Sugar Loaf, a high sand hill on the peninsula seven miles north of Fort Fisher. As it turned out, there was little to do. The Federals made a landing, but their half-hearted attack did little more than create a good deal of excitement among the Confederate defenders. On December 28 Bragg notified Davis of the Federals' withdrawal.[27]

Butler's abrupt departure left the Confederates confused and, worse, cocky. "The movements of the enemy are not clear to me," Whiting reported. "We could not have damaged them so seriously as to cause this rapid abandonment of the attack. . . . That great and irreparable disaster did not overtake us we owe to God." Butler could hardly be equated with the deity, but that is precisely to whom Whiting was actually obliged. Butler lost his nerve and his wits, and upon learning of the approach of Hoke's Division on December 25, he called off the assault, returning to Hampton Roads as quickly as weather permitted. For his pains,

26 *OR*, XLII (pt. 3), 1056, 1283, 1301–2; (pt. 1), 979; Wightman, *From Antietam*, p. 222. For full discussion of the attacks on Fort Fisher and Wilmington, see Wise, *Lifeline*; Rod Gragg, *Confederate Goliath: The Battle of Fort Fisher* (New York, 1991).

27 *OR*, XLII (pt. 3), 1303, 1334; William Lamb, "The Defense of Fort Fisher," in *Battles and Leaders*, IV, 642.

or the pains he created for others, Grant had him relieved of duty and sent home to Massachusetts.[28]

Other people were more willing than Whiting to look for mortal beings to praise for the results of this attack. "Gen. Bragg is credited with the repulse of the enemy at Wilmington," Jones reported on December 30, and three days later he repeated, "Gen. Bragg is applauded here for this successful defense." John Forsyth congratulated Bragg on his achievement, declaring, "I am delighted that you were there and had that opportunity." Basking in the glow of this praise, Bragg shared it with his subordinate officers and his soldiers. "One of the most formidable expeditions yet organized by the enemy . . . has accomplished no other object than a fruitless landing on a barren coast, followed in forty-eight hours by a hasty re-embarkation," he crowed. "Thus another gigantic effort of a powerful enemy has come to naught."[29]

Bragg erroneously and fatally believed the assault had afforded the Confederacy a profitable lesson. He declared it "proves that the superiority of land batteries over ships of war . . . has been re-established by the genius of the engineer; and the weaker party on the defensive may still defy the greater numbers and mechanical resources of an arrogant invader."[30] This boasting echoes that following the defeat of the Federal forces at Manassas in 1861, rhetoric that allowed Southerners to believe themselves invincible. The easy repulse of the enemy from Fort Fisher in December seems to have created a mind-set among the Confederate high command that made it easier for the next Federal expedition, sent out a few weeks later under a competent and determined commander, to succeed.

Whiting may have been nearly the only one not to fall into this fatal frame of mind. He began his report with the comment that "this account [is] of the failure *for the present* of the very formidable combined attack of the enemy." He attributed the Confederate

[28] *OR*, XLII (pt. 1), 996; Faust, *Encyclopedia*, p. 100.
[29] J. B. Jones, *Rebel War Clerk's Diary*, II, 369, 373; John Forsyth to Bragg, January 17, 1865, Bragg Papers, Western Reserve; *OR*, XLII (pt. 1), 999.
[30] *OR*, XLII (pt. 1), 999.

success to bad weather and Federal mismanagement but warned, "We cannot always hope for such aid from weather or the blunder of the enemy." No sooner did the Federal fleet disappear into the mist than Whiting and Colonel William Lamb, commander of Fort Fisher, began working furiously to repair the damage and prepare for the Federals' return.[31]

As Whiting made ready for the next assault, his superiors exhibited little concern for Wilmington's safety. Bragg wanted him to spend precious time and resources rescuing the cargo from a grounded blockade-runner, while officials in Richmond sat on their hands on other matters. Whiting believed the ocean inlets should be obstructed and asked permission to do so. His communication made the rounds of various officials, the last of whom noted, "No further disposition required, Fort Fisher having fallen." Bragg's request regarding the independent status of the signal officers received the same treatment. After three weeks in the labyrinths of officialdom, the final endorser remarked, "The closing of the port of Wilmington renders a further discussion of this question unnecessary."[32]

The three-week respite between attacks allowed Bragg an opportunity to indulge himself in his favorite pastimes—griping and carping. He complained about the length of time involved in moving Hoke's Division from Virginia to North Carolina, attributing the delay to imbecility. He also groused about the lack of cooperation from the West. He believed the only viable source of aid for his department was the "large unemployed army in the Trans-Mississippi," and all that was needed to secure it was "tact, energy, and will." Enamored of his little homily to the officials of South Carolina and Georgia a few weeks earlier, he rephrased it and trotted it out again. "If the East is lost, the West must follow," he burbled; "if the East is saved, the West can be redeemed." Bragg wrote this letter to his military secretary and confidant, John B. Sale. The final sentence, "Use this for our cause," sug-

[31] *Ibid.*, 993, 996, author's emphasis; Wise, *Lifeline*, p. 207.
[32] *OR*, XLII (pt. 3), 1345; XLVI (pt. 2), 1000–1002; 1004–5.

gests that Bragg may still have harbored ambitions for the Trans-Mississippi command.[33]

The relationship between Bragg and Whiting began showing signs of wear. Whiting took exception to Bragg's order of December 24 assigning him to command the defenses at the mouth of the river. After the emergency abated, Whiting, somewhat incoherently, "beg[ged] leave to state that I entirely but respectfully object to [the orders] . . . issued after I had proceeded to that portion of my command most immediately threatened, as far as the order concerns myself, as altogether unnecessary, the defenses of the mouth of the river being a part, and a part only, of my care." Bragg failed to see anything objectionable in the orders and chastised Whiting for his disrespectful tone and language.[34]

All too soon the breathing spell came to an end. As Bragg and Whiting wrangled, a second expedition, under General Alfred Howe Terry, left Virginia for Wilmington on January 4, 1865. Terry had been aboard for the December assault and had learned from Butler what not to do. While the navy provided covering fire from the fleet, Federal forces established a beachhead above Fort Fisher's landface and built strong works across the upper neck to prevent Hoke's force from aiding the fort. Bragg had helped the Federals secure this position by failing to prepare in advance. Not until January 12 did he order Hoke to Sugar Loaf to construct defensive works. This did not leave much time, as that night Bragg received the first reports of the return of the enemy fleet. It appears the troops did not even have the tools with which to construct these works, as three days later Bragg asked that Hoke be supplied with 200 spades and shovels.[35]

Sometime prior to midnight of January 12 Bragg notified Lee that the Federal fleet had returned, this time having the advantage of good weather and smooth seas. Bragg ordered Hoke to make every effort to prevent a landing of the enemy, but if the enemy

[33] *Ibid.*, XLII (pt. 3), 1344, 1358.
[34] *Ibid.*, 1303, 1356, 1358–59; XLVI (pt. 2), 1046.
[35] *OR*, XLVI (pt. 2), 1043, 1063.

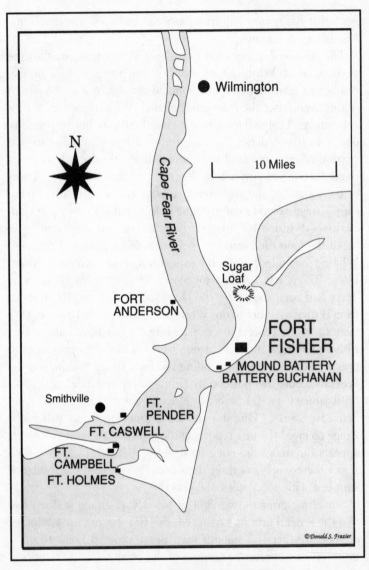

THE VICINITY OF FORT FISHER

had already landed, Hoke should take up the position they had decided upon during the December fiasco. Bragg promised to join him when the Federals' intentions became clear. The orders sent to the commander of one of the forts along the river proved much more forceful, decreeing that the posts must be defended "at every hazard and to the last extremity."[36]

On January 13 enemy forces landed and dug in. Early in the day Whiting, at Fort Fisher, warned Bragg that the garrison was too weak to resist an assault or to prevent the enemy's advance. He urged Bragg to attack at once. He repeated this during the day, and by 8:00 P.M. became completely exasperated. "Enemy are on the beach," Whiting fumed, "where they have been all day. Why are they not attacked?" Hoke, meanwhile, spent the day at Sugar Loaf fearing that the enemy might attack him. He failed to mention his own plans, if any, for an offensive. At 2:00 P.M. Bragg went to Sugar Loaf to supervise in person.[37]

January 14, another day Bragg spent in relative inactivity, proved no more successful for the Confederates. At 8:00 P.M. Bragg informed Lee that after examining the enemy lines, Hoke considered it too risky to assault with his inferior force. Yet at midnight Bragg decided it was of primary importance to break the Federal line. Hoke's feeble efforts failed to make an impression upon the enemy or to relieve the pressure on Fort Fisher. Throughout the day Whiting had pleaded with Hoke and Bragg for some relief. "Sooner you attack the enemy the better," he declared at 11:45 A.M. At 1:30 he openly criticized his commander. "I have received dispatches from you stating that the enemy had extended to the riverbank. This they never should have been allowed to do; and if they are permitted to remain there the reduction of Fort Fisher is but a question of time." Despite Bragg's failures, Whiting promised, "I will hold this place till the last extremities; but unless you drive that land force from its position I cannot answer for the security of this harbor."[38]

[36] *Ibid.*, 1042, 1044, 1045, 1050.
[37] *Ibid.*, 1046, 1048, 1049.
[38] *Ibid.*, 1053, 1059.

On January 15, shortly before the Federals began their final and successful assault against Fort Fisher, a thoroughly frustrated Whiting pressed Bragg, "Is Fisher to be beseiged, or you to attack?" Bragg replied that "Hoke is moving on enemy, but I am confident you will repel him with your infantry." Incredibly, at exactly the same time, Bragg informed Lee that little would be done, as Hoke believed the effort would fail, and at a heavy sacrifice. Bragg artfully worded his report to align Lee with his own way of thinking, referring to Hoke as "the commander of *your* troops."[39]

Because of Bragg's and Hoke's reluctance to expose the Virginia troops to danger, when the Federals moved against the fort, it did not take long to overpower the undersoldiered garrison. At 6:30 P.M. Whiting informed Bragg, "The enemy are assaulting us by land and sea. Their infantry outnumber us. Can't you help us?" He also announced that he had been slightly wounded. Pleas for help continued to emanate from the beleaguered fort.[40]

Bragg, choosing to accept Hoke's timidity, left Fort Fisher to its own devices. Although at 8:00 P.M. he assured Major Robert Strange in Wilmington that the rumors of Fisher's fall were entirely unfounded, at 10:30 P.M. an observer telegraphed, "All at once firing has ceased; also signals; and the whole fleet are now throwing rockets up—all colors. It is fully believed that the fort has surrendered." As indeed it had. At 11:15 the observer announced men constantly arriving from Battery Buchanan (adjacent to Fort Fisher and the last refuge of the garrison there) who stated that the fort had surrendered. Five minutes later he reported having spoken to two officers who confirmed the fort's surrender and the capture of Whiting and Lamb. Unwilling to believe these accounts of disaster, at 11:30 Bragg ordered that someone reliable be sent by boat to the fort to ascertain the facts. "Let him say to the commander of Fort Fisher General Bragg orders him not to surrender." The commander charged with

[39] *Ibid.*, 1064, 1061, author's emphasis.
[40] *Ibid.*, 1064, 1065, 1066–67.

sending out the party replied that the "last information is that
Fort Fisher has surrendered," and he awaited further orders. At
midnight, after having had an hour and a half to digest the disagreeable news, Bragg swallowed it and countermanded the order
to send someone to the fort, "as [the] place seems to have surrendered."[41]

Bragg's activities before and during the attack on Fort Fisher
and his comments on its fall indicate his serious misjudgment of
what had occurred in December. Lamb later reported that, even
though the Confederates were aware of the impending attack,
Bragg had withdrawn Hoke's troops from Sugar Loaf, marched
them to a camp sixteen miles away, and there held a grand review.
Indeed, Bragg did not order them back to Sugar Loaf until just
hours before the Federals landed. His report to Lee indicated just
how secure the December fiasco had rendered him when he professed himself mortified by the unexpected capture of Fort
Fisher.[42]

Bragg submitted his official report on January 20, a masterpiece
of distortions and innuendoes concocted to show that he could not
be blamed, although circumstances disallowed overt placement of
blame on his immediate subordinates. Bragg did not believe Fort
Fisher faced much danger, "if boldly defended by a vigilant garrison." As the garrison had been under attack for only two days
and on duty but one night, he had not felt the slightest apprehension for its safety. Bragg stated that he failed to attack with his
outnumbered forces at Sugar Loaf, as this would have "exhausted
our means to aid the fort, and thereby not only have insured its
ultimate fall, but have opened the country behind it." Remember-
ing the cooperation of the weather in December, Bragg insisted
that it would be only a matter of time before the enemy's "early
and complete discomfiture, as the first change of weather would
drive off the fleet and leave him unsupported and cut off from
supplies." Incredibly, he included in his report two of Whiting's

[41] *Ibid.*, 1063, 1069, 1070, 1071.
[42] Lamb, "Defense of Fort Fisher," pp. 646–47; *OR*, XLVI (pt. 2), 1078.

pleas for help, claiming that they dispelled all apprehension. These supposedly reassuring dispatches cried, "The enemy are assaulting us by land and sea. Their infantry outnumbers us. Can't you help us?" and, "We still hold the fort, but are sorely pressed. Can't you assist us from the outside?" Just how these messages dispelled his apprehensions Bragg did not explain.

Bragg's greatest dilemma was how to divert blame from himself. The report reveals his quandary. "All accounts agree that the courage and devotion of . . . Whiting and . . . Lamb were most conspicuous; they both fell pierced by severe wounds, at the head of their men." In other words, these men had become heroes, and Bragg knew better than to attack heroes. "Without better information than is now possessed," he concluded, "no opinion should be hazarded as to how this misfortune was brought about." Along with his report, however, Bragg sent copies, without comment, of statements from an early party he had sent to Fort Fisher to ascertain details regarding rumors of its fall. The party's observations included disparaging statements regarding the soldiers, a strategy designed covertly to put blame on Lamb and Whiting. "I think there were . . . 300 or 400 men, and many of them drunk," wrote General A. H. Colquitt, while his aide-de-camp Lieutenant Hugh H. Colquitt reported, "All of our men were in a state of panic and demoralization; no organization, no guns, nothing but confusion and dismay. The only man I saw with a gun was a drunken Irish marine, who cocked it and presented it at me." Ordnance officer Harry Estill confirmed this report. "Whilst upon the point I saw but one of our men armed," he claimed. "He was a drunken marine, and offered to shoot Lieutenant Colquitt." Lieutenant George L. Washington insisted, "No officer seemed to be in command, nor could any one give any collected account of the bombardment or evacuation. I saw no arms in the hands of the men. They appeared to have given up all idea of making resistance, and there was no possible means of escape." By the time this group arrived at the fort, the Federals had entered it. Speaking briefly to the wounded Lamb, they fled before seeing Whiting, who had also been wounded.[43] They left Lamb and Whiting behind to be captured with the rest of the garrison.

In a letter to his brother five days after Fort Fisher fell, Bragg repeated his innuendoes, citing enemy reports to confirm the statements regarding the condition of Fisher's garrison. "They assert that they walked into the fort without resistance, not a shot being fired at them, our men all being in the *bomb-proofs*. That after they got in a small force was rallied and fought them very gallantly, inflicting a heavy loss, but they soon overcame them and captured most of our officers and men without arms." Both Union and Confederate official reports put the lie to these charges. Bragg also insinuated to his brother that Whiting and others had been in league with the blockade-runners and now declared, "Blockade running has cured itself," as though he were content to lose the Confederacy's last port if that solved the problems of dealing with people he despised. Bragg also revealed that he had never intended to hold the fort indefinitely. "The defense of the fort ought to have been successful against *this* attack," he asserted, "but it had to fall eventually." One wonders just when Bragg would have felt it proper for the fort to be lost. He ended his account with the usual bid for sympathy. "But enough for the present," he sighed. "I am both tired and sad."[44]

Bragg's diversionary tactics failed to deflect blame from himself. Whiting, to Bragg's misfortune, survived his wounds and imprisonment long enough to write scathing criticisms of his commander. Two days after his capture, Whiting dictated a report for Lee. "The garrison of Fort Fisher had been coolly abandoned to its fate," he charged. "I think that the result might have been avoided . . . if the commanding general had have done his duty. I charge him with this loss; with neglect of duty in this, that he either refused or neglected to carry out every suggestion made to him in official communications by me for the disposition of the troops . . . [and that] he moves them twenty miles from the point

[43] *OR*, XLVI (pt. 1), 432–34, 443, 445, 446, 447.
[44] *Southern Historical Society Papers*, X (1882), 349, 362–63.

of landing in spite of repeated warnings. . . . I charge him further with making no effort whatever to create a diversion in favor of the beleaguered garrison during the three days' battle." So incensed was Whiting that he demanded "a full investigation be had of this matter and these charges which I make; they will be fully borne out by the official records." Hesitating to send the report through enemy lines, Whiting did not forward it to Lee until February 19, at which time, having had time to reconsider his remarks, he had not changed his mind. "In all his career of failure and defeat from Pensacola out," Whiting asserted, "there has been no such chance missed, and no such stupendous disaster." His rage at Bragg induced Whiting to cooperate with Butler in the Federal general's attempts to justify his inability to capture Fort Fisher in December. In reply to questions put to him by Butler, Whiting commented that it was only due to the "supineness of the Confederate general" that the Federal land attack had not been destroyed.[45]

Lamb concurred with Whiting, charging that Bragg "abandoned us to our fate" and that "no assault would have been practicable in the presence of Bragg's force, had it been under a competent officer." He charged that Bragg, despite an unparallelled opportunity to witness the movements of the enemy, "hid away in the undergrowth of safe sand hills, [and] gathered his news of the condition of the most important part of his command from rumors. . . . The women, children and old men, who watched the battle from the farm houses across the river, knew more about what was going on in his command than did General Braxton Bragg." Writing in response to the 1881 publication of Bragg's letter to his brother, Lamb contended that Bragg's statements showed one of two things: "that his defeat had seriously affected his mind, or that he distorted the facts to justify himself to his brother."[46]

Civilians also blamed Bragg for Fisher's fall. Mary Chesnut reported that Whiting's aide "denounces Bragg for sacrificing Gen-

[45] OR, XLVI (pt. 1), 439–42; XLII (pt. 1), 980.
[46] Lamb, "Defense of Fort Fisher," pp. 653, 654; Southern Historical Society Papers, X (1882), 350, 352, 359.

eral Whiting at Fort Fisher." Edmonston complained, "So will it ever be where Bragg commands. Bragg the Unlucky is a Millstone which Mr Davis persist in tying around our necks!" War clerk Jones summed it up succinctly: "Alas for Bragg the unfortunate! He seems to be another BOABDIL the Unlucky."[47]

Despite the ensuing controversy about the fall of Fort Fisher, some people gave Bragg the benefit of the doubt. His friend General Robert C. Tyler expressed great confidence in Bragg, believing him "infinitely the superior of any Genl the Confederacy can boast of." Tyler also assured his friend, "I do Esteem you as a peerless Commander, the gallant Soldier, the Self Sacrificing Patriot—My beau ideal of a soldier."[48]

[47] Chesnut, *Civil War*, p. 817; Edmondston, *Secesh Lady*, p. 657; J. B. Jones, *Rebel War Clerk's Diary*, II, 388. Boabdil is a reference to the last Moorish king of Granada (in southern Spain), who, upon his defeat by Ferdinand and Isabella in 1492, returned to Africa, where he died in battle. Washington Irving used Boabdil as a prominent character in *The Alhambra* (1832).

[48] Edmonston, *Secesh Lady*, p. 663; Edson J. Harkness, "The Expeditions against Fort Fisher and Wilmington," in *Military Essays and Recollections: Papers Read before the Commandery of the State of Illinois, Military Order of the Loyal Legion of the United States* (Chicago, 1894), II, 178; Robert C. Tyler to Bragg, January 22, 1865, Bragg Papers, Western Reserve.

CHAPTER XIII

Most sad and humiliating

January, 1865–September, 1876

W HEN THE FEDERALS CAPTURED Fort Fisher on January 15, 1865, the Confederacy had less than 100 days of token existence remaining. To those maneuvering in North Carolina the outcome seemed obvious—inevitable defeat; to those cloistered in Richmond the outcome appeared equally obvious—eventual victory. The last several weeks of Bragg's field command saw the general and his fellow commanders carrying out orders issued through an aura of unreality by the Richmond authorities, including the new general-in-chief, Robert E. Lee.

With Fort Fisher gone, Bragg turned his attention to containing the disaster as far as possible. Davis, ever the dreamer, asked, "Can you retake the fort?" Bragg lost no time informing the president that the enemy fleet could destroy them, let alone the land forces. In fact, he announced, the most he hoped for was to hold the position around Sugar Loaf.[1] And Bragg did manage to hold that line, although not for long, as he busied himself with efforts to diminish the effects of the fort's loss and the inevitable fall of Wilmington.

Bragg first soothed the fears of civilians in the area. In response to a request for soldiers from Mayor John Dawson, Bragg assured him that no effort would be spared to protect the citizens of Wilmington. Within a week he informed Governor Vance that a gubernatorial visit would boost morale, assuring him, "The usual despondency following a disaster is giving place to a better feeling even now." Bragg also used Elise to improve morale. He refused to send her away, as he "feared it would look badly for me to send

[1] *OR*, XLVI (pt. 2), 1078.

her off in the panic. . . . It has had a good effect on the weak and
nervous."[2]

One of Bragg's duties, however, did not promote good relations
with civilians. Confederate authorities, anxious about the cotton
stockpiled in Wilmington for blockade-running, charged Bragg
with preventing any of it from falling into Union hands. Immediately after Fort Fisher fell, Seddon ordered Bragg to remove
government stores of cotton to Raleigh and to encourage civilians
to do the same. Bragg's encouragement took the form of threats,
announcing that any cotton not removed within a reasonable time
would be seized and destroyed. He promised, however, to give
every assistance to private owners. After the removal of government cotton, he ordered the railroads to give preference to that in
private hands over all other goods. At the same time he directed
that a spot be selected where remaining cotton could be burned
without endangering the city.[3]

Bragg also attended to personnel matters. Mrs. S. C. Lamb,
wife of the captured colonel, wished to return to her home in the
North. Bragg recommended she be allowed to do so, and within a
few days permission was granted, and Mrs. Lamb and the children left Wilmington.[4]

Other problems proved more difficult to resolve. Before the fall
of Fort Fisher, Whiting had complained to Bragg of troops tres-
passing and committing depredations throughout the area. After
the loss of the fort, conditions failed to improve. Bragg ordered
General Louis Hebert to send the cavalry to arrest stragglers. Several days later Bragg informed Hoke that his hospitalized soldiers
had committed numerous depredations and were deserting to an
alarming extent. On January 25 Bragg complained to Hoke about
the behavior of General Johnson Hagood's troops, large numbers
of whom were "straggling off home, plundering indiscriminately
as they go." That was bad enough, but worse still, Bragg received
reports that the army's subsistence stores were being wasted and

[2] Ibid., 1108, 1130; Southern Historical Society Papers, X (1882), 349.
[3] OR, XLVI (pt. 2), 1085, 1095, 1104, 1108–9; XLVII (pt. 2), 1189, 1119–20.
[4] Ibid., XLVII (pt. 2), 1099, 1111.

destroyed. To remedy the situation, Bragg directed that guards be posted to protect property, and if necessary, the entire command should be kept under arms at all times.[5]

Bragg not only had trouble controlling the troops, he had difficulties even hanging on to them. Lee, oblivious to the situation around Wilmington, began badgering Bragg about sending off some of his small force. On February 4 Lee asked Bragg if he could send reinforcements to Beauregard at Columbia. Bragg explained that he was greatly outnumbered by the enemy but laid the responsibility for troop movement at Lee's feet. "Should you think otherwise I will detach any portion you think may be spared." Lee proved too wily to step into this position of responsibility and tried again to force Bragg to shoulder it. "Can the Second South Carolina Cavalry be spared for defense of South Carolina?" he asked. Again, Bragg threw the issue back into Lee's hands. "The enemy landed more troops at Fisher yesterday," he warned, "including cavalry. Our force of this arm is very small." Later in the day he turned the tables, informing Lee, "You will see by my dispatch of this morning that more cavalry is required here."[6]

The lack of soldiers once again brought up the question of arming Negroes. In December Bragg believed that emancipating slaves to provide a resource from which to conscript soldiers "would be fatal." He was not, however, averse to using them as laborers. Fearing the loss of valuable property to the Federals, he directed that "all able-bodied male negroes, cattle stock, provisions, &c." be secured before the enemy arrived. If necessary, this would be done forcibly. Shortly after the fall of Fisher, Bragg sent soldiers to the area plantations with instructions to collect all able-bodied male slaves that owners were willing to turn over to the military. Not surprisingly, with their emancipators so close, large numbers of Negroes had run away from their masters, and Bragg was offering plantation owners a measure of security for their

[5] *Ibid.*, XLVI (pt. 2), 1021, 1108, 1138, 1164.
[6] *Ibid.*, XLVII (pt. 2), 1098, 1103, 1139.

more valuable property by sending their able-bodied men within his lines. He did not appear, however, to have been concerned with those of lesser value—the women and the children.[7]

Many owners did not appreciate Bragg's solicitude for their property, complaining to Davis that the army damaged their human investments, and in early February Bragg sent the president an apologia on their treatment by the army. He listed several factors as contributing to complaint, only a small part of which was due to mismanagement and inattention. He cited hazardous work as a factor but pointed out that white troops had performed the same tasks. Lack of sufficient food played a part, as did want of suitable clothing and proper hospital accommodations. He promised that if owners made their complaints known to him, he would do what he could to satisfy them. Some planters simply took matters into their own hands. "Desertions are constant," Whiting had reported in January, "and I have no doubt that their owners encourage it, especially when the negro has been impressed."[8]

With Fort Fisher in Union hands, it became a matter of time until the port city fell. Judith Brockenbrough McGuire, whose adult daughters were refugees and whose son was in a Northern prison, reflected the sentiments of most people when she declared in January, "Fort Fisher has fallen; Wilmington will of course follow." Throughout the rest of January and into the beginning of February, Bragg received reports of Federal movements and small skirmishes along the peninsula between Fort Fisher and Wilmington as the Federals moved in to accomplish what all awaited.[9]

As the lifeline of the Confederacy unraveled, so too did Bragg's military career. During the time he spent in Wilmington, Bragg continued to act as military adviser through the staff he left in Richmond under Sale's direction. In late January, however, Con-

[7] *Ibid.*, XLII (pt. 3), 1358; XLVI (pt. 2), 1036, 1097, 1121, 1139.
[8] *Ibid.*, XLVII (pt. 2), 1137–38; XLVI (pt. 2), 1031.
[9] K. M. Jones, *Heroines of Dixie*, pp. 168–69; *OR* XLVI (pt. 2), 1096, 1102, 1105, 1114, 1115, 1154, 1164, 1167; XLVII (pt. 2), 1103–4, 1114–15, 1119, 1130–31, 1228.

gress passed a bill creating an official general-in-chief, with the understanding that Lee be assigned the post, and Davis signed it. The bill not only forced Davis to replace Bragg with Lee, it also deprived Bragg of his Richmond staff. At about the same time, Seddon resigned as secretary of war, to be replaced by General John C. Breckinridge, who, for good reason, hated Bragg. Jones reported that Breckinridge required the removal of Northrop, and that "Bragg is also named."[10] Bragg, however, was not removed from command of the forces left in North Carolina—at least not yet.

Lee's appointment created a flurry of excitement among Bragg's Richmond staff as they sought to maintain safe staff positions for themselves. On January 26 Sale reported to Bragg the approval of the bill "creating generalissimo." He pointed out that, as it repealed the law allowing Bragg a Richmond staff, his own and other positions were in jeopardy. He suggested Bragg come to Richmond to take care of turning the office over to Lee. Bragg replied the next day that it was impossible for him to visit the capital and suggested that Sale see Davis and request orders to join Bragg. Sale promptly responded, "I do not know how your presence can be dispensed with. . . . Consultation seems necessary." However, Bragg still insisted that he could not leave Wilmington, but "I wish nothing more than for my personal staff to be re-appointed as General Lee's was, to save them from going out."[11]

By February 2 Sale had convinced Davis that Bragg's presence in Richmond was essential. "President is fully disposed to do all you wish," Sale wrote Bragg. "Your presence would save all and do other good. The President thinks you should come." Bragg now communicated directly with Davis, asking that his staff be sent to him, explaining, "I would prefer seeing you in person on this and other matters, but do not feel authorized to leave here in the present condition of affairs." At the same time he informed

[10] OR, XLVI (pt. 2), 1205; J. B. Jones, *Rebel War Clerk's Diary*, II, 395.
[11] OR, XLVI (pt. 2), 1142, 1153, 1156.

Sale, "Have telegraphed the President. . . . My absence from here now could only be justified by orders." Here, finally, was what Bragg had been angling for all along with his complaints of not being able to leave Wilmington—he wanted orders so as to cover himself when disaster struck, and the ploy worked. On February 9 Bragg received the much-desired order, and he left for Richmond on the tenth. Remaining in the capital a full week, he accomplished at least one thing—Sale received orders to report to Bragg at Wilmington. By the time Sale joined him, however, Wilmington had fallen to the Federals, and they met instead in Goldsboro, North Carolina.[12]

As he traveled back to Wilmington, Bragg wired ahead asking Hoke, in command during Bragg's absence, to advise him of anything important. Upon his arrival, he found that, indeed, something of importance had occurred—the Confederates had withdrawn from Wilmington, and communications to the south had been cut. As he resumed command of the department on February 21, Bragg made it clear he could not be held responsible for the loss of Wilmington. "I find on arrival," he wrote to Lee, "that our forces are driven from the west bank of Cape Fear." Beauregard also received the message from Bragg that the disaster had already occurred "on my arrival." To General L. S. Baker he wired, "Enemy had driven our forces across the river when I arrived." He also asked Baker to see that Elise, who would leave that evening, got off for Raleigh all right.[13]

After Bragg withdrew under the cover of darkness on the morning of February 22, Lee urged him to concentrate his forces and harry the Federals. As Bragg retreated along the Wilmington and Weldon Railroad, he tried to do just that. Headquartering successively at North East, Burgaw, and Teachey's Depot, Bragg issued orders for the destruction of the railroad, authorized the impressment of horses for pickets, and called for temporary volunteers to protect vital shops and services.[14] A week after leaving

[12] Ibid., XLVII (pt. 2), 1083, 1088, 1129, 1138, 1154, 1214, 1216, 1293.
[13] Ibid., 1227, 1241, 1242, 1244, 1245.
[14] Ibid., 1249, 1262, 1263, 1270, 1294–95.

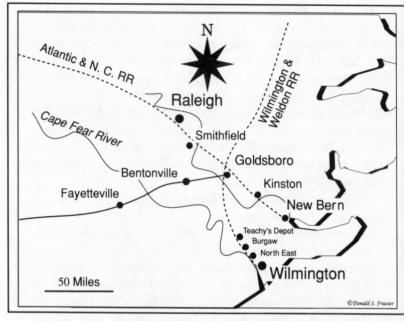

THE NORTH CAROLINA FRONT

Wilmington, Bragg established his headquarters at Goldsboro, the junction of the Wilmington-Weldon Railroad and the Atlantic-North Carolina Railroad running out of the port of New Bern.

In spite of his efforts to deflect blame from himself, Bragg's compatriots would have none of it. Edmondston reported that her husband brought "sad news of inefficiency & bad management on Bragg's part in the evacuation of Wilmington." A rumor of some troops being captured prompted her to remark, "Would that Bragg had been with them."[15]

By now Bragg had lost Fort Fisher, his post as military adviser, most of his staff, and Wilmington. Another blow fell in the form of General Joseph E. Johnston, whom Bragg had had relieved of duty in July 1864. On February 23 Lee, as general-in-chief, assigned Johnston to command the remnants of the Army of Ten-

[15] Edmonston, *Secesh Lady*, p. 672.

nessee, as well as the troops in the Department of South Carolina, Georgia, and Florida. In addition, "Should your operations bring you within reach of the troops under General Bragg . . . of course you will direct their movements." Perhaps nothing else signified Bragg's fall from grace and authority within the Confederacy as poignantly as this humiliation. Rubbing salt into the wound, Johnston immediately applied for the services of Archer Anderson, who had been Bragg's chief adjutant-general since December 25, 1864. Bragg demurred, explaining, "Lieutenant-Colonel Anderson is the only officer of the department on duty with me, and the only one of any field experience now available. When his place can be supplied I will not object to his joining General Johnston. My staff is very deficient," he pointed out, "my aides-de-camp having been legislated out of service." With Sale's arrival, however, Bragg agreed to allow Anderson to report to Johnston.[16]

Bragg could not allow these changes in his position and authority to go unheeded. The full force of his feelings became apparent in a letter to Davis on March 5. As his command had been incorporated within those of Lee and Johnston, "it fairly terminates the temporary command to which you assigned me," he informed the president. "For this and other reasons which present themselves to your mind as forcibly as I could express them, I beg that you will relieve me from the embarrassing position." So anxious was he to get out of this contretemps, he asked for no immediate reassignment. Bragg admitted that "the circumstances constraining me to make this request are painful in the extreme, but I cannot blindly disregard them. You will find many abler servants to fill my place," he assured Davis, "but I feel the country has had none more sincerely devoted."[17]

Davis clearly wished to accommodate his friend. In January congressional representative Thomas Lowndes Snead of Missouri reported that a strong effort was being made on the part of

[16] *OR*, XLVII (pt. 2), 1256–57, 1263, 1274, 1278; XLII (pt. 3), 1305; Archer Anderson to Bragg, February 28, 1865, Bragg Papers, Western Reserve.
[17] *OR*, XLVII (pt. 2), 1328.

Louisianians to replace Kirby Smith with Bragg, but most of the other Trans-Mississippi representatives were violently opposed. Despite the opposition, Davis saw this appointment as a solution to his and Bragg's problem. On March 22 the president wrote a long letter to Lee explaining why he could not rely upon Smith to send troops from west of the Mississippi, citing Smith's consistent failure to carry out, or even acknowledge, orders to cross the river. He believed the only hope of getting any of the Trans-Mississippi troops to the East would be to send a commander "who knows the necessities on this side of the river, and whose views were sufficiently comprehensive to embrace the whole question of defense in the Confederate States." Not surprisingly, in Davis's judgment "General Bragg fulfills the conditions here enumerated."[18] Events, however, precluded the necessity of a decision.

The Federals had not been sitting idly by. After forcing Bragg out of Wilmington, Federal general John Schofield decided that New Bern, with its connection to the Atlantic–North Carolina Railroad, would provide a more viable port of entry for opening a line of communications to Goldsboro, Sherman's anticipated objective for a junction of forces. Keeping one corps at Wilmington, Schofield sent the other steaming toward New Bern under the command of General Jacob Cox.

The sorely pressed Confederates frantically sought measures to repel the enemy, who rapidly diminished the area still to be defended within a pincerlike grip. Suggestions flew back and forth among various commanders regarding when and where who should unite with whom. On March 6 Bragg reported Cox's movement from New Bern toward Goldsboro in heavy force. He urged the enemy be met immediately. "A few hours would suffice to unite the forces at Smithfield with mine & insure a victory," he pressed. Johnston, who had taken command of the North Carolina troops (and Bragg), agreed, ordering troops to Bragg's assistance. Throughout March 7 they moved toward a concentration at Kinston, where Hoke and Bragg impatiently awaited

[18] *Ibid.*, XLVIII (pt. 1), 1321; XLIX (pt. 2), 1140–41.

their arrival. When they finally arrived, Bragg had about 8,000 soldiers to oppose the Federals' 13,000.[19]

At midnight on March 8 Bragg issued his orders for the coming battle. Troops under D. H. Hill would hold the enemy's front on Southwest Creek while Hoke moved to attack his left flank. When Hoke's assault caused the enemy line to waver, Hill was to make a frontal assault. The battle began promisingly. About one mile from the Federal main line Hoke surprised a small post of the enemy, who broke for the rear. Mistaking this retreat for a rout of the whole enemy force, Hoke asked Bragg to send Hill after them. Bragg did so, allowing Hill to go off on a fruitless mission rather than linking up with Hoke to push the enemy farther eastward. Although Hoke's attack netted about 1,000 prisoners, little more was accomplished. Throughout March 9 Bragg searched futilely for another breakthrough point. His dispatches and orders that day indicate his usual battlefield confusion and lack of focus. At 2:15 A.M. he requested reinforcements, later in the day decided he did not need all that had been forwarded, but at 5:45 P.M. changed his mind again. By 8:30 P.M. he informed the Goldsboro quartermaster to "hold ready necessary transportation for transfer of troops *from* Kinston." Sometime during this bewildering day he ordered Hill and Hoke to cooperate in another attack, reminding them, "The attack must be vigorous and determined, as success must be achieved."[20]

But success was not achieved, and at 9:30 A.M. on March 10 Johnston began demanding that the troops return to Goldsboro to aid in repelling Sherman's inland advance. By late afternoon Bragg concurred, and the next day he arrived in Goldsboro, leaving Hoke to arrange a rear guard.[21]

The results at Kinston proved less than hoped, but more than

---

[19] *Ibid.*, XLVII (pt. 2), 1271, 1272, 1279, 1281, 1283, 1292, 1314, 1320, 1339, 1340, 1341, 1342–43, 1346; (pt. 1), 1078; Faust, *Encyclopedia*, p. 418.

[20] *OR*, XLVII (pt. 2), 1350, 1355, 1356, 1359–60; Faust, *Encyclopedia*, pp. 418–19; Foote, *Civil War*, III, 823, author's emphasis. For a fuller discussion of the battle at Kinston, see Connelly, *Autumn of Glory*, p. 524.

[21] *OR*, XLVII (pt. 2), 1363, 1364, 1379.

should have been expected. Historian Thomas Connelly pointed out that, although the battle was "fruitless and wasteful," Bragg had inflicted 1,200 casualties while losing only 200 of his own soldiers. Bragg's contemporaries expected more. "Our joy," insisted Edmondston upon hearing the first news of a victory at Kinston, "is damped by the fact that Bragg is Com in Cheif [*sic*]. Some contre temps will be sure to happen & some how or other we will lose the fruit of a victory gained by him." A few days later she wailed, "As I feared, Bragg's evil genius is in the ascendant!" A Union artillery major had heard that Bragg reported Kinston a Confederate victory, but soon learned otherwise. "It is a query," he remarked, "whether Bragg lies to Davis officially, or whether these dispatches are only intended for the people, 'to fire the Southern heart.'"[22]

Johnston instructed Bragg to remain in Goldsboro until Sherman's route of advance from Fayetteville could be determined, but on March 13 he changed his mind and ordered Bragg to transfer his command to a more centralized position at Smithfield. When he got there on March 14, Bragg took command of all the troops in the vicinity, but by the eighteenth Johnston arrived and took over. Sherman had divided his force after marching through Fayetteville, and Johnston now determined to strike the wing proceeding on the single road from Fayetteville to Goldsboro via Bentonville, at a point just south of the village of Bentonville where the road bisected a patch of dense woodland and thickets. Johnston laid his plans carefully and skillfully. Bragg's troops constituted the left wing, with its line astride the Goldsboro Road; Hardee (when he arrived) would form the center; A. P. Stewart extended Hardee's line, with Wade Hampton's cavalry at the farthest extension to Stewart's line. Most of the Confederate line lay parallel to the Goldsboro Road in the hopes of utterly surprising and routing the Federals with a broadside attack.[23]

---

[22] Connelly, *Autumn of Glory*, p. 524; Edmondston, *Secesh Lady*, pp. 676–77; Thomas Osborne, *The Fiery Trail: A Union Officer's Account of Sherman's Last Campaigns*, ed. Richard Harwell and Philip N. Racine (Knoxville, 1986), p. 186.
[23] *OR*, XLVII (pt. 2), 1377, 1388, 1389, 1394, 1397; Connelly, *Autumn of Glory*,

Unfortunately for the Confederates, the battle did not proceed according to plan. The trouble began when the Federals arrived before Hardee did. Bragg's forces managed to throw them back, but from then on Johnston's carefully laid plans went awry. Bragg appealed for reinforcements, and as the lead units of Hardee's troops arrived, Johnston diverted them to Bragg rather than to the position originally reserved for them. With Hardee's remaining soldiers finally in place by midafternoon, the battle continued. Hardee and Stewart attacked the Union left flank with some success, but Bragg, instructed to advance against the center in concert with them, failed to move out promptly. He delayed so long that the original drive by Hardee and Stewart had already lost its momentum. When Bragg did belatedly advance, his troops suffered heavy casualties in unsuccessful charges against the Federal log barricades. Hardee, too, blundered by further dividing his force and ordering some of his troops to make repeated attacks upon an entire Union corps. Connelly places the blame for the failure at Bentonville squarely upon Hardee's and Bragg's delays, panics, and blunders.[24]

It is difficult to believe that any of the Confederate participants had harbored expectations of a brilliant victory at Bentonville, or even sincerely hoped to much delay the enemy. "Of course," Hampton contended, "General Johnston's only object in making this fight was to cripple the enemy and impede his advance." It did not even accomplish that for long. After hanging around for two more days in hopes of retrieving something of value from the disaster, Johnston withdrew under cover of darkness toward Smithfield. By then Goldsboro had been evacuated by the Confederates and occupied by a large Federal force.[25]

News reached Richmond on March 21 that Johnston had checked one of the Federal columns. Jones found this "a great

---

p. 526. For a fuller discussion of the battle at Bentonville, see Connelly, *Autumn of Glory*, pp. 526–29.

[24] Connelly, *Autumn of Glory*, p. 527; B. Davis, *Sherman's March*, p. 236.

[25] Wade Hampton, "The Battle of Bentonville," in *Battles and Leaders*, IV, 705; OR, XLVII (pt. 2), 1453.

relief—more as an indication of what is to follow, than for what is accomplished." He apparently believed that since "Sherman has three [Confederate] full generals in his front," it was just a matter of time before all this talent crushed the invader. This array of brass, however, may have contributed to the disarray of the Confederate forces and plans. One of the few things that Johnston, Hardee, and Bragg agreed on was their thorough dislike, distrust, and jealousy for one another. A more disagreeable trio could hardly be found throughout the Confederate command, and now they were expected to work together in a last-ditch effort to save the rapidly diminishing Southern nation. Jones concluded his diary entry, "A few days more will decide [Sherman's] fate—for immortality or destruction."[26] His belief that the remotest possibility existed that Sherman could be destroyed reveals much about the feeble grasp on reality current in the capital.

The war was rapidly drawing to a close. On March 25 Bragg established his headquarters at Raleigh, from which he sent and received messages regarding possible, although ultimately futile, efforts to protect the few bits left of the Confederacy. With little else to do, he again complained to Davis about the embarrassment of his position. "Finding myself with nothing but a small division in the field," he groused, "and virtually ignored in regard to that, . . . I asked and was allowed to turn over Hoke's division to him." In a snit, he continued, "I have retired to this point where I have nothing to do but mourn over the sad spectacle hourly presented of disorganization, demoralization, and destruction." He reported many stragglers "living at free quarters on the people. It is a most sad and humiliating picture. Officers seem paralyzed, men indifferent to everything but plunder, and the people, as they well may," he admitted, "appear disgusted and dismayed. This state of things cannot last," he declared, "and no one is so blind as not to see the inevitable result." Little did he realize that Davis did indeed remain "so blind" and would continue so for some time. Bragg pointed out that the troops facing Sherman numbered only

[26] J. B. Jones, *Rebel War Clerk's Diary*, II, 455.

"12,000 effectives, as they are erroneously called." In all, "With no duty to perform, I shall remain quietly here awaiting events, and fall back toward the south as necessity may require. My position is both mortifying and humiliating," he lamented, "but the example of your more trying one warns me to bear it with resignation." In closing he warned the president, "You should not permit yourself to hope . . . for any result here, and in your movements, official and personal, you should be governed accordingly." Bragg, understanding what had to take place in a very near future, thus warned his president and friend to consider possible escape routes from Richmond, perhaps even from a soon-to-be-defeated South.[27]

Davis replied on April 1, just hours before the evacuation of Richmond, in a letter that revealed the extent of his disconnection from reality. "Our condition," he asserted, "is that in which great generals have shown their value to a struggling State. Boldness of conception and rapidity of execution have often rendered the smaller force victorious." So narrow had his view become that he declared that if the army in Virginia could be fed, "the problem would be, even in the worst view of it, one of easy solution." He assured Bragg that because of their long and pleasant association, "I have desired to see you employed in a position suited to your rank and equal to your ability." However, he stated, "I do not desire to subject you to unfair opposition, when failure may be produced by it, and will not fail on the first fitting occasion to call for your aid in the perilous task which lies before us."[28]

Davis very likely continued to consider the Trans-Mississippi as the place for Bragg, and for himself in the unlikely event that the government was forced out of Richmond. The president had apparently discussed these possibilities with his wife. A week after fleeing Richmond, Varina Howell Davis suggested to her husband that it appeared the Trans-Mississippi would be their

[27] OR, XLVII (pt. 3), 686, 694, 697, 702, 703, 711, 717, 722, 723, 730, 739, 754; LIII, 415–16.
[28] Ibid., XLVII (pt. 3), 740.

ultimate destination. "Though I know you do not like my interference," she wrote, "let me entreat you not to send B. B. to command there. I am satisfied that the country will be ruined by its
internecine feuds if you do so. . . . If I am intrusive," she apologized, "forgive me for the sake of the love which impels me [,] but
pray long and fervently before you decide to do it."[29]

Varina need not have worried. Davis no longer had the power,
nor the Confederacy the resources or the will, to continue the
fight for independence. By the end of December 1864 the Confederate armies held fewer than 50 percent of those on their rolls,
with only 196,016 out of 400,787 present for duty. By April 1865
the percentage fell even lower, the figures showing only 160,198
out of 358,692. In those few months, the Confederates had not
only lost over 40,000 troops, but those remaining were deserting
or reporting ill at a higher rate than ever. To some people the
result seemed obvious. One Southerner explained to his sister
that "i hev conkludid that the dam fulishness uv tryin to lick shur-
min Had better be stoped. we hav bin gettin nuthin but hell &
lots uv it ever since we saw the dam yankys & i am tirde uv it. . . .
and its no use tryin to whip em. . . . the dam yankees [are] . . .
thicker an lise on a hen and a dam site ornraier."[30]

Field soldiers appeared more aware of what was happening than
did Richmond's inhabitants. A visitor to the capital reported that,
even as its government crammed the trains with loot and archives,
Richmonders believed their city could not fall to the enemy, having "erected for themselves a fancied invincibility for the City,"
and they seemed to think "Heaven will interfere." A Federal believed he knew the cause of the Confederates' failure to acknowledge the truth. "It is evident now that the boss Rebels made some
very important miscalculations in going to war," he explained.
"They overestimated their powers and underestimated ours. Pride

[29] Varina Howell Davis to Jefferson Davis, April 7, 1865, Edwin M. Stanton
Papers, Library of Congress.
[30] *OR*, Series 4, III, 989, 1182; Spenser Glasgow Welch, *A Confederate Surgeon's
Letters to His Wife* (Marietta, Ga., 1954; orig. ed., 1911), p. 121.

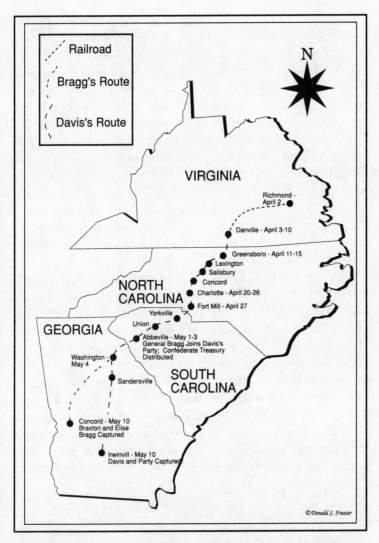

Railroad

Bragg's Route

Davis's Route

N

VIRGINIA

Richmond - April 2

Danville - April 3-10

Greensboro - April 11-15
Lexington
Salisbury
Concord

NORTH
CAROLINA

Charlotte - April 20-26
Fort Mill - April 27

Yorkville

GEORGIA

Union

Abbeville - May 1-3
General Bragg Joins Davis's
Party; Confederate Treasury
Distributed

Washington -
May 4

SOUTH
CAROLINA

Sandersville

Concord - May 10
Braxton and Elise
Bragg Captured

Irwinvill - May 10
Davis and Party Captured

©Donald S. Frazier

FLIGHT AND CAPTURE OF CONFEDERATE GOVERNMENT

now prevents them from admitting it. To cave in after such blood-curdling vows and execrations will be doubly humiliating."[31]

The Confederate government, led by Davis, left Richmond on April 2, leading an itinerant existence as it plunged deeper and deeper into the Carolinas, attempting to elude its pursuers and reach the Trans-Mississippi. Bragg did not catch up with Davis for a month, finally joining the much-depleted party near Abbeville, South Carolina, on May 1. He came just in time to see the final breakup of the party and to distribute the money left in the Confederate treasury. He also used his influence to force Davis to acknowledge the fact of defeat. On May 4 in Washington, Georgia, Davis held his last cabinet meeting, with Bragg in attendance, at which he finally accepted the inevitable. Bragg and Elise left the president's party the next day as Davis and a small cavalry escort rode toward capture.[32]

After leaving Davis, Bragg and Elise traveled west with a small party of two staff officers, a black servant, three wagons, and an ambulance. On May 10 the Fifteenth Pennsylvania Volunteer Cavalry caught up with them near Concord, Georgia. The officer in charge, Lieutenant Samuel Phillips, paroled Bragg on the spot. While the two men discussed the parole, some of the cavalry troopers searched the belongings of the party. When they opened Elise's trunk, "She opened her batteries by reminding us who we were, and said that she had never been so insulted in all her life as to have her effects searched by a set of Yankee hirelings." Another Federal reported that Elise "was not altogether amiable. She scolded our men and applied all sorts of epithets to them, but the

[31] Thomas Conolly, *An Irishman in Dixie: Thomas Conolly's Diary of the Fall of the Confederacy*, ed. Nelson D. Lankford (Columbia, S.C., 1988), p. 83; John Haley, *The Rebel Yell and the Yankee Hurrah: The Civil War Journal of a Maine Volunteer*, ed. Ruth L. Silliker (Camden, Maine, 1985), p. 237.

[32] Basil W. Duke, "Last Days of the Confederacy," in *Battles and Leaders*, IV, 764–66; W. C. Davis, *Breckinridge*, pp. 519–20, 522; Burke Davis, *The Long Surrender* (New York, 1985), pp. 106, 126; K. M. Jones, *Heroines*, p. 234; Mrs. J. J. Robertson, "Reminiscences of Jefferson Davis's Visit to Washington, Georgia, in 1865," (1902), Last Cabinet Chapter, United Daughters of the Confederacy, Washington, Georgia; *Southern Historical Society Papers*, XXXIX (1911), 24–25; *ibid.*, X (1882), 141; *Confederate Veteran*, XXV (1917), 258–59.

principal burden of her song was the disgrace of having been captured by a Philadelphia fireman." This may have been a ploy on
her part, as "while she was giving vent to her eloquence she was at
the same time tearing up a letter of dispatch into very small
pieces, and by the time her tirade was exhausted the ground was
covered with small bits of paper." A corporal escorting the Bragg
party to Federal general James H. Wilson found Bragg "pleasant
company, but reserved and very much of a gentleman." Elise "had
nothing to say . . . she had expressed her opinion to the Yanks an
hour before."[33]

It is unclear just how far the escort should have accompanied
the Braggs. Some people claimed that he was to report to General
James H. Wilson in Macon, but on May 19 Wilson declared he
had heard nothing of him. A week later Union soldiers remained
on the lookout for him, and a unit in Montgomery, Alabama, was
alerted to arrest him if possible, as he had failed to report as promised. Long after the war Wilson denied that he expected to see
Bragg at his headquarters. Upon hearing of the arrest, Wilson
contended, "I sent word to him he could go on home, provided he
would remain there on his parole of honor to abstain from all acts
of hostility to the United States."[34]

The final year of the war had not improved Bragg's visage or
image. One observer during the final days reported that "his
shaggy eyebrows and piercing eyes made him look like a much
greater man than he ever proved himself to be," while a Georgia
woman found him the ugliest man in the Confederacy, declaring
that "he looks just like an old porcupine." Her opinion, however,
may have been prejudiced, for she admitted, "I never was a special
admirer of his." Mary Chesnut reported overhearing attacks on
the leaders and government of the Confederacy. Although she left
the room, she could still hear "loud screams of vituperation and

---

[33] Bragg, Parole, May 10, 1865, Braxton Bragg Papers, Chicago Historical Society; Suzanne Colton Wilson, *Column South: With the Fifteenth Pennsylvania Cavalry from Antietam to the Capture of Jefferson Davis* (Flagstaff, Ariz., 1960),
pp. 308–10.
[34] *OR*, XLIX (pt. 2), 840, 894; Seitz, *Bragg*, p. 542.

insult; 'Jeff Davis's stupidity, . . . Bragg's insanity.'" During a train journey Kate Cumming, who had nursed many of Bragg's Army of Tennessee soldiers, remarked that a friend of hers "believed General Bragg was one of our best generals; and a gentleman answered, that my friend must be deranged."[35]

Elise, though, appears to have preserved her looks throughout the four years of worry and turmoil. One of her captors found her "good looking, had black hair and eyes; in fact, a perfect type of a Southern brunette"[36]—gracious words from one whom she had so thoroughly abused.

Peace settled heavily upon Braxton and Elise. In late 1862 their plantation, Bivouac, now called Greenwood, located near Thibodaux, Louisiana, had been confiscated by the Federal army. For a time it served as the Bragg Home Colony for Freedmen under the auspices of the Freedmen's Bureau, until January 3, 1866, when it was sold at the Merchant's and Auctioneer's Exchange in New Orleans. "I am living almost out of the world," Bragg explained to a friend, "without mental or social occupation, and struggling hard for a subsistence, after the complete wreck of my future." He compared his situation with that of the defunct Confederacy, declaring that "now, as in our lost cause, I shall never despair as long as a ray of hope is left."[37]

Braxton and Elise settled down on his brother's plantation in Lowndesboro, Alabama. Here they lived in the former overseer's cabin, in which "by moving about [one] can find a dry spot when it rains," while Bragg supervised "thirty demoralized Negroes

[35] John S. Wise, *The End of an Era* (New York, 1899), p. 415; Eliza Francis Andrews, *The War-Time Journal of a Georgia Girl, 1864–1865* (New York, 1908), p. 206; Chesnut, *Civil War*, p. 812; Cumming, *Kate*, p. 198.

[36] S. C. Wilson, *Column South*, p. 310.

[37] *Richmond Daily Dispatch*, December 27, 1862; *Confederate Veteran*, IV (1896), 102; Bragg to William T. Sherman, January 25, 1867, David F. Boyd Papers, Walter L. Fleming Collection, Louisiana State University Archives; Edgar L. Erickson, ed., "With Grant at Vicksburg: From the Civil War Diary of Captain Charles E. Wilcox," *Journal of the Illinois State Historical Society*, XXX (1938), 443–44; Conveyance Record, 1808–1920, vol. 9, 548–52, Lafourche Parish Court House, Thibodaux, Louisiana; Bragg to unknown, n.d., Jones Papers.

trying to make cotton." He complained of "finding that *all*, *all* was lost, except my debts, and that not even *sympathy* much less assistance was extended to me." This lack of sympathy pained him. He thought his lot particularly difficult, as others "did not fall so far." He did acknowledge that perhaps Davis and a few others, imprisoned by the U.S. authorities, were experiencing hardship, but they at least "are receiving the support which sympathy and condolence always give." He lamented the lack of "food for the mind. . . . To cultivated minds, a life without books, papers, or society is next to purgatory." They lacked more than literature: "Not a human being has ever called to see us."[38]

Unhappy in seclusion, Bragg soon left Alabama for hopefully greener pastures and congenial society, but his propensity for controversy continued to plague him. In January 1867 the New Orleans, Opelousas, and Great Western Railroad seemed willing to hire him if he could use his influence to improve its financial status. But the job did not last, and in August 1867 Bragg became superintendent of the New Orleans waterworks, only to be "superseded upon the accession of reconstructionists to power by a colored man." In late 1869 his old friend Jefferson Davis came to his rescue, offering him a job as district agent in the Carolina Life Insurance Company, of which Davis was president. Although Bragg seemed pleased to be remembered by Davis and he accepted the job, within four months he again became restless, confessing that "this life Insurance business is not suited to my taste and, what is more important, does not pay."[39]

By April 1870 Bragg considered trying his fortunes in Egypt. In response to an inquiry about his going there as a commander in

[38] Bragg to P. W. Alexander, December 10, 1865, P. W. Alexander Papers; Bragg to W. H. Walter, April 8, 1866, Walter Papers.
[39] Bragg to William T. Sherman, January 25, 1867, Boyd Papers; Snow, *Lee and His Generals*, p. 360; Orville Hickman Browning, *The Diary of Orville Hickman Browning*, ed. Theodore Calvin Pease and James G. Randall (2 vols., Springfield, Ill., 1925), II, 124; Stout, *Reminiscences*, p. 19; Bragg to Jefferson Davis, December 1, 1869, Letterbook, December, 1869–January, 1871, Bragg Papers, Rosenberg Library; Bragg to D. W. Adams, April 12, 1870, Confederate Personnel, Louisiana Historical Association Collection.

the viceroy's army, Bragg admitted that his inability to speak and write French held him back. However, he had contemplated a move to Egypt for a different purpose. He regarded Egypt as a field of opportunity: the soil and climate, he pointed out, were ideal for growing cotton and sugar, and with the "introduction of Scientific cultivation, with machinery for labor saving and preparing the crops," Egypt would soon control the European markets for those products.[40]

Despite his excitement about the future of Egypt, Bragg remained in his homeland, his contentiousness continuing to color everything he did. In August 1871 the city of Mobile employed him to improve the river, harbor, and bay, a job he lost through disagreement with a "combination of capitalists." In November 1873 he had become so desperate that he began to look "outside of these conquered provinces," inquiring of an acquaintance in St. Louis about the prospects of employment. This, too, failed to provide anything.[41]

In 1874 Bragg decided to try his luck in Texas, where his career ran no more smoothly than it had elsewhere. In July 1874 the Gulf, Colorado, and Santa Fe Railroad appointed him chief engineer. For the next several months Bragg worked hard and accomplished much, but in April 1875 he became embroiled in a controversy with the company's directors. Bragg later wrote that although he should have been receiving $400 per month, he had been paid irregularly "for want of funds." He contended that during discussions in April with a committee of the company's directors the question of his salary came up. Bragg explained that he had declined asking for it in the past as he knew the company "had no money," and that the railroad owed him $1,600. He told the committee he was willing to take $500 in cash and some shares of stock in lieu of the $1,600. On May 5 the secretary of the company

[40] Bragg to Adams, April 12, 1870, Confederate Personnel, Louisiana Historical Association Collection.

[41] Stout, *Reminiscences*, p. 19; Bragg to D. M. Frost, November 12, 1873, Richard Graham Papers, Frost Collection, Missouri Historical Society; Dunbar Bragg to Bragg, July 24, 1872, Bragg Papers, Rosenberg Library.

called at Bragg's office with a check for $500 and a receipt, which
Bragg signed "without examination, never doubting the integrity
of the Committee's action." A few days later, when Bragg inquired
of the secretary about his shares of stock, he was told, "You are
not a stockholder, never having subscribed, and you have never
been called on or paid any installment." The committee, Bragg
complained, had "simply reported to the Board in favor of paying
me $500 in full for past services," and, the secretary told him,
"even that amount had been objected to." The receipt Bragg had
signed stated that he accepted the $500 as full payment for past
services. Bragg promptly replied that the receipt was "a fraud
fraudulently obtained, and would be disputed," and he immediately hired an attorney.[42]

Although this caused a breach in his relationship with the company, Bragg did not leave at once. It was not until June 5 that he
informed the company's president that there seemed to be a "want
of confidence in the proceedings" of the company. "If my withdrawal as Chief Engineer will produce more concert of action," he
wrote, "I beg the Board of Directors will designate some one to
relieve me in the duties of this office." Bragg had used this same
ploy, a sort of calling for a vote of confidence from his superiors,
during the Civil War—successfully on some occasions, disas-
trously on one memorable occasion. This proved to be another
unsuccessful attempt. In a second letter written later the same
day, Bragg offered to work at a "much lower rate, even, than you
have assigned to my successor," and he threatened to expose what
he considered some wrongdoing on the part of the company.
Bragg's appeal and threat went for naught; the directors accepted
his resignation. But that did not end his association with the railroad. Within a year, having been appointed inspector of railroads
for the state of Texas, Bragg examined the roadbed of the Gulf,
Colorado, and Santa Fe. If Bragg hoped to grab a measure of
revenge through this assignment, he was sadly disappointed; he

[42] Bragg to H. Rosenberg, June 5, 1875, Bragg Papers, Western Reserve; Braxton Bragg, "Memo: Bragg in Santa Fe R[ail]w[ay] Co.," Bragg Papers, Western
Reserve.

had to report the construction as satisfactory.[43] Bragg held the post of railroad inspector for the remaining few months of his life.

During the postwar years Bragg kept in touch with old comrades, sometimes contributing to controversies that no longer mattered, at other times exchanging news and complaints. One letter in particular pleased him. E. T. Sykes informed Bragg that Sale had named his son Braxton Bragg. Bragg remarked, perhaps only half jesting, about the child's "fate . . . —it may be his misfortune—to bear my name." In addition to keeping in touch with friends, Bragg aided in the founding of the Southern Historical Society in New Orleans in 1868, chairing the initial meeting. The society's purpose was to provide a platform for the airing of information regarding all aspects of the recent war, and Bragg proved a valuable member. He served first as vice president of the new organization, then as president, and he actively solicited material for the society's publication, the *Southern Historical Society Papers*.[44]

Although Bragg seemed anxious to have the South's story told by Southerners, he appeared reluctant to write his own story. He confessed to P. W. Alexander that he "could not be impartial," but to another correspondent he declared, "*I dare not tell the truth, and I dare not tell lies.*" As to accepting an offer from a New York firm, he avowed he would not do business with a concern that "acted for the Atrocious Sherman & Beast Butler."[45]

---

[43] Bragg, Letter Book, April 1874–September 1876, 13, Bragg Papers, Rosenberg Library; Richard Coke to Bragg, June 29, 1876, Bragg Papers, Western Reserve.

[44] C. B. Richardson to Bragg, October 23, 1865; Bragg to P. W. Alexander, December 10, 1865, P. W. Alexander Papers; Bragg to Walter, April 8, 1866, Walter Papers, Southern Historical Collection; Bragg to D. W. Adams, April 12, 1870, Confederate Personnel, Louisiana Historical Association Collection; Bragg to E. T. Sykes, February 8, 1873, Southern Historical Society Collection; Bragg to William Preston Johnston, July 5, 1873, Albert Sidney and William Preston Johnston Papers, Barret Collection, Louisiana Historical Association Collection; E. T. Sykes to Bragg, January 25, 1873; Bragg to E. T. Sykes, February 8, 1873, Southern Historical Society Collection; *Southern Historical Society Papers*, XVIII (1890), 349–55; Frank E. Vandiver, *Ploughshares into Swords: Josiah Gorgas and Confederate Ordnance* (Austin, Tex., 1952), p. 293.

[45] Bragg to Alexander, December 10, 1865, P. W. Alexander Papers; Bragg to My dear Major, February 18, 1873, Southern Historical Society Collection.

To the end of his life Bragg remained bitter, with characteristic impartiality, toward both Confederates and Federals. He explained to one correspondent that he knew the Southern cause was lost "from the moment I saw the government go into the hands of our *old, trading politicians and demogogues*," particularly those in the War Department. Regarding the North, he asserted, "The war is over, but there is no peace, and never can be between two such people." As Reconstruction proceeded, he became more vociferous, castigating parties on all sides. Reporting the recent adjournment of the "Semi-Negro, Semi-Military legislature with which we are cursed," Bragg remarked that "our people have not only submitted to these outrages, but seem to have welcomed them." Five years later he declared that Egypt offered a more congenial atmosphere than the South, as it "is ruled by an enlightened and honorable chief from whom may be expected the freedom and justice long withheld from our people."[46]

At 9:00 A.M. on September 27, 1876, while walking with L. E. Trezevant from the Galveston Custom House, Post Office, and U.S. Court building to their business office, Bragg leaned against his companion and then fell "at full length in the street . . . without uttering a word." Within fifteen minutes he was pronounced dead. From the circumstances of his death and from the impaired memory, headache, and tendency to sleep described by Elise, a physician who had treated Bragg for several years believed Bragg had "died by the brain," probably due to the degeneration of his cerebral blood vessels. Ironically, after creating so much controversy and turmoil during his lifetime, Braxton Bragg died quietly and with a minimum of fuss at the age of fifty-nine. Galveston paid its respects in the grand manner that Bragg deserved and would have appreciated. A steamer then carried his remains to Mobile, where he was interred in Magnolia Cemetery with "grand

[46] Bragg to Walter, April 8, 1866, Walter Papers, Southern Historical Collection; Bragg to Alexander, December 10, 1865, P. W. Alexander Papers; Bragg to General D. W. Adams, April 12, 1870; Bragg to Dr. D. W. Adams, June 25, 1875, Confederate Personnel, Louisiana Historical Association Collection.

civic and military honors." Elise did not join him there until 1908, surviving him for thirty-two years.[47]

Bragg's death saved him from a final ignominy at the hands of the U.S. government. In 1881 Congress refused an appropriation to purchase his papers.[48]

[47] *Galveston Weekly News*, October 2, 1876; Dr. Hanford E. Chaille to Elise Bragg, November 22, 1876, Bragg Papers, Western Reserve; *Galveston Daily News*, September 28, 1876; *New Orleans Daily Picayune*, September 29, 1876; *Marion* (Alabama) *Commonwealth*, October 5, 1876; *New Orleans Times-Democrat*, September 26, 1908.

[48] W. T. Walthall to Marcus J. Wright, February 9, 1881; William Preston Johnston to Wright, March 3, 1881; Elise to Wright, March 12, 1881; Elise to Wright, July 5, 1881, Wright Papers.

CHAPTER XIV

Determined devotion

Braxton Bragg and Confederate Defeat

B RAXTON BRAGG is unique in his Civil War experiences. Throughout the four years of the Confederacy's existence,
no other prominent person held such a range of positions and
responsibilities. In charge of Gulf Coast fortifications at the start
of the war, Bragg later served as a corps commander and chief of
staff in the Army of Tennessee before moving up to command the
army, a post he held longer than anyone else. With his 1864 appointment as Jefferson Davis's military adviser, Bragg became one
of only two Southerners assigned the duties of general-in-chief.
By the time the war wound down, Bragg once again found himself in the field and, once again, in a subordinate position.
Throughout this cycle of service Bragg contributed much to the
Confederate cause and to Confederate defeat; indeed, he epito-
mized several factors that contributed to the inability of Southerners to establish their independence, either through his own
activities or characteristics, or through the people and events im-
pacting upon him.

Students of war have compiled various lists of the traits a successful commander must possess. high intelligence, intuition,
determination, and physical and moral courage rank high on these
lists. If events during battle conspire to convince a commander
that a wrong decision has been made, he must have the courage
and the determination to uphold his convictions. In addition, a
commander's role consists of two important facets: the mainte-
nance of group solidarity and the coordination of operations.[1]

[1] Howard, *Clausewitz*, p. 32; Gwynne Dyer, *War* (New York, 1985), p. 136;
Wendell J. Coats, *Armed Force as Power: The Theory of War Reconsidered* (New York,
1966), pp. 157–58; Hajo Holborn, "The Prusso-German School: Moltke and the

Bragg met some of these criteria admirably and competently. He clearly displayed intelligence and determination in his services to the Confederacy. His administrative skills, when properly focused, proved admirable. Although many paid lip-service to co-operation and concentration of force, Bragg unhesitatingly sent troops to other commanders whenever necessary. He drove him-self in pursuit of perfection for his soldiers, sometimes perform-ing too many duties himself that should have been delegated to staff officers. General Manigault declared that Bragg was full of energy, an indefatigable worker, and a firm and impartial admin-istrator. He believed that the army under Bragg's command at-tained its highest state of efficiency. Indeed, Bragg achieved greater successes with the Army of Tennessee than did any other Western general.[2]

But Bragg also proved seriously wanting in several qualities. His abilities in organizing and disciplining leave no doubt that Bragg possessed a good mind, but it failed to enable him to achieve success on the battlefield, the real testing ground of an army commander. One contemporary described him as "routine in intellect rather than operative," while another "doubted that he had a mind fitted to his tasks." E. P. Alexander, Longstreet's artil-lery chief, accused Bragg of being "simply muddle headed," to the point where he could not even understand a map. Bragg also lacked imagination, a serious drawback that caused inflexibility during crises. This rigidness and lack of imagination led him to turn to others to help him out of battlefield dilemmas. "In a word," charged a subordinate, "he was no tactician to execute his own strategic combinations." Part of his problem came from his habit of calling a council of war to help him alter plans on the spur of the moment, often following the advice of others when he clearly would have, or should have, decided otherwise. So pro-

---

Rise of the General Staff," in *Makers of Modern Strategy from Machiavelli to the Nu-clear Age*, ed. Peter Paret (Princeton, N.J., 1986), p. 290.

[2] McWhiney, *Bragg*, pp. 176–77, 198–202, 180–81, 266, 178–79, 279–80; Manigault, *A Carolinian*, p. 158; Connelly, *Autumn of Glory*, p. 278.

nounced was this habit that Buckner charged that Bragg would "lean upon the advice of a drummer boy." And, most damning of all, Bragg failed to learn from his mistakes.[3]

Bragg's most serious shortcoming may have been his inability to establish and maintain group solidarity within the army. This defect had not been a problem when Bragg held a small command. During his months at Pensacola early in the war, Bragg established a close relationship with his army, creating long-lasting and loyal friendships. His command of the Army of Tennessee, however, failed to instill the same feelings within the army or among his subordinates. Although many of his soldiers respected their commander and most followed and obeyed him, they did not feel warmth for or from him. Widely admired for his ability to discipline an army, Bragg at times seemed to go beyond the bounds of reason and necessity in his efforts to instill professional standards in volunteer troops, even to the point of tyranny. Bragg's harshness may have been prompted by fears of his own inadequacy.[4] His unreasonable efforts to discipline and organize his soldiers may have provided him some measure of comfort as a way of making up for his inadequacies on the battlefield.

With his subordinate officers, Bragg fared even worse—they failed even to follow and obey. One subordinate reported, with fine understatement, "Bragg was not well supported by his generals, on whom he had every reason to rely." Commenting on this idea, a student of the Civil War asserted that it is important for commanders to know the people under them, to understand how they think, and to recognize who can be trusted and who needs to be guarded against. Bragg failed in this respect, leaving himself vulnerable to his subordinates through his neglect to appreciate their own personalities and ambitions. Liddell asserted that Bragg

[3] Liddell, *Record*, p. 150; Polk, *Leonidas Polk*, II, 308; E. P. Alexander, Manuscript, E. P. Alexander Papers; Archer Jones, *Confederate Strategy from Shiloh to Vicksburg* (Baton Rouge, 1961), p. 108; Richard O'Connor, *Thomas: Rock of Chickamauga* (New York, 1948), p. 26; *Nashville Banner*, December 4, 1909; McWhiney, *Bragg*, pp. 240, 251, 390–91.

[4] McWhiney, *Bragg*, pp. 185–86, 192–94; *Southern Historical Society Papers*, XXXIX (1911); Hagerman, *Origins*, p. 68; Putnam, *Richmond*, p. 260.

was a poor judge of character, and Mackall maintained that Bragg did not know his friends from his enemies, taking subserviency as a sign of friendship. "Bragg could handle an army command," one critic stated, "but he couldn't handle the individuals in his command." This evaluation seems to sum Bragg up succinctly—he could manage everything but people.[5]

Liddell also asserted, "No man needed friends more than Bragg," attributing it to Bragg's manner, which created "malignant enemies and indifferent, callous friends." But it was difficult to be a friend to Bragg. He seemed to decide early on whether a person was worthy of his friendship, apparently determined by the degree to which people humbled themselves before him. Liddell testified that with Bragg, neither service, enterprise, nor zeal counted for much—only favoritism led to credit and promotion. Bragg also delighted in punishing those who were not his favorites. One of Kate Cumming's patients confided to her that Bragg had taken a personal dislike to him and thus tried to "annoy him in every possible way."[6] Indeed, Bragg's personality was perhaps his greatest shortcoming.

Another important factor in the makeup of a successful general is the health of the individual; Bragg's was appalling. Migraine headaches, dyspepsia, boils, and rheumatism headed the list of his complaints and infirmities. He proved particularly vulnerable to illness during periods of stress, indicating that much of his frailness may have been psychosomatic (which is not to be confused with hypochondria). Psychosomatic illnesses are very real and debilitating, often brought on by difficult, intolerable, or frightening situations, of which Bragg faced many during the war years. By early 1863 he appeared so debilitated that biographer Grady McWhiney asserted that Bragg "had lost touch with reality."[7]

[5] Liddell, *Record*, pp. 98, 117; William W. Mackall to My dearest Mimi, October 5, 1863, Mackall Papers; Barrie Almond to author, May 10, 1988; McWhiney, *Bragg*, pp. 327–28, 383–84.
[6] Liddell, *Record*, p. 106; Cumming, *Kate*, p. 103.
[7] McWhiney, *Bragg*, pp. 179, 294–95, 388–89; Steven Stowe to author, July 18, 1985; Oliver Sacks, *Migraine: Understanding a Common Disorder* (Berkeley,

To relieve his many and varied symptoms, Bragg turned to the popular remedies of the day. A particularly nasty and dangerous staple in the medicine chest was calomel, a mercurial purgative, which in the intestines breaks down into highly poisonous components. Continued use caused severe gastrointestinal irritation (Bragg's dyspepsia?) and central nervous system symptoms of lethargy or restlessness. To make matters worse, antebellum Southern doctors maintained that the dosages of calomel needed to be large, often twice as large as that administered in the North, to arouse therapeutically the "torpid livers" of Southerners, which were subjected to "continued excitement" by the climate. Bragg indeed admitted to a friend in 1855 that every summer he suffered from his "old Florida complaint of the *liver*" (most likely a side effect of malaria), and declared, "I can now only keep about by almost living on Mercury (Blue Mass & Calomel)." And he was right when he stated, "No constitution can stand it."[8]

Americans also indulged themselves in opiates to deal with pain and illness. With few effective therapeutic techniques, physicians routinely dispensed opium to their patients for its analgesic and tranquilizing properties. It is unclear whether or not Bragg indulged in this palliative; if he did not, he was unusual for his place and time, as Southerners had the highest rate of addiction in the country—perhaps one of the highest in the world. One historian

Calif., 1985), p. 186; Edward Weiss and O. Apurgeon English, *Psychosomatic Medicine: The Clinical Application of Psychopathology to General Medical Problems* (Philadelphia, 1943), pp. 8–10.

[8] Guenter B. Risse, Ronald L. Numbers, and Judith Walzer Leavitt, eds., *Medicine without Doctors: Home Health Care in American History* (New York, 1977), p. 98; William G. Rothstein, *American Physicians in the Nineteenth Century: From Sects to Science* (Baltimore, 1972), pp. 49–52; James Harvey Young, *The Toadstool Millionaries: A Social History of Patent Medicines in America before Federal Regulation* (Princeton, N.J., 1972), pp. 61–65; John Harley Warner, "The Idea of Southern Medical Distinctiveness," in *Sickness and Health in America: Readings in the History of Medicine and Public Health*, ed. Judith Walzer Leavitt and Ronald L. Numbers (Madison, Wis., 1978), p. 54; John Harley Warner, *The Therapeutic Perspective: Medical Practice, Knowledge, and Identity in America, 1820–1885* (Cambridge, Mass., 1986), p. 71; Stewart Brooks, *Civil War Medicine* (Springfield, Ill., 1966), pp. 64–65; Bragg to William T. Sherman, June 3, 1855, William T. Sherman Papers, Library of Congress.

suggested that Bragg's behavior under stress, when he would be most likely to feel the need for relief, was perhaps opium induced. Despite his elaborately organized army and his carefully laid plans, as battle developed he seemed to lose track of what he wanted to accomplish and appeared unable to adapt to changing situations on the battlefield. His grandiose early reports of victory on some of his defeats or retreats or draws, such as Murfreesboro, the Tullahoma campaign, Fort Fisher, and Kinston, may have been prompted by an opium fog. One historian believed Bragg's "skewed visions of success, his paranoia toward his officers after each defeat," may have resulted from his medical care.[9] And the paranoia toward his subordinates may have come from the fact that Bragg truly did not know what had occurred during battle.

Braxton Bragg, then, exemplified much of what went wrong for the South. His poor health was shared by many of his fellow Confederates, and his penchant for quarreling matched that of great numbers of his compatriots. Through much of the war Bragg's talents were wasted. In the early months he proved himself an excellent trainer of recruits, but he was soon thrust into army command, a position beyond his emotional capabilities and his physical stamina. His appointment as military adviser, the role to which he was most suited, did not last long enough for him to complete the work he had begun in streamlining the South's military institutions. Instead, Davis sent Bragg back to field command, where he had already proved himself particularly inept. Bragg's Civil War career clearly illustrates the Confederates' failure to use their human resources effectively. The context in

---

[9] David T. Courtwright, "Opiate Addiction as a Consequence of the Civil War," *Civil War History*, XXIV (June 1978), 108; Brooks, *Civil War Medicine*, p. 70; Mark A. Quinones, "Drug Abuse during the Civil War (1861–1865)", *International Journal of the Addictions*, X (1975), 1016; Robert Wilson, "Medicine in the Days of the Confederacy," *Journal of the South Carolina Medical Association*, LXVI (1970), 172; *OR*, Series 4, I, 1041; II, 13, 14, 79, 442, 467, 569, 1021, 1024; III, 533; David T. Courtwright, "The Hidden Epidemic: Opiate Addiction and Cocaine Use in the South, 1860–1920," *Journal of Southern History*, XLIX (1983), 57; Stowe to author, July 18, 1985; James Street, Jr., "Under the Influence," *Civil War Times Illustrated*, XXVII (1988), 31–35.

which Bragg found himself enmeshed merely frustrated his good
qualities, while emphasizing his poor points.

In 1863, shortly after the humiliating defeat at Missionary
Ridge, a soldier from Mississippi praised Bragg. He insisted that
some historian in the future would recognize Bragg's "cool courage, consummate bravery, and determined devotion to the cause
he espoused and served so well."[10] Sadly, the Braxton Bragg of
the battlefield lacked the cool courage and the consummate bravery so necessary to a field commander. What remained was
Bragg's determined devotion to the Confederate cause, the Confederate president, and the Confederate people.

[10] Mayer, Note, c. December 1863, owned by Harold S. Mayer, New Orleans.

BIBLIOGRAPHY

Manuscripts and Collections

Alexander, Edward Porter, Papers, Southern Historical Collection, University of North Carolina, Chapel Hill.
Alexander, P. W., Papers, Columbia University, New York.
Allen, Dwight, Papers, Duke University Library, Durham, North Carolina.
Ayers, Alexander M., Papers, Centenary College of Louisiana, Shreveport.
Bailey Diary, Louisiana Historical Association Collection, Tulane University, New Orleans.
Bartlett-Basore Papers, *ibid*.
Beatty, Taylor, Diary, Southern Historical Collection, University of North Carolina.
Beauregard, Pierre Gustave Toutant, Papers, Duke University Library.
Boyd, David F., Papers, Walter L. Fleming Collection, Louisiana State University Archives, Baton Rouge.
Bragg, Braxton, Papers, Chicago Historical Society.
—— Papers, Duke University Library.
—— Papers, Henry E. Huntington Library, San Marino, California.
—— Papers, Library of Congress, Washington, D.C.
—— Papers, Lincoln National Life Foundation Archives, Fort Wayne, Indiana.
—— Papers, Rosenberg Library, Galveston, Texas.
—— Papers, Samuel Richey Confederate Collection, Miami University, Oxford, Ohio.
—— Papers, University of Texas, Austin.
—— Papers, William K. Bixby Collection, Missouri Historical Society, St. Louis.
—— Papers, Western Reserve Historical Society, Manuscript Collection No. 2000, Cleveland, Ohio.
Breckinridge Family Papers, Library of Congress.
Brent, George W., Papers, Louisiana Historical Association Collection.

Buckner, Simon Bolivar, Papers, Henry E. Huntington Library.

Bullock, John, Papers, Duke University Library.

Butler, Thomas, and Family, Papers, Louisiana State University Archives.

Callaway, Joshua K., Papers, University of Texas.

Cameron Family Papers, Southern Historical Collection, University of North Carolina.

Campbell, George Washington, Papers, Library of Congress.

Capers, Ellison, Papers, Duke University Library.

Chalaron Papers, Louisiana Historical Association Collection.

Cheatham, Benjamin Franklin, Papers, Southern Historical Collection, University of North Carolina.

—— Papers, Tennessee State Library and Archives, Nashville.

Chickamauga National Military Park Collection, Chickamauga, Georgia.

Civil War Collection, Henry E. Huntington Library.

Civil War Manuscript Series, Louisiana Historical Association Collection.

Civil War Miscellany, University of Texas.

Claiborne, J. H., Papers, University of Virginia, Charlottesville.

Claiborne, John Francis Hamtramck, Papers, Southern Historical Collection, University of North Carolina.

Coleman, D., Diary, *ibid.*

Confederate Generals and Staff Officers, Compiled Service Records, National Archives and Records Administration, Washington, D.C.

Confederate Personnel, Louisiana Historical Association Collection.

Confederate Sketches, Southern Historical Collection, University of North Carolina.

Confederate States of America, Records, University of Texas.

Confederate States of America Army Archives, Miscellany, Duke University Library.

Corr Family Papers, Virginia Historical Society, Richmond.

David, Pritchard Von, Papers, University of Texas.

Davis, Jefferson, Papers, Duke University Library.

—— Papers, Louisiana Historical Association Collection.

—— Papers, Museum of the Confederacy, Richmond, Virginia.

Edmonston, Katherine Ann Devereux, Diary, North Carolina Department of Archives and History, Raleigh.

Ellis, E. John, Thomas C. W., and Family, Papers, Louisiana State University Archives.

Fairfax, John Walter, Papers, Virginia Historical Society.

Fouche, Simpson, Papers, Southern Historical Collection, University of North Carolina.

Graham, Richard, Papers, Frost Collection, Missouri Historical Society.

Gray, R. M., "Reminiscences," Southern Historical Collection, University of North Carolina.

Hale, J. N., Typescript, Confederate Sketches, Southern Historical Collection, University of North Carolina.

Hammond, James J., Papers, Library of Congress.

Heartsill, W. W., Memoir, University of Texas.

Hill, Daniel Harvey, Papers, North Carolina Department of Archives and History.

——— Papers, Southern Historical Collection, University of North Carolina.

Jernigan, Albert, Letter, University of Texas.

Johnston, Albert Sidney, and William Preston, Papers, Barret Collection, Louisiana Historical Association Collection.

Johnston, J. Stoddard, Military Papers, Filson Club, Louisville, Kentucky.

Johnston, Joseph E., Papers, Henry E. Huntington Library.

Jones, Howard F., Papers, North Carolina Department of Archives and History.

Jones, Joseph, Manuscript, Joseph Jones Collection, Louisiana Historical Association Collection.

Kendall, W. D., Papers, Henry E. Huntington Library.

Leverich, Charles E., Diary, Louisiana State University Archives.

Longstreet, James, Papers, Duke University Library.

Lovell, Mansfield, Papers, Henry E. Huntington Library.

Mackall, William Whann, Papers, Southern Historical Collection, University of North Carolina.

McLaws, Lafayette, Papers, *ibid.*

Martin, William T., Letters, University of Texas.

Mercer, George Anderson, Diary, Southern Historical Collection, University of North Carolina.

Metts, E. S., Papers, Duke University Library.

Miles, William Porcher, Letter, University of Texas.

Polk, Leonidas, Papers, Library of Congress.

——— Papers, University of the South, Sewanee, Tennessee.

Rare Book Collection, Southern Historical Collection, University of North Carolina.

Reid, Samuel Chester, Family Papers, Library of Congress.

Rosecrans, William S., Papers, Special Collections, Research Library, University of California, Los Angeles.

Ruffin, Francis Gildart, Papers, Virginia Historical Society.

Seddon, James A., Papers, Duke University Library.

Semple, Henry C., Papers, Southern Historical Collection, University of North Carolina.

Sherman, William T., Papers, Library of Congress.

Southern Historical Society Collection, Eleanor S. Brockenbrough Library, Museum of the Confederacy, Richmond.

Stanton, Edwin M., Papers, Library of Congress.

United States Army Military History Institute, Carlisle Barracks, Pennsylvania.

Venable, Charles Scott, Papers, Southern Historical Collection, University of North Carolina.

Verdery, Eugene, Jr., and James Paul, Papers, Duke University Library.

Walker, William H. T., Papers, *ibid.*

Walter, Harvey W., Papers, Southern Historical Collection, University of North Carolina.

Ward, J. W., Family Correspondence, University of Texas.

Watson, Clement Stanford, Family Papers, Louisiana Historical Association Collection.

Wigfall Family Papers, University of Texas.

Wigfall, Louis Trezevant, Family Papers, Library of Congress.

Wiswell, James H., Papers, Duke University Library.

Wright, Marcus J., Papers, Southern Historical Collection, University of North Carolina.

Newspapers

Galveston Daily News
Galveston Weekly News
Marion (Alabama) *Commonwealth*
Mobile Daily Advertiser and Register
Montgomery Weekly Mail
Nashville Banner
New Orleans Daily Picayune
New Orleans Times-Democrat
Richmond Daily Dispatch
Richmond Enquirer
Richmond Sentinel
Richmond Whig

Published Primary Sources

Akin, Warren. *Letters of Warren Akin, Confederate Congressman.* Edited by Bell Irvin Wiley. Athens, Ga., 1959.

Alexander, E. P. *Military Memoirs of a Confederate: A Critical Narrative.* New York, 1907.

Anderson, Archer. "Address of Col. Archer Anderson on the Campaign and Battle of Chickamauga," *Southern Historical Society Papers,* IX (1881), 386–418.

Andrews, Eliza Francis. *The War-Time Journal of a Georgia Girl, 1864–1865.* New York, 1908.

Batchelor, Frank, and George Turner. *Batchelor-Turner Letters, 1861–1864, Written by Two of Terry's Texas Rangers.* Annotated by H. J. H. Rugeley. Austin, Tex., 1961.

Battles and Leaders. See Johnson, Robert Underwood, and Clarence Clough Buel, eds. *Battles and Leaders of the Civil War.*

Beatty, John. *Memoirs of a Volunteer, 1861–1863.* Edited by Harvey S. Ford. New York, 1946.

Beers, Fannie A. *Memories: A Record of Personal Experience and Adventure during Four Years of War.* Philadelphia, 1889.

Bird, Edgeworth, and Sallie Bird. *The Granite Farm Letters: The Civil War Correspondence of Edgeworth and Sallie Bird.* Edited by John Rozier. Athens, Ga., 1988.

Blackford, Susan Leigh. *Letters from Lee's Army, or, Memoirs of Life in and out of the Army in Virginia during the War between the States.* New York, 1947.

Blackford, W. W. *War Years with Jeb Stuart.* New York, 1945.

Blackmore, Bettie Ridley. "Behind the Lines in Middle Tennessee, 1863–1865: The Journal of Bettie Ridley Blackmore." Edited by Sarah Ridley Trimble. *Tennessee Historical Quarterly,* XII (1953), 48–80.

Browning, Orville H. *The Diary of Orvill Hickman Browning.* Edited by Theodore Calvin Pease and James G. Randall. 2 vols. Springfield, Ill., 1925.

Buck, Irving A. *Cleburne and His Command.* New York, 1908.

—— *Cleburne and His Command.* Edited by Thomas Robson Hay. Jackson, Tenn., 1959.

Carter, Howell. *A Cavalryman's Reminiscences of the Civil War.* New Orleans, n.d.

Chesnut, Mary Boykin. *A Diary from Dixie.* Edited by Ben Ames Williams. Boston, 1949.

—— *Mary Chesnut's Civil War.* Edited by C. Vann Woodward. New Haven, Conn., 1981.

Collins, R. M. *Chapters from the Unwritten History of the War between the States.* St. Louis, 1893.

Conolly, Thomas. *An Irishman in Dixie: Thomas Conolly's Diary of the Fall of the Confederacy.* Edited by Nelson D. Lankford. Columbia, S.C., 1988.

Cumming, Kate. *Kate: The Journal of a Confederate Nurse*. Edited by Richard Barksdale Harwell. Baton Rouge, 1959. Orig. ed., 1866.

Daniel, Frederick S. *The Richmond Examiner during the War; or, The Writings of John M. Daniel. With a Memoir of His Life*. New York, 1868.

Duke, Basil W. "Last Days of the Confederacy," in *Battles and Leaders*, IV, 762–67.

—— *Reminiscences of General Basil W. Duke, C.S.A.* New York, 1911.

Edmondston, Catherine Ann Devereux. *"Journal of a Secesh Lady": The Diary of Catherine Ann Devereux Edmondston, 1860–1866*. Edited by Beth G. Crabtree and James W. Patton. Raleigh, N.C., 1979.

Erickson, Edgar L., ed. "With Grant at Vicksburg: From the Civil War Diary of Captain Charles E. Wilcox," *Journal of the Illinois State Historical Society*, XXX (1938), 441–503.

Fleet, Betsy, and John D. P. Fuller, eds. *A Virginia Plantation Family during the Civil War: Green Mount*. Charlottesville, Va., 1962.

Foster, Samuel T. *One of Cleburne's Command: The Civil War Reminiscences and Diary of Capt. Samuel T. Foster, Granbury's Texas Brigade, C.S.A.* Edited by Norman D. Brown, Austin, Tex., 1980.

Fremantle, Arthur James Lyon. *The Fremantle Diary; Being the Journal of Lieutenant Colonel Arthur James Lyon Fremantle, Coldstream Guards, on His Three Months in the Southern States*. Edited by Walter Lord. New York, 1960.

Glenn, William Wilkins. *Between North and South: A Maryland Journalist Views the Civil War: The Narrative of William Wilkins Glenn, 1861–1869*. Edited by Bayly Ellen Marks and Mark Norton Schatz. Teaneck, N.J., 1976.

Gordon, John B. *Reminiscences of the Civil War*. New York, 1903.

Gorgas, Josiah. *The Civil War Diary of General Josiah Gorgas*. Edited by Frank E. Vandiver. University, Ala., 1947.

Grant, U. S. *Personal Memoirs of U. S. Grant*. 2 vols. New York, 1885.

Grebner, Constantin, trans., and Frederic Trautmann, ed. *"We Were the Ninth": A History of the Ninth Regiment, Ohio Volunteer Infantry, April 17, 1861, to June 7, 1864*. Kent, Ohio, 1987.

Haley, John. *The Rebel Yell and the Yankee Hurrah: The Civil War Journal of a Maine Volunteer*. Edited by Ruth L. Silliker. Camden, Maine, 1985.

Hampton, Wade. "The Battle in Bentonville," in *Battles and Leaders*, IV, 700–705.

Hardin, Lizzie. *The Private War of Lizzie Hardin: A Kentucky Confederate Girl's Diary of the Civil War in Kentucky, Virginia, Tennessee, Alabama, and Georgia*. Edited by G. Glenn Clift. Frankfort, Ky., 1963.

Harkness, Edson J. "The Expeditions against Fort Fisher and Wilmington," in *Military Essays and Recollections: Papers Read before the*

Commandery of the State of Illinois, Military Order of the Loyal Legion of the United States, II, 145–88. Chicago, 1894.

Heartsill, W. W. *Fourteen Hundred and Ninety-One Days in the Confederate Army: A Journal Kept by W. W. Heartsill for Four Years, One Month, and One Day; or, Camp Life; Day by Day, of the W. P. Lane Rangers from April 19, 1861, to May 20, 1865.* Edited by Bell Irvin Wiley. Jackson, Tenn., 1953.

Hill, Daniel Harvey. "Chickamauga—the Great Battle in the West," in *Battles and Leaders,* III, 638–62.

Hoffman, John. *The Confederate Collapse at the Battle of Missionary Ridge: The Reports of James Patton Anderson and His Brigade Commanders.* Dayton, Ohio, 1985.

Holborn, Hajo. "The Prusso-German School: Moltke and the Rise of the General Staff," in *Makers of Modern Strategy from Machiavelli to the Nuclear Age,* ed. Peter Paret. Princeton, N.J., 1986.

Hough, Alfred Lacey. *Soldier in the West: The Civil War Letters of Alfred Lacey Hough.* Philadelphia, 1957.

Johnson, Robert Underwood, and Clarence Clough Buel, eds. *Battles and Leaders of the Civil War.* 4 vols. New York, 1956.

Johnston, Joseph E. *Narrative of Military Operations Directed, during the Late War between the States.* Bloomington, Ind., 1959.

Jones, John B. *A Rebel War Clerk's Diary at the Confederate States Capital.* Edited by Howard Swiggett. 2 vols. New York, 1935.

Jones, Katherine M., ed. *Heroines of Dixie: Winter of Desperation.* St. Simons Island, Ga., 1975.

Kean, Robert Garlick Hill. *Inside the Confederate Government: The Diary of Robert Garlick Hill Kean, Head of the Bureau of War.* Edited by Edward Younger. New York, 1957.

Key, Thomas J., and Robert J. Campbell. *Two Soldiers: The Campaign Diaries of Thomas J. Key, C.S.A., December 7, 1863–May 17, 1865, and Robert J. Campbell, U.S.A., January 1, 1864–July 21, 1864.* Edited by Wirt Armistead Cate. Chapel Hill, N.C., 1938.

Lamb, William. "The Defense of Fort Fisher," in *Battles and Leaders,* IV, 642–54.

Lee, Robert E. *Lee's Dispatches: Unpublished Letters of General Robert E. Lee, C.S.A., to Jefferson Davis and the War Department of the Confederate States of America, 1862–65.* Edited by Douglas Southall Freeman. New York, 1915.

Lee, Susan P. *Memoirs of William Nelson Pendleton, D. D.* Philadelphia, 1893.

Liddell, St. John Richardson. *Liddell's Record.* Edited by Nathaniel C. Hughes. Dayton, Ohio, 1985.

282 BIBLIOGRAPHY

Longstreet, James. *From Manassas to Appomattox: Memoirs of the Civil War in America.* Bloomington, Ind., 1960. Orig. ed., 1896.

Mackall, William W. *A Son's Recollections of His Father.* New York, 1930.

Manigault, Arthur Middleton. *A Carolinian Goes to War: The Civil War Narrative of Arthur Middleton Manigault, Brigadier General, C.S.A.* Edited by R. Lockwood Tower. Columbia, S.C., 1983.

Medical and Surgical History of the War of the Rebellion. 4 vols. Washington, D.C., 1870–1888.

Mosman, Chesley A. *The Rough Side of War: The Civil War Journal of Chesley A. Mosman, 1st Lieutenant, Company D, 59th Illinois Volunteer Infantry Regiment.* Edited by Arnold Gates. Garden City, N.Y., 1987.

Nugent, William L. *My Dear Nellie: The Civil War Letters of William L. Nugent to Eleanor Smith Nugent.* Edited by William M. Cash and Lucy Somerville Howorth. Jackson, Miss., 1977.

Opdycke, Emerson. "Notes on the Chickamauga Campaign," in *Battles and Leaders,* III, 668–71.

Osborne, Thomas. *The Fiery Trail: A Union Officer's Account of Sherman's Last Campaigns.* Edited by Richard Harwell and Philip N. Racine. Knoxville, 1986.

Owen, William Miller. *In Camp and Battle with the Washington Artillery of New Orleans.* Boston, 1885.

Patrick, Robert Draughon. *Reluctant Rebel: The Secret Diary of Robert Patrick, 1861–1865.* Edited by F. Jay Taylor. Baton Rouge, 1959.

Pember, Phoebe Yates. *A Southern Woman's Story.* Edited by Bell Irvin Wiley. Covington, Ga., 1977.

Polk, W. M. "General Polk at Chickamauga," in *Battles and Leaders,* III, 662–63.

Putnam, Sallie Brock. *Richmond during the War: Four Years of Personal Observation.* New York, 1867.

Quintard, Charles Todd. *Doctor Quintard, Chaplain C.S.A. and Second Bishop of Tennessee, Being His Story of the War (1861–1865).* Edited by Arthur Howard Noll. Sewanee, Tenn., 1905.

Ross, Fitzgerald. *Cities and Camps of the Confederate States.* Edited by Richard Barksdale Harwell. Urbana, Ill., 1958.

Ruffin, Thomas. *The Papers of Thomas Ruffin.* Edited by J. G. de Roulhac Hamilton. 4 vols. Raleigh, N.C., 1920.

Seaton, Benjamin M. *The Bugle Softly Blows.* Edited by Harold B. Simpson. Waco, Tex., 1965.

Smith, Private. *Private Smith's Journal: Recollections of the Late War.* Edited by Clyde C. Walton. Chicago, 1963.

Sorrel, G. Moxley. *Recollections of a Confederate Staff Officer.* Dayton, Ohio, 1978. Orig. ed., 1905.

Stout, L. H. *Reminiscences of General Braxton Bragg*. Hattiesburg, Miss., 1942.

Sykes, E. T. *Walthall's Brigade: A Cursory Sketch, with Personal Experiences of Walthall's Brigade, Army of Tennessee, C.S.A., 1862–1865.* N.p., n.d.

Truxall, Aida Craig, ed. *"Respects to All": Letters of Two Pennsylvania Boys in the War of the Rebellion*. Pittsburgh, 1962.

Urquhart, David. "Bragg's Advance and Retreat," in *Battles and Leaders*, III, 600–609.

Villard, Henry. *Memoirs of Henry Villard, Journalist and Financier, 1835–1900*. 2 vols. Boston, 1904.

War of the Rebellion: A Compilation of the Official Records of the Union and Confederate Armies. 128 vols. Washington, D.C., 1880–1901.

Watkins, Sam R. *"Co. Aytch": A Side Show of the Big Show*. New York, 1979.

Welch, Spenser Glasgow. *A Confederate Surgeon's Letters to His Wife*. Marietta, Ga., 1954. Orig. ed., 1911.

Wightman, Edward King. *From Antietam to Fort Fisher: The Civil War Letters of Edward King Wightman, 1862–1865.* Edited by Edward G. Longacre. Rutherford, N.J., 1985.

Wilson, Suzanne Colton. *Column South: With the Fifteenth Pennsylvania Cavalry from Antietam to the Capture of Jefferson Davis*. Flaggstaff, Ariz., 1960.

Worsham, W. J. *The Old Nineteenth Tennessee Regiment, C.S.A.* Knoxville, 1902.

Young, John Russell. *Around the World with General Grant*. 2 vols. New York, 1879.

Secondary Sources

Adams, George Worthington. *Doctors in Blue: The Medical History of the Union Army in the Civil War*. New York, 1952.

Berry, Mary Frances. *Military Necessity and Civil Rights Policy: Black Citizenship and the Constitution, 1861–1868*. Port Washington, N.Y., 1977.

Boatner, Mark Mayo, III. *The Civil War Dictionary*. New York, 1959.

Bridges, Hal. *Lee's Maverick General: Daniel Harvey Hill*. New York, 1961.

Brooks, Stewart. *Civil War Medicine*. Springfield, Ill., 1966.

Cleaves, Freeman. *Rock of Chickamauga: The Life of General George H. Thomas*. Norman, Okla., 1948.

Coats, Wendell J. *Armed Forces as Power: The Theory of War Reconsidered*. New York, 1966.

Coffman, Edward M. *The Old Army: A Portrait of the American Army in Peacetime, 1784–1898.* New York, 1986.

Connelly, Thomas Lawrence. *Army of the Heartland: The Army of Tennessee, 1861–1862.* Baton Rouge, 1967.

—— *Autumn of Glory: The Army of Tennessee, 1862–1865.* Baton Rouge, 1971.

Connelly, Thomas Lawrence, and Archer Jones. *The Politics of Command: Factions and Ideas in Confederate Strategy.* Baton Rouge, 1973.

Courtwright, David T. "The Hidden Epidemic: Opiate Addiction and Cocaine Use in the South, 1860–1920," *Journal of Southern History,* XLIX (1983), 57–72.

—— "Opiate Addiction as a Consequence of the Civil War," *Civil War History,* XXIV (1978), 101–11.

Cummings, Charles M. *Yankee Quaker, Confederate General: The Curious Career of Bushrod Rust Johnson.* Teaneck, N.J., 1971.

Cunningham, H. H. *Doctors in Gray: The Confederate Medical Service.* Baton Rouge, 1958.

Daniel, Larry J. *Cannoneers in Gray: The Field Artillery of the Army of Tennessee, 1861–1865.* University, Ala., 1984.

Davis, Burke. *The Long Surrender.* New York, 1985.

—— *Sherman's March.* New York, 1980.

Davis, William C. *Breckinridge: Statesman, Soldier, Symbol.* Baton Rouge, 1974.

Dowdey, Clifford. *Lee's Last Campaign: The Story of Lee and His Men against Grant—1864.* New York, 1960.

Dufour, Charles L. *Nine Men in Gray.* Garden City, N.Y., 1963.

Durden, Robert F. *The Gray and the Black: The Confederate Debate on Emancipation.* Baton Rouge, 1972.

Dyer, Gwynne. *War.* New York, 1985.

Dyer, John P. *"Fightin' Joe" Wheeler.* Baton Rouge, 1941.

Eckenrode, H. J., and Bryan Conrad. *James Longstreet, Lee's War Horse.* Chapel Hill, N.C., 1936.

Evans, Eli N. *Judah P. Benjamin: The Jewish Confederate.* New York, 1988.

Faust, Patricia L., ed. *Historical Times Illustrated Encyclopedia of the Civil War.* New York, 1986.

Foote, Shelby. *The Civil War: A Narrative.* 3 vols. New York, 1963.

Freeman, Douglas Southall. *Lee's Lieutenants: A Study in Command.* 3 vols. New York, 1943.

Fuller, J. F. C. *The Conduct of War, 1789–1961.* N.p., 1961.

Gallagher, Gary W. *Stephen Dodson Ramseur, Lee's Gallant General.* Chapel Hill, N.C., 1985.

Goff, Richard D. *Confederate Supply.* Durham, N.C., 1969.

Govan, Gilbert E., and James W. Livingood. *A Different Valor: The Story of General Joseph E. Johnston, C.S.A.* New York, 1956.

Gow, June I. "Chiefs of Staff in the Army of Tennessee under Braxton Bragg," *Tennessee Historical Quarterly*, XXVII (1968), 341–60.

—— "The Johnston and Brent Diaries: A Problem of Authorship," *Civil War History*, XIV (1968), 46–50.

—— "Military Administration in the Confederate Army of Tennessee," *Journal of Southern History*, XL (1974), 183–98.

—— "Theory and Practice in Confederate Military Administration," *Military Affairs*, XXXIX (1975), 119–23.

Gragg, Rod. *Confederate Goliath: The Battle of Fort Fisher.* New York, 1991.

Hagerman, Edward. *The American Civil War and the Origins of Modern Warfare: Ideas, Organization, and Field Command.* Bloomington, Ind., 1988.

Hartje, Robert G. *Van Dorn: The Life and Times of a Confederate General.* Nashville, 1967.

Hattaway, Herman. *General Stephen D. Lee.* Jackson, Miss., 1976.

Hattaway, Herman, and Archer Jones. *How the North Won: A Military History of the Civil War.* Chicago, 1983.

Hay, Thomas Robson. "The Battle of Chattanooga," *Georgia Historical Quarterly*, VIII (1924), 121–41.

—— "Braxton Bragg and the Southern Confederacy," *Georgia Historical Quarterly*, IX (1925), 267–316.

—— "The Campaign and Battle of Chickamauga," *Georgia Historical Quarterly*, VII (1923), 213–50.

—— "Davis, Bragg, and Johnston in the Atlanta Campaign," *Georgia Historical Quarterly*, VIII (1924), 38–48.

—— "The Davis-Hood-Johnston Controversy of 1864," *Mississippi Valley Historical Review*, XI (1924), 54–84.

Heck, Frank H. *Proud Kentuckian, John C. Breckinridge, 1821–1875.* Lexington, Ky., 1976.

Henry, Robert Selph. *"First with the Most" Forrest.* New York, 1944.

Holland, Cecil Fletcher. *Morgan and His Raiders: Biography of the Confederate General.* New York, 1943.

Horn, Stanley F. *The Army of Tennessee.* Norman, Okla., 1941.

Howard, Michael. *Clausewitz.* Oxford, 1983.

Hughes, Nathaniel Cheairs, Jr. *General William J. Hardee, Old Reliable.* Baton Rouge, 1965.

James, Alfred P. "General Joseph Eggleston Johnston, Storm Center of the Confederate Army," *Mississippi Valley Historical Review*, XIV (1927), 342–59.

Jimerson, Randall C. *The Private Civil War: Popular Thought during the Sectional Conflict.* Baton Rouge, 1988.

Johnston, William Preston. *The Life of Gen. Albert Sidney Johnston, Embracing His Services in the Armies of the United States, the Republic of Texas, and the Confederate States.* New York, 1879.

Jones, Archer. *Confederate Strategy from Shiloh to Vicksburg.* Baton Rouge, 1961.

Jones, Charles T., Jr. "Five Confederates: The Sons of Bolling Hall in the Civil War," *Alabama Historical Quarterly,* XXIV (1962), 133–221.

Jordan, Thomas, and J. P. Pryor. *The Campaigns of Lieut.-Gen. N. B. Forrest, and of Forrest's Cavalry.* New Orleans, 1868.

Klein, Maury. *Edward Porter Alexander.* Athens, Ga., 1971.

Koeniger, A. Cash. "Climate and Southern Distinctiveness," *Journal of Southern History,* LIV (1988), 21–44.

Krick, Robert K. "'I Consider Him a Humbug . . .'—McLaws on Longstreet at Gettysburg," *Virginia Country Civil War,* V (1986), 28–30.

Lamers, William M. *The Edge of Glory: A Biography of General William S. Rosecrans, U.S.A.* New York, 1961.

Leavitt, Judith Walzer, and Ronald L. Numbers, eds. *Sickness and Health in America: Readings in the History of Medicine and Public Health.* Madison, Wis., 1985.

Livermore, Thomas L. *Numbers and Losses in the Civil War in America, 1861–1865.* Dayton, Ohio, 1986.

Long, E. B., and Barbara Long. *The Civil War Day by Day: An Almanac, 1861–1865.* Garden City, N.Y., 1971.

Lytle, Andrew. *Bedford Forrest and His Critter Company.* New York, 1931.

McKinney, Francis F. *Education in Violence: The Life of George H. Thomas and the History of the Army of the Cumberland.* Detroit, 1961.

McMurry, Richard M. "'The *Enemy* at Richmond': Joseph E. Johnston and the Confederate Government," *Civil War History,* XXVII (1981), 5–31.

—— *John Bell Hood and the War for Southern Independence.* Lexington, Ky., 1982.

—— *Two Great Rebel Armies: An Essay in Confederate Military History.* Chapel Hill, N.C., 1989.

McPherson, James M. *Battle Cry of Freedom: The Civil War Era.* New York, 1988.

McWhiney, Grady. *Braxton Bragg and Confederate Defeat.* Vol. I, *Field Command.* New York, 1969.

McWhiney, Grady, and Perry D. Jamieson. *Attack and Die: Civil War Military Tactics and the Southern Heritage.* University, Ala. 1982.

Mathes, James Harvey. *General Forrest.* New York, 1902.

Millet, Allan R., and Peter Maslowski. *For the Common Defense: A Military History of the United States of America.* New York, 1984.

Morris, Roy. "That Improbable, Praiseworthy Paper: The *Chattanooga Daily Rebel,*" *Civil War Times Illustrated,* XXIII, no. 7 (1984), 16–24.

O'Connor, Richard. *Thomas: Rock of Chickamauga.* New York, 1948.

Paludan, Phillip Shaw. *"A People's Contest": The Union and Civil War, 1861–1865.* New York, 1988.

—— *Victims: A True Story of the Civil War.* Knoxville, 1981.

Paret, Peter, ed. *Makers of Modern Strategy from Machiavelli to the Nuclear Age.* Princeton, N.J., 1986.

Parks, Joseph Howard. *General Edmund Kirby Smith, C.S.A.* Baton Rouge, 1954.

—— *General Leonidas Polk, C.S.A.: The Fighting Bishop.* Baton Rouge, 1962.

Patrick, Rembert W. *Jefferson Davis and His Cabinet.* Baton Rouge, 1944.

Patterson, Gerard A. *Rebels from West Point.* New York, 1987.

Piston, William Garrett. *Lee's Tarnished Lieutenant: James Longstreet and His Place in Southern History.* Athens, Ga., 1987.

Polk, William M. *Leonidas Polk, Bishop and General.* 2 vols. New York, 1915.

Purdue, Howell, and Elizabeth Purdue. *Pat Cleburne, Confederate General.* Hillsboro, Tex., 1973.

Quinones, Mark A. "Drug Abuse during the Civil War (1861–1865)," *International Journal of the Addictions* (1975), 1007–20.

Ramage, James A. *Rebel Raider: The Life of General John Hunt Morgan.* Lexington, Ky., 1986.

Risse, Guenter B., Ronald L. Numbers, and Judith Walzer Leavitt, eds. *Medicine without Doctors: Home Health Care in American History.* New York, 1977.

Robertson, James I., Jr. *Soldiers Blue and Gray.* Columbia, S.C., 1988.

Robertson, William Glenn. *Back Door to Richmond: The Bermuda Hundred Campaign, April–June 1864.* Newark, Del., 1987.

Rothstein, William G. *American Physicians in the Nineteenth Century: From Sects to Science.* Baltimore, 1972.

Sacks, Oliver. *Migraine: Understanding a Common Disorder.* Berkeley, Calif., 1985.

Sanger, Donald Bridgman, and Thomas Robson Hay. *James Longstreet.* Baton Rouge, 1952.

Schiller, Herbert M. *The Bermuda Hundred Campaign.* Dayton, Ohio, 1988.

Seitz, Don C. *Braxton Bragg, General of the Confederacy*. Columbia, S.C., 1924.

Shanks, Henry T. "Disloyalty to the Confederacy in Southwestern Virginia, 1861–1865," *North Carolina Historical Review*, XXI (1944), 118–35.

Shryock, Richard H. "A Medical Perspective on the Civil War," *American Quarterly*, XIV (1962), 161–73.

Snow, William P. *Lee and His Generals*. New York, 1982. Orig. ed., 1867.

Sommers, Richard J. *Richmond Redeemed: The Siege at Petersburg*. Garden City, N.Y., 1981.

Starr, Stephen Z. *The Union Cavalry in the Civil War*. 3 vols. Baton Rouge, 1985.

Stickles, Arndt Mathias. *Simon Bolivar Buckner: Borderland Knight*. Chapel Hill, N.C., 1940.

Stillwell, Lucille. *John Cabell Breckinridge*. Caldwell, Idaho, 1936.

Street, James, Jr. "Under the Influence," *Civil War Times Illustrated*, XXVII (1988), 30–35.

Swanson, Guy R., and Timothy D. Johnson. "Conflict in East Tennessee: Generals Law, Jenkins, and Longstreet," *Civil War History*, XXXI (1985), 101–10.

Swiggett, Howard. *The Rebel Raider: A Life of John Hunt Morgan*. Garden City, N.Y., 1937.

Thomas, Wilbur. *General George H. Thomas: The Indomitable Warrior*. New York, 1964.

Thomason, John W., Jr. *Jeb Stuart*. New York, 1941.

Tucker, Glenn. *The Battle of Chickamauga*. Harrisburg, Pa., 1981.

—— *Chickamauga: Bloody Battle in the West*. Dayton, Ohio, 1984.

Vandiver, Frank E. "Jefferson Davis and Unified Army Command," *Louisiana Historical Quarterly*, XXXVIII (1955), 26–38.

—— *Ploughshares into Swords: Josiah Gorgas and Confederate Ordnance*. Austin, Tex., 1952.

—— *Rebel Brass: The Confederate Command System*. Baton Rouge, 1956.

Warner, Ezra J. *Generals in Gray: Lives of the Confederate Commanders*. Baton Rouge, 1959.

Warner, John Harley. "The Idea of Southern Medical Distinctiveness: Medical Knowledge and Practice in the Old South," in *Sickness and Health in America: Readings in the History of Medicine and Public Health*, ed. Judith Walzer Leavitt and Ronald L. Numbers. Madison, Wis., 1985.

—— *The Therapeutic Perspective: Medical Practice, Knowledge, and Identity in America, 1820–1885*. Cambridge, Mass., 1986.

Weiss, Edward, and O. Apurgeon English. *Psychosomatic Medicine: The Clinical Application of Psychopathology to General Medical Problems*. Philadelphia, 1943.

Wiley, Bell Irvin. *The Life of Johnny Reb: The Common Soldier of the Confederacy*. Baton Rouge, 1982.

Williams, T. Harry. *P. G. T. Beauregard: Napoleon in Gray*. Baton Rouge, 1955.

Wilson, Robert. "Medicine in the Days of the Confederacy," *Journal of the South Carolina Medical Association*, LXVI (1970), 169–72.

Wise, John S. *The End of an Era*. New York, 1899.

Wise, Stephen R. *Lifeline of the Confederacy: Blockade Running during the Civil War*. Columbia, S.C., 1988.

Wyeth, John Allan. *That Devil Forrest: Life of General Nathan Bedford Forrest*. New York, 1959.

Yearns, Wilfred Buck. *The Confederate Congress*. Athens, Ga., 1960.

———, ed. *The Confederate Governors*. Athens, Ga., 1985.

Young, James Harvey. *The Toadstool Millionaires: A Social History of Patent Medicines in America before Federal Regulation*. Princeton, N.J., 1961.

Pickett, George E., 182
Pidgeon Mountain, 54
Pillow, Gideon, 31, 35, 36, 115
Polk, Leonidas, 13, 16, 17, 18, 20,
21, 25, 26, 31, 40, 44, 53,
61–62, 68, 71, 75, 77, 79, 80,
82, 83, 84, 89–98, 103, 104,
109, 118, 213–14; background
of, 9; incompetent in command,
9, 17–18, 61–62, 71–74, 78,
90–91
Polk, Lucius, 152
Polk, W. N., 62
Porter, David, 229
Preston, John S., 166, 178
Preston, William, 44, 67, 80, 96,
104–6, 166; background of, 42–
43
Prison conditions, 171–72
Prisoners-of-war, 116, 171–72
Pugh, James, 89
Pyle, William, 64

Raccoon Mountain, 123
Randolph, George W., 198
Ransom, Robert, 172
Reconstruction, 265
Red House Ford, Ga., 84
Reed's Bridge, Ga., 80
Reid, Samuel Chester, 162
Rennolds, Edwin, 146
Reynolds, A. W., 142
Richardson, T. G., 155, 171
Richmond Enquirer, 214–15
Richmond Examiner, 152, 214, 215
Ringgold, Ga., 33–34, 53, 70
Robertson, Felix G., 188–89
Rock Spring, Ga., 60–61
Roddey, Philip D., 35, 45, 51,
110–12, 153; background of, 43–
44
Rome, Ga., 49, 52

Rosecrans, William S., 4, 6, 8,
13–27 passim, 28, 29, 34, 39,
40, 44–47, 51–54, 57, 60, 62,
66, 67, 78, 81, 84, 85, 86, 88,
109–22 passim

Sale, John B., 93, 166, 198, 225,
227, 228, 232, 245–49, 264
Sand Mountain, 54
Schofield, John, 250
Second South Carolina Cavalry,
244
Seddon, James A., 39, 40, 91, 95,
107, 121, 163, 165, 170–71,
172, 173, 174, 176–77, 200,
204–6, 207, 210, 212, 223, 224,
243, 246; background of, 204–5;
health of, 204–5
Semmes, Thomas, 88
Sequatchie Valley, Tenn., 111
Shelbyville, Tenn., 16, 24, 141
Sherman, William T., 112, 129,
131, 135, 190, 192–93, 201,
224–27, 250–55, 264
Slaves, 244–45; army use of,
179–80; proposed enlistment of,
179–81, 244
Smith, Edmund Kirby, 167, 186,
228, 250
Smith, W. N. H., 176
Snead, Thomas Lowndes, 249
Snodgrass Hill, Ga., 75
Sorrel, Moxley, 125
Southern Historical Society Papers,
264
Steven's Gap, Ga., 54, 58–59
Stevenson, Carter L., 131–34, 162
Stevenson, Tenn., 20
Stewart, Alexander P., 17, 41–42,
68, 78, 118, 140, 188, 252–53;
background of, 11
Strange, Robert, 236

298 INDEX

About the Author

Judith Lee Hallock received her master's and doctoral degrees in history from the State University of New York at Stony Brook.